Curated Stories

Curated Stories

The Uses and Misuses of Storytelling

Sujatha Fernandes

OXFORD
UNIVERSITY PRESS

OXFORD

UNIVERSITY PRESS

Oxford University Press is a department of the University of Oxford. It furthers
the University's objective of excellence in research, scholarship, and education
by publishing worldwide. Oxford is a registered trademark of Oxford University
Press in the UK and certain other countries.

Published in the United States of America by Oxford University Press
198 Madison Avenue, New York, NY 10016, United States of America.

© Oxford University Press 2017

CIP data is on file at the Library of Congress
ISBN 978–0–19–061804–9 (hbk.)
ISBN 978–0–19–061805–6 (pbk.)

9 8 7 6 5 4 3 2 1

Paperback printed by Webcom, Inc., Canada
Hardback printed by Bridgeport National Bindery, Inc., United States of America

For Shaad, my budding storyteller

CONTENTS

ACKNOWLEDGMENTS

This book was conceived, researched, and written within a rich community of scholars, students, friends, organizers, and artists in New York City and at the City University of New York (CUNY). I am very grateful to my colleagues who shaped the project from the beginning, especially Kandice Chuh and Jim Jasper. They both read early drafts of proposals, gave detailed feedback as I wrote, asked the important questions, and steered me in directions that would end up being crucial in the final shape of the book. I appreciate Jim's work as a series editor for Oxford in helping to bring this book to publication.

I am grateful to all of those colleagues and friends who read various proposals and chapters and gave helpful and detailed feedback: Marnia Lazreg, Lila Abu-Lughod, Karen Miller, Don Mitchell, Walter Nicholls, Alfonso Gonzales, Ruth Milkman, Francesca Polletta, AK Thompson, and the late and dearly missed Juan Flores. Thanks to Josie Saldaña, Hisham Aidi, Mark Nowak, Chris Colvin, Michelle Farrell, and Fanny Lauby, who provided materials, research tips, and directions for my work. Greg Grandin, John Beverley, and Carol Greenhouse have always been crucial interlocutors and I'm grateful for their support. I would like to thank my new colleagues at the University of Sydney, especially Adam David Morton, who discussed the project with me in detail over Skype and whose suggestions I incorporated in these pages. *Mil gracias* also to my friends in Venezuela, Yajaira Hernandez, Johnny Moreno, and Ricardo Guerrero, who helped provide contacts and materials for my Venezuela chapter.

This book was made possible by the hard work and dedication of my research assistant, Courtney Frantz. Courtney first approached me as a volunteer and then became my graduate student, lending her keen intelligence and impressive research skills to the project for five years. I also thank my other graduate student assistants, Jacob Lederman, Kathleen Dunn, Shirley Leyro, Tom Buechele, and Christie Sillo, for their help with the project over the years.

I am grateful to all of the people and centers who provided support for this book: Don Robotham, Ruthie Gilmore, David Harvey, Mary Taylor, Gary Wilder, Aoibheann Sweeney, Kendra Sullivan, Anahi Viladrich, Ron Hayduk, Phil Kasinitz, the Committee on Globalization and Social Change, the Center for Place, Culture and Politics, the Advanced Research Collaborative, and the Center for the Humanities at the CUNY Graduate Center. While a fellow at each of these various centers, I presented work from this book, and I am grateful to the seminar leaders and participants for their incisive and critical comments that helped me to revise the manuscript. Thanks also to my stellar Department chair, Andy Beveridge at Queens College, who has always been a strong advocate for me. I was thankful to receive grants from the Queens College Research Enhancement Committee and the Immigration Studies Working Group at Queens College, and the University of Sydney Research Assistance Support Scheme. I am especially grateful to the Professional Staff Congress–City University of New York Research Foundation for funding this project for seven years, covering all aspects of research, writing, and publication.

I had the opportunity to present this work at various seminars and conferences that helped me to rethink and revise my ideas. I thank the Sociology Colloquium at Rutgers University; Victoria Pitts-Taylor and the Center for the Study of Women and Society at the CUNY Graduate Center; Tony Spanakos and the participants of "The Politics of the Popular in Latin America" at NYU; Fernando Montero and the Americas South Seminar at Columbia University; Marcy Schwartz and the participants of the "Media and Culture in Venezuela" seminar at Rutgers University; the organizers and participants of the Politics and Protest Workshop at the CUNY Graduate Center; Pamela Calla and the participants of "Racisms in Comparative Perspective" at NYU; Ron Zboray, Lara Putnam, and the participants of the Cultural Studies Annual Common Seminar at the University of Pittsburgh; the organizers and participants of the "Urban Spatial Practices in Contemporary Latin America" conference at the CUNY Graduate Center; and the Political Economy and Anthropology Seminars at the University of Sydney.

I would like to express a special thanks to the social movement organizers and workers who have left a deep imprint on me and whose thoughts and ideas animate the pages of this book. These include Terri Nilliasca, Rob Robinson, Nastaran Mohit, Ninaj Raoul, Linda Oalican, Bhairavi Desai, and Javaid Tariq, as well as the current and former members of Domestic Workers United—Christine Lewis, Pat Francois, Samantha Lee, Joyce Gill-Campbell, Carolyn DeLeon, and Erline Brown. I was very fortunate to be a co-leader along with Colette Daiute and Jeanne Theoharis of a Mellon-funded seminar on Public Engagement and Collaborative Research entitled "Narrating

Change," at the Center for the Humanities. Over a series of three events, including a Domestic Workers working group, a working group called "Whose Movement Is It?", and a political education workshop, we brought together domestic workers and other migrant workers, as well as scholars and students to discuss the questions of storytelling, advocacy, the role of foundations, and our visions for social change. These working groups had a profound impact on my work, and they have forced me to think about how I can always make my work relevant to and in dialogue with social justice struggles on the ground.

I thank the editors and publishers of two journals for permission to republish earlier versions of chapters 3 and 4, and I thank the reviewers of those pieces for their excellent comments, which are reflected in this book also: "Stories and Statecraft: Afghan Women's Narratives and the Construction of Western Freedoms," *Signs: Journal of Women in Culture and Society*; and "Out of the Home, into the House: Narratives and Strategies in Domestic Worker Legislative Campaigns," *Social Text*.

My editor at Oxford University Press, James Cook, has believed in this book and has been an important source of encouragement and guidance. It has also been a pleasure to work with Amy Klopfenstein, who provided crucial editorial support. I would also like to thank the reviewers of the manuscript for their careful reading and extensive comments that have helped to make this a much better book.

There are no words to thank my family, who have always provided the crucial emotional and physical support that make possible everything that I do. My parents, Sylvie and Joe Fernandes, have always supported me in my work, and they provide unlimited love, childcare, and food to our family. My father-in-law, Tom Walsh, built me a study complete with shelves for all of my books, so that I could have a "room of my own," in which to write amidst the chaos of family life. I don't know what we would do without Abba Tom. Just like she did for my other books on Cuba and then Venezuela, my sister Deepa introduced me to the key people, domestic workers and activists, who would shape my research on the ground. A fearless, brilliant reporter and storyteller, Deepa founded the Community News Production Institute of People's Production House, which provided the means for domestic workers, street vendors, and other workers to learn the tools by which to create and tell their own stories.

A large amount of credit must go to my spouse, Mike Walsh, who took on much of the labor of childcare on top of his own academic work, while I was writing this book. His love and companionship were a constant throughout the solitary process of writing. Every night at dinner he asks me, "What did you work on today?" and I'm sure he's glad to see the book finished so that we can finally talk about something else.

I began the work on this book right before giving birth to my second child, and it has grown and developed alongside two toddlers who have now blossomed into curious and compassionate children. It was through my kids, Aisha and Shaad, that I rediscovered the joys of storytelling. Not content with the books on their shelves, they wanted me to tell them stories. On the way to their daycare, I would make up stories to entertain and intrigue them. I was reminded of my late grandmother Nana Harris—when I was a child she would tell me that her pocket was full of stories. Like a conjuror she would pull out her never-ending handkerchief of tales from her native Karnataka. Her memory and my children give me hope that we can find our way back to an art of storytelling.

Curated Stories

CHAPTER 1
Curated Storytelling

Malala Yousafzai grew up in the northwestern Swat district of Pakistan, about 50 miles from the Afghan border. She was the daughter of an educator who ran a chain of private schools in the area. When the militant Taliban group took over the Swat valley and banned girls' education in 2008, the eleven-year-old Malala was enlisted to write a blog under a pen name for the BBC, recounting her experiences. She spoke about education rights to American officials and to grassroots organizations. As Malala began to address national and international media, her identity was revealed and she received numerous death threats. On October 9, 2012, she was shot in the head by a Taliban gunman while returning home on a bus after taking an exam. She survived after numerous rounds of reconstructive surgery and rehabilitation, and went on to complete her schooling in Birmingham, England.

In the wake of her shooting, Malala has been the recipient of numerous awards and honors, including the Nobel Peace Prize. She has received honorary citizenships and doctorates, was featured by *Time* magazine as one of the 100 most influential people in the world, has met with many heads of state, and has been the subject of a documentary, *He Named Me Malala*. She has been iconized as the girl who was shot by the Taliban for seeking an education.

In the geopolitical crosscurrents of American military intervention in the Middle East, a rising wave of protest from the Arab revolutions, and criticism of the surveillance of Muslim populations in Western countries, Malala's story was one that could provide reassurance and comfort to a Western public that America was doing the right thing. Media pundits, politicians, and advocacy organizations worked to create an image of Malala as a symbol of women's rights under attack by the Taliban, a situation requiring

Western military intervention. In constructing this narrative about Malala, talk show hosts and marketing teams did not mention Malala's opposition to the war, and they ignored her indictments of American intelligence agencies as having fostered the idea of jihad and arming the Taliban. She is presented as a deserving empathetic subject; nonconfrontational compared to the angry Muslims who dominate Western media coverage.[1]

The refashioning of Malala's story has become possible within an emergent culture of storytelling that presents carefully curated narratives with predetermined storylines as a tool of philanthropy, statecraft, and advocacy. Contemporary life is saturated with such initiatives from the phenomenon of TED talks and Humans of New York to the plethora of story-coaching agencies and strategists that have emerged to sustain this culture. It is no coincidence that the rise of this curated storytelling takes place in an era of Facebook, which a *New Yorker* article notes is a medium which promotes the "quick and cavalier consumption of others."[2] Just as Malala is depicted as a typical teen in *He Named Me Malala*, giggling at a picture of Brad Pitt, the popular stories in news feeds and timelines of social media are those that are accessible. Histories, ambiguities, and political struggles are erased in an effort to create warm and relatable portraits of others who are "just like us."

This mode of curated storytelling has extended deep into contemporary social life and political culture and institutions. The Harvard lecturer and political strategist Marshall Ganz was called upon in 2007 to provide storytelling workshops for Barack Obama's election campaign, and his Public Narrative trainings have since been used widely by advocacy organizations, nonprofits, nongovernmental organizations (NGOs), and immigrant rights groups. "Tell your story!" has become an inspirational mantra of the self-help industry. Narrative research centers have emerged to look at the benefits of storytelling in a range of areas from treating depression to helping new immigrants build community. Philanthropic organizations and foundations produce storytelling manuals and offer trainings to their grantees in nonprofit storytelling. The US Department of Defence sponsors a project known as "Narrative Networks,"[3] looking at the strategic implications of narrative for defense missions, and the US State Department has sponsored story workshops as a means of cultural diplomacy in places like Afghanistan.

What is behind this contemporary boom of instrumental storytelling? What accounts for the wide diffusion of a storytelling model, as a set of globally available trainings, toolkits, and protocols? Although most of the literature about storytelling has focused on the multiple gains to be had from telling stories, this book takes a more critical look at the storytelling boom. Alongside a broader shift to neoliberal and financialized economies, storytelling is being reconfigured on the model of the market to produce entrepreneurial, upwardly mobile subjects and is leveraged toward strategic and measurable goals driven by philanthropic foundations. Curated personal stories shift the focus away from structurally defined axes of oppression and help to defuse the confrontational politics of social movements. Under what conditions do stories reproduce dominant relations of power, and when can they be subversive? What are the stakes, and for whom, in the crafting and mobilization of storytelling? Rather than being the magical elixir we imagine, might curated stories actually inhibit social change?

This book presents different cases of curated storytelling as used in the online Afghan Women's Writing Project (AWWP), the domestic workers movement in New York, and the undocumented student Dreamer movement. These three examples together illustrate some of the ways that storytelling has been reconfigured in a neoliberal era and, more specifically, they show how curated stories were part of broader efforts to absorb and redirect global antiwar opposition, activism among marginal sectors of workers, and a rising migrant rights movement. Although these cases are exemplary of the trend I identify, they are not unique, and we could see these dynamics playing out in any number of other sites. I conclude with the case of the Misión Cultura storytelling project in Venezuela, as containing the possibility for a more transformative kind of storytelling. These examples provide an opportunity to examine how the varied arenas of online, legal, media, and movement storytelling produce different kinds of narratives and subjectivities, as well as possibilities for critique or outright dissent.

In his seminal essay "The Storyteller," Walter Benjamin decried the loss of the craft of oral storytelling marked by the advent of the short story and the novel. Whereas the multiple retellings contained in oral traditions reveal a "slow piling one on top of the other of thin, transparent layers," modern society abbreviated storytelling.[4] Like Benjamin, I continue to believe in the need for more deeply contextualized and complex storytelling. The affinity between stories and the ethos of late capitalist culture is not inevitable. The instrumentality of contemporary storytelling is not inherently negative, as some of the most deeply affecting stories have also had the aim of moving people toward some kind of action or goal. The testimony of Rigoberta Menchú, a Guatemalan indigenous woman whose family suffered atrocities at the hands of the military for their work in organizing poor indigenous communities in the 1980s, played a crucial role in building international solidarity with oppressed indigenous peoples. The consciousness-raising groups of the US feminist movement in the 1970s used personal stories as a way to give depth to their analyses of patriarchy. My critique is not of instrumentality per se, but rather of a utilitarian approach to stories that seeks to reduce experiences and histories to easily digestible soundbites in service of limited goals. We need to reclaim storytelling as a craft that allows for the fullness and complexity of experience to be expressed and which seeks to transform rather than reproduce global hierarchies and structures of power through movements for social change.

The reinvention of storytelling in a contemporary era has involved constructing a genealogy of an essentialized, universal formula out of what are fairly diverse oral traditions and narrative practices. Scholarly and popular nonfiction works, storytelling manuals, and storytelling strategists often extrapolate from the Western experience to present the idea of storytelling as universal and timeless. Jonathan Gottschall's popular work *The Storytelling Animal* draws on neuroscience and evolutionary biology to prove that the "master formula" of story—including character, predicament, and attempted extrication—is a fundamental part of human psychology.[5] A storytelling strategy guide for organizations similarly asserts that "storytelling is hardwired into our brains."[6] Another work of popular nonfiction, *Winning the Story Wars* by Jonah Sachs, refers to stories as "ancient mythological formulas" that are "deeply engrained in our DNA."[7] Sachs projects a seamless trajectory from thousands of years old oral traditions of pre-Colombian Americans, ancient Greeks, and Chinese dynasties to what he calls the "digitoral era" of social media and digital technology. Scholarly accounts also participate in this reification of a universal storytelling mode. One scholar calls for a "recognition of the universality of stories."[8] Another suggests that all stories from Hopi creation myths to James Joyce's *Ulysses* share a "commonly held narrative code."[9] The construction of a genealogy of an essentialized storytelling reduces disparate practices across vast time periods and reifies discourses that are often inseparable from everyday rituals and relationships.

Scholarly and popular works attempt to pin down the key elements of a prototypical story. For the narrative psychologist Jerome Bruner, a story includes characters as free agents with expectations about the world, a breach in the expected state of things, efforts by the character to come to terms with that breach, and then a resolution or outcome.[10] Gottschall argues for a universal grammar of stories that is based on trouble as the key ingredient. Sachs similarly asserts that "Without a conflict, there is no story."[11] But this construction of a prototypical story formula as based in conflict is also highly reductive of the vast oral and narrative practices that it purports to represent. What different people around the world refer to as some sort of story may all look very different from one another. One of the celebrated stories in the Western literary canon, "Why Don't You Dance?" by Raymond Carver, has no plot or conflict. A man sets up his bedroom furniture on the lawn outside his house. A young couple passing by stops and buys some of the items. They all dance. When we look at what constitutes a story outside the West, which is the focus of most sociological studies of storytelling, we see even less adherence to the master formula of story. For example, in the Japanese story form kishōtenketsu, there is no recognizable conflict. There is usually a twist sometime late in the story, but the narrative is driven by elements other than conflict. The anticipation of the reader is encouraged less through expectations about future events and more toward an appreciation of the predicament of the current situation.[12] The notion of a prototypical, conflict-driven story is a construct, which serves to impose order on what is an incoherent, widely divergent set of narrative practices.

The construction of a universal model of conflict-driven stories has emerged alongside the idea that storytelling should be employed to give a voice to those who are marginal, powerless, and silent. Rather than having advocates and others speaking for them, there is the notion that people can now speak for themselves. Personal testimony assumes a privileged relation to the truth because it is spoken by those affected.[13] The Afghan women, domestic workers, barrio residents, and undocumented students who narrate their stories in this book are all assumed to be silent, silenced, invisible, and voiceless sectors of society. By learning how to tell their story, it is suggested that they will have a voice. Advocates and story workshop leaders use such terms as "coming out of the shadows" and "coming out from behind the veil." But this claim of invisible and silenced people gaining a voice through stories is itself a rhetorical construction that amplifies some voices at the expense of others. Those who are able to make their personal experiences legible to the mainstream through drawing on dominant narratives and devices are given a platform while other voices are silenced.

The purpose of this construction of storytelling through notions of genealogy, prototype, and voice is to instrumentalize it, even if just to show, as scholars have done, that stories can help sustain human life and humanity, create empathy, mobilize people in support of social change, and share meaning within social movements. In this book, I do not treat stories and storytelling as predetermined, universal categories and objects of analysis, but rather I examine the ways in which genealogies of storytelling, story prototypes, and voice are themselves constructed by different actors. How people tell stories, what they think stories should be like, and what they propose as prototypical narratives can provide insight into the political role of narrative.[14] This involves a close examination of both the story as a text and the protocols and instruments through which stories are produced.

Analyzing stories as texts requires examining the discourses, devices, and constructs used in the stories. A story is a text that contains several different kinds of discourse units, including narrative, description, and argumentation.[15] Stories can be classified by literary genre, such as autobiography, the Latin American *testimonio*, and anecdote. We can look at the collective myths that shape stories, the narrative models like conversion narratives, epic narratives, or narratives of uplift through education, and the construction of typologies such as "deserving immigrants." We can trace the genealogy of some tropes such as "caring masters" and "individual victims," which date back to slavery and colonialism. The use of myths, narrative models, tropes, and so on in stories situates them within a web of power relations. Patricia Ewick and Susan Silbey argue that "the structure, content, and the performance of stories as they are defined and regulated within social settings often articulate and reproduce existing ideologies and hegemonic relations of power and inequality."[16] The countless personal stories that we tell and are told create a polyvocal fabric that insulates the master narrative from critique.

Stories are narrated using different modes, what Alessandro Portelli refers to as the personal, the collective, and the political.[17] The personal storytelling mode includes accounts of private and family life, as well as the life cycle of birth, marriage, children, and death. The collective register encompasses the life of the community or neighborhood, and it can extend to the workplace and collective participation. The political mode refers to global and national historical context, and the political sphere. Narrators create coherence in their stories by combining these different levels, but one level is usually dominant. Portelli argues that the shift between these different registers of narration is done strategically by the narrator, depending on what he or she wants to achieve with the narrative. For instance, in his main case of the Italian steelworker Luigi Trastulli, Portelli argues that when describing the contested circumstances surrounding his death, younger political organizers shifted from the political to the personal mode in order to avoid a message of collective powerlessness.[18]

Drawing on Portelli's insights, I suggest that the contemporary boom of storytelling in legislative campaigns, cultural diplomacy, and advocacy has involved a shift in emphasis away from the collective and political modes of narration toward the personal mode. Those relating their stories are individuals rather than members of a class or community, and they enter into conflict with individual employers or spouses instead of dominant classes or patriarchal structures. If there is a shift to the political in these stories, it is usually a predetermined slogan or campaign messaging, and not an interrogation of the structural conditions that shape one's life story. Narrators may avoid giving a political framing to their stories for fear of reprisal or because they are directed away from such framing by legal advocates or protocols. Or they may employ a dominant political framing to protect themselves from the more critical implications of the stories that they tell. But when stories shift to include the community or structural-political modes, they have the potential to be subversive stories. As Ewick and Silbey argue, "subversive stories recount particular experiences as *rooted* in and part of an encompassing cultural, material, and political world that extends beyond the local."[19] Through semiotic analysis of discourses, constructs, and modes, we can probe these deeper significations of stories as text.

I also distinguish between the story as a text and storytelling as a practice. The anthropologist Michael Jackson emphasizes the importance of studying storytelling as the action of meaning-making: "the social process rather than the product of narrative activity."[20] The focus on storytelling takes us beyond the study of how the text is constructed to the places where stories are staged, stories as performance, the protocols that guide their telling, the trainings and workshops where they are composed, and the audiences to whom they are told. We must supplement the semiotic meanings of stories as texts with an understanding of where and how they are brought into social life and the impacts they have there.

"Let's face it, my presence on this stage is pretty unlikely." Barack Obama opened his speech to the 2004 Democratic National Convention (DNC) with his personal story. "My father was a foreign student, born and raised in a small village in Kenya. He grew up herding goats, went to school in a tin roof shack. His father, my grandfather, was a cook, a domestic servant to the British. But my grandfather had larger dreams for his son. Through hard work and perseverance, my father got a scholarship to study in a magical place—America—that is shown as a beacon of freedom and opportunity to so many that had come before."[21]

Obama's story of uplift, one that confronted the underpinnings of the white, wealthy political establishment, would become the basis for his 2008 bid for the presidency. Appealing to a multiracial base of community organizers, students, and hip-hop activists, the Obama campaign motivated them to mobilize others in support of his electoral bid. Political strategists worked with Marshall Ganz to devise an electoral campaign that reached out to volunteers and potential voters through sharing stories. In a series of workshops known as Camp Obama, volunteers studied Obama's 2004 DNC speech and used his story—of the son of an African immigrant who might one day become president of the United States—as a model for their own two-minute stories, which they deployed when canvassing voters.

The 2008 election of Obama as the son of a Kenyan immigrant and as an African American presented the spectacle of a major challenge to the racial

underpinnings of the American nation and a seismic shift in America's geopolitical role. From the mid-2000s, there were growing frustrations with
the neoconservative agenda of interventionist wars to secure markets and
resources, and the criminalization of Muslims, African Americans, and
undocumented workers domestically. There was much frustration among
African Americans as racialized poverty, unemployment, and homelessness
increased during the years of the George Bush administration. Following
Bush's deliberate negligence in his handling of the crisis in the Gulf Coast
caused by Hurricane Katrina in 2005, his approval ratings fell dramatically
among black people.[22] Antiwar sentiment was growing and vocal Afghan
women leaders like Malalai Joya were calling for American troops to pull
out of her country. Antimigrant legislation was passed in the US Congress
in the mid-2000s, leading to a migrant rights movement that mobilized millions of undocumented workers and students in mega marches across the
country.

The Obama election campaign tapped into the energies and frustrations
of these various disaffected communities, especially those who had been
marginalized economically and politically like undocumented migrants
and African Americans. But then, as William Robinson argues, the campaign channeled this passion into the electoral arena, demobilizing and
weakening the insurgency, and ultimately betraying its aspirations.[23] Once
in office, Obama continued his predecessor George Bush's military policies.
He deported more than 2.5 million people in his second term in office, and
he did not address persistent economic inequality or the criminalization of
black Americans. The election of Obama resembled what Antonio Gramsci
has called "*trasformismo,*" or a process of class formation involving "the
gradual but continuous absorption, achieved by methods which varied in
their effectiveness, of the active elements produced by active groups—and
even of those which came from antagonistic groups and seemed irreconcil-
ably hostile."[24] An Obama administration offered up the prospect of change,
but incorporated and defused those who were a voice of opposition.

The Obama administration proposed a new direction that promised to
engage with Muslim populations at home and abroad, and to draw immigrant groups into a project of civic education and participation. In 2007, the
US Muslim Engagement Project spearheaded by the former US Secretary of
State Madeleine Albright was entitled "Changing Course: A New Direction
for US Relations with the Muslim World."[25] The strategy document notes
the growing antipathy toward the United States in Iraq and Afghanistan,
opposition to the global war on terror at home and abroad, and the negative
image of the United States as a human rights violator, given wide publicity
about the abuses of prisoners in Abu Ghraib and Guantanamo detention
facilities. The document proposed using cultural exchanges with musicians

and artists, educational exchanges with young Muslims who have the potential to be future leaders, and others who could influence public opinion in their home countries, with priority given to places like Iran, Iraq, and Afghanistan. After Obama was elected, there was a turn to these strategies of soft power.[26] The US government used hip-hop diplomacy programs abroad to rebrand America's image and outreach to Muslim communities.[27] The instruments of soft power also included public diplomacy, exchange programs, and disaster relief. Deepa Kumar suggests that Obama's rhetorical shift to speaking about improving relations with Muslim countries such as Iraq and Afghanistan was a shift to a liberal imperialism that relied on engagement and dialogue as a way of reasserting dominance in an increasingly multipolar world.[28] The post-Bush strategy appealed to populations in the Middle East and United States by promoting a convincing storyline about the benevolence of American intervention.

Similar efforts at courting and incorporating disaffected immigrant groups were being launched domestically by labor groups, church groups, think tanks, and foundations in the United States. Alfonso Gonzales argues that nonprofit professional activists and political operatives championed Obama's proimmigrant stance while defusing the potential of migrant rights groups and preparing Latinx communities to become a voter base for the Democratic Party.[29] The Democratic Party apparatus provided infrastructure and funds to channel the migrant rights movement away from street mobilizations and toward an electoral push, with slogans such as "Today we march, tomorrow we vote." With the election of Obama, Washington DC–based organizations sought to organize these migrant groups into a campaign-type structure to support Obama's push for legislative reforms.

Storytelling was one of the key vehicles of *trasformismo* in the Obama era. The same Camp Obama storytelling trainings that were developed by Ganz during the 2008 election campaign were used on a mass scale with immigrant rights groups, climate justice groups, immigrant worker organizations, and a range of nonprofits. The State Department sponsored creative writing programs and storytelling collaborations in countries where the United States was at war or sought to improve its image, such as Iraq, Afghanistan, and Venezuela.[30] In these various initiatives, mentorship and protocols were used to elicit the stories of individuals in brief, targeted formats that could then be reproduced on websites, in legal hearings, and in voter canvassing. Through learning how to tell curated stories, I argue that Afghan women, domestic workers, and undocumented students were redirecting their energies away from grassroots political organizing work toward foundation-driven advocacy and electoral channels. But they were also learning how to be new kinds of subjects, model citizens, and entrepreneurial actors who sought upward mobility rather than class conflict.

The story of Obama as the son of an immigrant who could one day become president was circulated through the Ganz trainings and was central to these projects of neoliberal self-making. Just like Obama's speech to the DNC, the story trainings and legislative campaigns reinforced tropes of the American Dream and the hard-working immigrant, and dominant myths such as the opportunity myth.

Most of the scholarly and popular literature extols the virtues of a prototypical and universal storytelling model, but it does not address the circuits of capital within which stories circulate or the situation of storytelling within broader neoliberal transformations. There are a few accounts that look at the structures of exchange and consumption in which stories are located.[31] Some studies examine the ways in which stories have become commodified[32] or drawn into marketing strategies.[33] But my analysis of storytelling looks beyond the commodification and marketization of stories to examine the ways in which storytelling in a neoliberal era comes to be guided by utilitarian logics. George Yúdice has described how under conditions of globalization, culture is recruited to goals of enhancing social capital, improving social conditions, and managing urban blight.[34] Storytelling has similarly been harnessed for such utilitarian goals: stories are leveraged to drive social impact and produce measurable gains that can be showcased in foundation reports, whether winning legislative victories or registering people to vote.

"Neoliberalism" is a term used to describe a broad constellation of practices, economic policies, modes of governance, discourses, and rationalities that take specific forms in different geohistorical contexts but still share enough features to retain analytical use. The neoliberal complex consists of ideas of free, enterprising individuals and competitive, unregulated markets, rooted in principles of classical liberal economic and political theory.[35] Since the 1970s, neoliberal theory has moved from the textbooks to restructure economies, everyday life, common sense, and modes of being through a series of encounters that involved coups, violent upheaval, structural adjustment, and seizures of state power. Neoliberal leaders played on social anxieties by promising strong leadership, regimes of law and order, competitive solutions to problems, and by mobilizing affective and religious moral economies. Neoliberalism has become a hegemonic project, although one that must be constantly reworked and reinvigorated, opening it up to multiple contradictions and fissures in its operation.

To describe the remaking of storytelling in a context of neoliberalism, I have developed the concept of the "political economy of storytelling." The concept refers to two intertwined activities. The first is the production, circulation, and consumption of stories that are mobilized toward certain utilitarian ends, such as building the political capital of organizations and bolstering electoral and legislative goals. Stories are structured through protocols and workshops to provide soundbites that can be easily delivered in a newspaper interview, voter recruitment drive, or legal hearing. Disembedded from the social networks and everyday life of the storyteller, these stories are circulated in legislative and electoral campaigns, and online forums. A political economy of storytelling is concerned with the conditions of production of stories within neoliberal orders.

The second activity involves the deployment of stories in processes of subject-making. Scholars of literature have shown how under liberal modernity, the story form provided the technology by which social outsiders acquired the capacity to become citizen-subjects.[36] Genres such as autobiography produced modern liberal notions of the self as rational, unitary, and assured of its free agency, with origins in the eighteenth-century Enlightenment and colonial capitalism. Through a process of self-knowledge, the historically marginalized individual moved toward becoming the Enlightenment subject capable of participation in civic life. This teleology of development is also apparent in the examples I discuss in this book; however, in a neoliberal era, Nikolas Rose argues that subjects of rule are specified in a new way: "as active individuals asking to 'enterprise themselves,' to maximize their quality of life through acts of choice."[37] The individual is seen as an "active agent in the fabrication of their own existence."[38] For Wendy Brown, neoliberal subjects are recalibrated as "rational, calculating creatures whose moral autonomy is measured by their capacity for 'self care'—the ability to provide for their own needs and service their own ambitions."[39] Feminist scholars have shown how the trope of upward mobility through work and education is also crucial to the production of the neoliberal subject, and given the trend of women entering into service occupations, meritocratic discourses of self-making are often tied to female subjects.[40]

Curated storytelling is a means of producing subjects who are guided by these principles of upward mobility, entrepreneurship, and self-reliance. They enter into a path of enlightenment and self-knowledge through the choices they make at key moments. Those who participate in this self-making often have aspirations of class mobility, due to their educational opportunities, niche position in the economy, or access to structures of funding. Yet despite the desire for individual personal advancement, the majority of those who tell their stories are not able to improve their conditions. This is one of the contradictions that could work to unravel the project of neoliberal subject-making.

One of the key technologies that both shapes the utilitarian nature of stories and guides subject formation is the storytelling workshop. In this book, I look at a range of formats and venues for storytelling workshops from the online creative writing workshops conducted by the Afghan Women's Writing Project (Chapter 3), and the Ganz Public Narrative workshops held with undocumented Dreamers (Chapter 5), to the Misión Cultura storytelling workshops organized under the government of Hugo Chávez in Venezuela (Chapter 6). In some cases the storytelling workshop is substituted by the protocols of the legal hearing, as is the case with the domestic workers movement (Chapter 4). The story workshop, the training manual, and the legal protocol have become a prime means of disciplining subjects and inculcating them with the narrative models, tropes, and myths that constitute their stories. For evidence of this, we can look to the framing given by mentors and storytelling guides, the narrative models provided in workshops, the protocols and formats that are made available, and the ends to which participants are instructed to direct their stories. The storytelling workshop is also intended to be used on a mass scale. "Train the trainer" sessions teach leaders how to carry out their own storytelling workshops and thus replicate the workshops in multiple settings. Participants are used to recruit other participants. Storytelling manuals are distributed to a wide range of organizations that adapt them for their own purposes.

While focusing on the political economy of storytelling, we must also take seriously the stories themselves—as representations of a life and as the public utterance of previously silenced experiences, which also involve certain self-conscious strategies of narration and performance on the part of the author. Stories can exceed the framings and protocols that try to contain them and direct them toward certain utilitarian goals. People's lived experiences, memories of collective struggle, deeply held feelings, and traumatic experiences may interject into their narrative in ways that disrupt the power of dominant discourses. Spaces of expression may open up within the text itself. It is the tension between the guided processes of storytelling and the stories themselves, between a global phenomenon and its local iterations, that lies at the heart of this book. The storytellers in state-sponsored and nonprofit storytelling initiatives sometimes, even if briefly, manage to break out of the utilitarian binds imposed on them to create alternative spaces of collective imagining.

The other response to the neoliberal capture of storytelling has been refusal or opting out. Some prefer to remain silent than to give in to the logic of the soundbite, the reduction of their selves and their stories to blurbs that can fit within the lines of a grant application or protocol. Some turn to their own networks and artistic skills to render their stories in different ways that give voice to alternative subjectivities and storylines, and include other kinds of narratives that go off script.

Although the subject matter of this book is wide ranging in terms of the locations and subjects I explore, I believe that it is necessary to bring together disparate phenomenon when studying the modes of subject-making and storytelling in a neoliberal era. I am concerned with tracing certain patterns and logics behind these phenomena. Each chapter looks at how the messy and inchoate experiences of everyday life are marshalled into compact and portable narratives that can be deployed by states and nonprofit organizations toward instrumental ends. I am concerned with the tropes and representations to be found in these narratives, often part of a deep history of associations stretching back to slavery and colonialism. The chapters look at narration as a means of liberal and neoliberal subject-making, where workshops and storytelling manuals guide individuals to think of themselves as entrepreneurial and upwardly mobile. In looking at these varied cases of storytelling in a neoliberal era, I also develop a broader claim: it is not just states and dominant classes who tell politically efficacious narratives; the personal stories of the marginalized can also be a site for constructing hegemony.

Chapter 2 aims to give an overview of how the storytelling turn occurred in recent decades. It is a chronicle of the broad shifts that led from the more deeply oppositional storytelling tactics of the 1960s and 1970s social movements to the transactional, therapeutic, and then market-based model of storytelling that currently predominates. It provides a background for the chapters to follow, which focus on contemporary modes of storytelling.

Chapter 3 examines the uses of storytelling in cultural diplomacy to engage an upwardly mobile strata of Afghan women as entrepreneurial actors aspiring to Western lifestyles, and to defuse opposition to interventionist war among women in the West who read their stories of subjugation under the patriarchal Taliban. I look at the Afghan Women's Writing Project (AWWP), a series of online creative writing workshops conducted by US-based mentors with Afghan women in English which seek to "give voice" to silent Afghan women who share their stories of abuse and hardship with readers across the globe. By disconnecting the personal experiences of Afghan women from the broader geopolitical context of war and military invasion, the stories tend to reinforce Orientalist stereotypes of traditional patriarchal culture as responsible for their situation. The chapter shows how stories can be drawn into strategies of imperial statecraft and create forms of Western liberal subjectivity among young Afghan women.

The next two chapters look at how storytelling was deployed by immigrant rights advocates and philanthropic foundations to channel oppositional movements into limited paths of legislative advocacy and electoral campaigns. Chapter 4 examines the use of storytelling in the campaign for a Domestic Workers Bill of Rights in New York State. It shows how the use of stories brought visibility and recognition to undervalued domestic workers, but the limited tropes and liberal framings available to them in the media and legal arenas led the campaign to embrace more pragmatic and constrained outcomes that led to few changes in the lives of domestic workers. Chapter 5 looks at the undocumented students known as Dreamers who told their stories to the legislature and the media in their campaign for a DREAM Act that would give them legal status. I describe the attempts by mainstream immigration organizations to redirect the energy of the movement through mass storytelling trainings, and the battles the students engaged in to win the right to define themselves on their own terms.

The book concludes with a case from my long-term research in Venezuela, where the radical left-wing leader Hugo Chávez came to power in 1998 with a platform and policies to reverse the neoliberal agenda of previous administrations. The example of Venezuela under Chávez, what I refer to as a hybrid post-neoliberal state, provides an opportunity to examine what kinds of storytelling might be available in a context of heightened social movements and a state that has been rolling back neoliberalism. Although the state-sponsored Misión Cultura storytelling program also promotes forms of subject-making and narrative based in dominant liberal tropes, at the same time it has given rise to other stories that might truly offer the potential to construct new forms of revolutionary subjectivity based in the everyday life and political struggles of poor communities.

I conducted the research for this book between 2010 and 2015 in New York City, although I have long-term relationships with several of the groups involved. Part of my research involved obtaining the texts of stories. Some were available on websites, but they were not all written down. My research assistants and I copied and transcribed hundreds of testimonies presented at legislative hearings and press conferences, and used in flyers, websites, broadsheets, and other outreach materials. We tracked down media reports that profiled stories. We also contacted individuals who had participated in these storytelling workshops, and they made available copies of their stories to us. I use discourse analysis for analyzing the stories themselves. The stories vary greatly in form, length, and style. Some are short and examine one brief episode, some group together a range of specific experiences in one document, and others are lengthy recountings of an entire life story.

To study the practice of storytelling, I look at the conditions under which stories are told. There are different settings in which stories were produced and circulated. Some were written in online workshops with instructors in another country. Some were written in local workshops, following guidebooks that were devised by an organization. And others were written for the purpose of legal hearings in response to particular legal protocols. They were shared on websites, and in press conferences, rallies, and media articles. Each chapter considers how the specific arenas in which stories were told impacted the kind of stories that were produced, for instance, submitting a story via an online workshop versus producing a story for the purposes of a legal hearing. I examine instructional materials such as storytelling manuals, legal protocols, and promotional materials. I was able to observe events and workshops in New York City that are described in the book. I also carried out in-depth, open-ended interviews with workshop directors, participants, and movement leaders.

The ideas in this book were often developed together with the actors that I describe in this book—the organizers, grassroots movements, and migrant workers who came to their own awareness of the ways that they were being drawn into storytelling strategies. Where possible, I conceived of the project as a work of collaboration, and shared drafts with organizers and domestic workers. Through a series of working groups, educationals, film showings, panel discussions, and articles in popular magazines, we debated the ideas that are reflected in these pages. Especially crucial was a working group that I organized at the CUNY Graduate Center on "Narratives and Strategies of Domestic Worker Activism" on March 20, 2015, where we were able to have an open and frank discussion between academics, domestic workers, and grassroots organizers. It is only through knowing and observing the activities of these groups for an extended period of time that I had the chance to see the processes described here unfold, and I am grateful for the unique opportunity to analyze these processes together with them. I hope that this book will prove useful in the rigorous work of social transformation ahead that faces all of us.

CHAPTER 2

Charting the Storytelling Turn

Rigoberta Menchú Tum was a Quiché woman from the mountainous Altiplano region of Guatemala. During the 1970s, she was a clandestine organizer with the Committee for Peasant Unity (CUC), which mounted an underground struggle against the US-backed military dictatorship. Forced to flee to exile in Mexico in 1981, the following year Menchú was touring in Europe as a spokesperson for the movement, and she told her story to a Venezuelan ethnologist, Elisabeth Burgos-Debray.

The testimony, edited by Burgos-Debray and published as *I, Rigoberta Menchú*, was translated into a dozen languages and sold more than half a million copies worldwide. The extended narrative recounts Menchú's childhood experiences working in the *fincas* or ranches with her family at the age of eight, and the humiliating encounters of indigenous people with non-Mayan Guatemalans or *ladinos*, for whom they worked as domestic laborers and agricultural workers. Her narrative is interspersed with detailed descriptions of a hardscrabble life in the Altiplano, marriage and harvest ceremonies, the strength of community and family networks, and local fiestas. It is punctuated with tales of early death of siblings due to poverty and murder of local peasant men and women at the hands of landowners and elites. Menchú connects her personal experiences to a broader account of political struggle, culminating in the horrifying persecution, capture, and death by torture of her younger brother and mother, and the perishing of her father in an occupation. Despite some later controversies over this account,[1] the testimony succeeded in drawing international attention to the genocidal actions of the Guatemalan army and created political pressure to bring about a negotiated end to the prolonged civil war.

I, Rigoberta Menchú was one of the more prominent narratives to emerge from the 1970s era of radical social movements in Latin America. It was part of a genre of first-person life narratives known as *testimonio*, which played a crucial role in building international support for embattled peasant and worker struggles. In the early 1980s, as US-backed counterrevolutionary forces and Central American militaries unleashed violent reprisals against local populations, the production and dissemination of *testimonios* were centered on the need to build solidarity abroad.[2] And although the stories were personal, they gestured toward broader collective struggles. As John Beverley suggests, testimonial narratives made a connection between the individual subject, chronicling her or his growth and transformation, and a broader struggle of a marginalized class or group.[3] Testimonial subjects were grounded in a community of oppressed people.

Similar kinds of storytelling were apparent in the consciousness-raising strategies of the feminist and antirape movements in the United States during the 1970s. Women's rights activists shared intimate details of their lives in small groups, which led to a critique of both internal and external forms of oppression.[4] Migrant farm workers in California also pioneered tactics of consciousness raising. The United Farm Workers (UFW) developed the strategy of "one-on-one" organizing, akin to the feminist consciousness-raising groups that put emphasis on small, intimate conversation and storytelling rather than political oratory.[5] Farm workers with their roots in radical organizing traditions in Mexico, along with US feminists such as Margaret Randall who were the transcribers of testimonies in Latin America, played a key role in exchanging tactics of consciousness raising as they were developing in multiple sites.

Over the period of the ensuing two decades as social movements went into a period of decline and neoliberal policies were imposed unevenly and differentially across the globe, social movement storytelling represented by Menchú's testimony and feminist consciousness-raising groups was repurposed by states, international agencies, and the culture industries. In truth commissions, courtrooms, and legislatures, stories were abstracted from the goals of building mass movements that confronted power, and they were reoriented toward transaction and negotiation. The method of consciousness raising was retooled as the sharing of personal stories in televised spectacles, and was divorced from the political. Stories were shorn of their nuance and complexity to become short texts that would fit in a report or could be easily recitable for the purposes of a legal hearing, daytime talk show, or civil litigation. Storytelling promoted reconciliation and/or catharsis rather than class-based antagonism. Telling your story was used as a form of individual healing that avoided questions of structural violence and a broader critique of power relations.

In the new millennium, with broader shifts from productive capital to finance capital and the intensification of market values in guiding vast spheres of personhood and practices,[6] storytelling has come to be configured more closely on the model of the market. Nonprofit storytelling and advocacy storytelling are increasingly defined by a business model that emphasizes stories as an investment that can increase competition positioning, help to build the organization's portfolio, and activate target audiences. Social change organizations that work within nonprofit structures are encouraged by foundations to use stories as a way of driving their social impact through measurable goals such as legislative wins and voter registration. Narrating one's story is also a process of neoliberal subject-making, as actors learn how to be entrepreneurial, self-reliant actors who seek upward mobility rather than building class consciousness.

This chapter aims to give an overview of how the storytelling turn occurred in recent decades.[7] I do not intend for it to be an in-depth political history, but rather a chronicle of the broad shifts that led from the more deeply oppositional storytelling tactics of the 1960s and 1970s social movements to the transactional, therapeutic, and then market-based model of storytelling that currently predominates. It provides a background for the chapters to come, which focus on contemporary modes of storytelling.

THE CULTURAL POLITICS OF CONSENSUS

The 1980s and 1990s era of pacts and agreements that ended decades of protracted conflict from Central America to South Africa inaugurated a new moment that foregrounded consensus and common interests. Jacques Ranciére refers to this moment as based upon "the idea that the old schemata of politics in terms of conflict, class war, emancipation, and so on, had collapsed."[8] The emergent notion of consensus, enshrined in such documents as the Washington Consensus, which declared that conservatives and progressives could reach agreement based on common interests, means rather, for Ranciére, that which is censored. He argues that a politics of consensus is about what he calls "the partition of the sensible," where the "sensible" refers to the configuration of the lived common world, the givens of a situation. Partitioning the sensible is the politics of how those lived experiences are structured to make certain speakers, places, and questions visible and to make others invisible. Consensus based on common interests can be achieved only through concealing deeper questions of power and inequality. The emergence of a consensual politics is similar to what Chilean cultural theorist Nelly Richard refers to as a shift from the politics of antagonism, understood as struggle against dictatorial regimes, to a politics of transaction, marked by formulas of arranged agreements, or *concertación* in the Chilean case.[9]

Truth commissions were one vehicle that enabled the shift from an era of contention between classes in struggle to a détente brokered by neoliberal elites. Greg Grandin and Thomas Klublock argue that truth commissions "indexed the shift from the global crisis of the 1970s—where escalating cycles of conflict and polarization often led to either repressive dictatorships or deadlocked civil wars—to the post–Cold War would-be *pax* neoliberal."[10] The pacification of unions and radical peasant and indigenous organizations facilitated the shift from state-managed economies to privatized and deregulated neoliberal economies. The emphasis within truth commissions on reconciliation and forgiveness rather than a true reckoning with the atrocities visited upon the population by armies and dominant groups was a reflection of the continued coercive power of the latter. Early truth commissions such as the National Commission on Disappeared People under President Raúl Alfonsín in Argentina in 1983 sought to prosecute the junta officers and soldiers responsible for the torture and disappearance of tens of thousands of Argentine citizens. But following a series of coup attempts by the Argentine military, Alfonsín was forced to halt these prosecutions, and by the time of his successor Carlos Menem, military officers were to be pardoned in the name of national reconciliation. The next major truth commission in Chile in 1990 was the first to be called a Truth and Reconciliation Commission (TRC), and it did not attempt to make targeted prosecutions a part of its activities. The prioritization of catharsis and forgiveness over punishment was a concession to the ongoing strength of the military.[11] The jettisoning of the idea of legal prosecution was a marker of the weaknesses of the post–Cold War order.

The use of storytelling within truth commissions was crucial in producing the consensus that underlay nascent neoliberal orders. Although truth commissions have taken varied forms, from nationally administered bodies to forums convened by international agents such as the United Nations, they have generally relied on individual testimonies from those affected by conflict situations.[12] Truth commissions enabled the shift to a politics of consensus through a regulation of the testimonies that were told. This regulation happened in different ways depending on the specific form, but it could include the protocols and questionnaires soliciting stories, the response of the commission, the nature of questions asked by commissioners, the power of commissioners to accept or cut short responses, and the writing up of the stories in a written report.[13] By presenting victims as individuals rather than collective political subjects, by leaving out the systemic dimensions of abuse such as state repression or apartheid, and by emphasizing the importance of national healing over justice, truth commission storytelling helped lay the groundwork for new modes of engagement that sought rapprochement rather than a challenge to dominant classes. The approach of truth commissions came from the international human rights movement, which helped bring an end to the worst abuses. But, as Naomi Klein argues in the case of Latin America's Southern Cone, human rights advocates, funded by foundations such as Ford who had trained the new economic elite, disguised the economic agenda of free market politics that underlay the vast repression by asking only how but not why the atrocities happened.[14]

The procedures of gathering testimonies and presenting them in legal hearings individualized the nature and meanings of suffering, disaggregating the collective social justice movements that had preceded the commissions. Describing the Argentine truth commission, Julie Taylor argues that only individual motivation was amenable to the relating of testimony.[15] The judicial process suppressed collective forms of memory and motivation not only of the perpetrators but of the victims as well, who, she says, "were defined as individuals whose human rights had been violated rather than as political activists." Taylor gives the example of a youth from a Basque family, who was abducted by the military along with several friends for their association with the guerrilla forces in Tucuman. When giving their testimony, his parents remembered that only their son had been abducted but not any of his acquaintances, erasing the existence of confrontation between different political forces.[16] The broader picture of class-based groups in combat, or state-sponsored terror against specific ethnic, political, or racial groups, was lost in the presentation of testimonies as the stories of individuals who had suffered specific violations for which they were seeking redress or simply wanted to be heard.

In general, the narratives in truth commissions left out questions of structural power. Fiona Ross describes how the Act that established the TRC in South Africa contained narrow definitions of violence and violation, and it "did not address forms of structural violence or the racial discrimination that characterized apartheid."[17] The commissions also excised history from their accounts of why terror happened. Rather than viewing terror as a campaign against democratic and socialist claims on state power, or as paving the way for neoliberal free market orders, truth commissions presented violence as a temporary breakdown in social relations.[18] The one exception to this was the Guatemalan Historical Clarification Commission (CEH), which actually chronicled in detail the social and political context of the conflict. Facing pressures from an emerging pan-Mayan cultural movement, the commission showed violence to be integral to the process of state formation.[19] But as the findings of the report were disseminated through school textbooks and USAID-sponsored *radionovelas* (radio soap operas), they became watered down from the original strong indictment of state repression and genocide to a more neutral "culture-of-peace" framework that reinterpreted the causes of the conflict as a "culture of violence." A sixth-grade textbook from 2001 argued that the conflict in Guatemala occurred because during thirty-six years of civil war people "practiced a culture of violence."[20] In Guatemala, the task of promoting reconciliation took place less through the commission itself and more through the circulation of its findings.

Reconciliation was one of the key aspects of consensual politics. The spectacle of national unity depended on the performance of opposed groups that had been reconciled. The orchestration of reconciliation drew on global therapeutic discourses that presented psychological healing through narrative as central to the peace-building process. Therapeutic discourses evolved in the West through the feminist movement and social institutions, and from there they were introduced to Global South nations.

THERAPEUTIC DISCOURSE AS DISCIPLINARY POWER

The "therapeutic turn" is generally associated with the feminist movement in the United States, which used psychotherapy to understand and analyze internalized oppression. One of the ways they did this was through consciousness-raising groups, which, as described earlier in this chapter, sought to expand consciousness of oppression through personal testimony, sharing one's experience, and generalizing individual stories.[21] Over the period of the 1980s, many feminist organizations began merging their activist work with service provision, gradually giving up their movement ties or focusing on therapeutic work as the key to social change.[22] Feminist writing workshops also became popularized around this time, with the idea that writing one's story could be an important way of working through trauma. This gradually morphed into the emerging field of professional feminist therapy.[23] The professionalization of social movements separated psychological healing and personal testimony from the analysis and confrontation of power that the feminist movement had insisted upon.

Scholars have argued that therapeutic discourse operates as a form of disciplinary power, whereby individuals come to blame themselves for their problems and seek solutions by adapting to rather than challenging the structures that create those problems.[24] Therapeutic discourse expanded into a whole range of social institutions in the United States, including workplace management, social work, education, and the media.[25] Commercial television entered the fray to redefine and exploit issues such as rape, drug use, and sex change through the medium of the issue-oriented daytime talk show, structured around the moral authority of a host and expert. Talk shows encouraged people to narrate stories about their traumatic experiences as a means to find psychic resolution. They fashioned guidelines for new kinds of public storytelling about previously silenced issues, using the frame of therapy as a means for individualizing broader class-based identities. They encouraged personal testimony and catharsis as a means for resolving social issues from domestic violence to child abuse, in contrast to the feminist political activism that had championed these causes in an earlier decade. Talk shows avoided a critique of racism, economic inequality, and patriarchy; rather, the therapeutic discourse comes to dominate over broader social critique.[26]

Therapeutic discourse and the language of trauma were fairly unknown in the Global South nations of Latin America and Africa, where they were introduced through mental health professionals and defenders of victims' rights who were placed on the frontlines of postconflict areas through humanitarian organizations.[27] As Christopher Colvin argues, trauma centers often run parallel to forms of political intervention, with trauma counsellors operating alongside peacekeeping troops and conflict resolution experts.[28] As a means of processing troubling instances of violence and abuse, therapy was applied partially and incompletely during and beyond the TRCs. Yet as a framework for narrating healing and closure for individual subjects and, more broadly, the nation, these discourses became deeply tied up with the relating of testimonies and the demonstration of psychic damage in return for compensation. Didier Fassin and Richard Rechtman argue that the language of trauma became the most effective way for people to have their stories heard in the international arena.[29] Violence could only be understood in the language of trauma and suffering, and not in terms of the broader structural violence of poverty, global inequality, and war.[30]

In various commissions such as the TRC in South Africa, stories were framed using typical trauma narratives. Colvin describes these narratives as follows: "traumatic event followed by, in various combinations, numbness, intrusion, denial, anxiety, a narrative 'working through' and, finally, acceptance and integration through storytelling."[31] Within this discourse, trauma is seen as a singular event that leaves a wound on the individual psyche. Unless this trauma is exorcised through confronting and reliving the memory, the wound will continue to fester. It is only by "mastering of a painful past" that the wounds can be cleansed, and individual as well as national healing can take place.[32] As the result of this usage of the language of trauma in truth commission storytelling, the vocabulary of trauma became widespread in both the TRC and post-TRC South Africa.

In the period after the South African TRC, groups who were disillusioned with the process began to meet and organize, such as the Khulumani Support Group in Cape Town that Colvin analyzes in his research. Despite their antipathy toward the TRC process, Khulumani members often adopted the format of brief stories of harm circulated in search of some form of redress.[33] This is akin to what Wendy Brown has described as "wounded attachments," or identity politics structured by a Nietschean politics of *ressentiment*.[34] This politics casts victims as those who have suffered the "injury" of social subordination and seek not emancipation for themselves but rather revenge on the perpetrator through appeal to the law as a neutral arbiter. As Brown argues, this politics structured by *ressentiment* legitimizes the law as the guardian of individuals and not capable itself of causing injury[35]—rather than critiquing the sovereign subject of accountability that liberal universalism presupposes.[36] Like Brown's wounded subject who can only make claims for itself by inscribing its pain in politics, the survivors of violence can only hold out their stories of pain in exchange for a promise of recognition or reparations.[37] They cannot go beyond this to enunciate alternative visions that see beyond the pain.

STORIES AS SCRIPTED PERFORMANCE

The models of the truth commission and talk show helped to develop a storytelling template and set of practices that would be replicated in later contemporary initiatives. The template included the use of protocols and coaching to elicit specific kinds of stories. It consisted of the promotion of storylines that emphasized forgiveness and reconciliation. Storytelling practices also involved the construction of typologies such as the "good victim" that resonated with audiences. The good victim was one who was innocent, helpless, and incapacitated, with whom audiences could empathize.

Talk shows and truth commissions created the illusion of people spontaneously and freely telling their own stories, whereas actually the narratives told were carefully controlled. Laura Grindstaff, who carried out a fine-grained participant observation of two talk shows as an intern and production assistant, notes that the idea of "real people telling real stories" is actually the product of intense planning and coordination between producers, guests, and others.[38] Similarly, the commissioners and officials involved in truth commissions often presented the sharing of testimonies as akin to local oral practices of telling stories. Some even naturalized the process as grounded in traditional modes of storytelling. Archbishop Desmond Tutu claimed during the South African TRC: "Storytelling is central, not only to many religious practices in this country but also to the African tradition of which we are a part." He quotes the parliamentarian Ellen Kuzwayo as saying that "Africa is a place of storytelling."[39] Yet despite these attempts to situate truth commission testimonies within a genealogy of oral traditions such as the storytelling of the African griots, truth commissions carefully proscribed the kinds of stories that could be told, how they could be told, the dominant tropes to be employed, and the topics that could be addressed.

The South African TRC did originally begin in early 1996 with few constraints on the ways that the testimonies were related. Alejandro Castillejo-Cuéllar describes these initial testimonies as "long, personal and detailed renderings of the context that surrounded particular incidents"; "there were little practical constraints regarding form and content"; and they "often constituted complex textures that wove time and space in a not necessarily linear fashion."[40] The testimonies did not only focus on the actual violations that occurred, but often talked about broader experiences. Castillejo-Cuéllar gives the example of one mother who described the murder of her son fairly briefly, but then went on to describe in great detail the repercussions of his death, including the dislocation of the family, financial hardships, loneliness, and so on.[41] By September 1996, investigators were frustrated with the slow pace of data collection, with statements taking hours to complete and running thirty to forty pages. Data analysts and lawyers criticized the stories as incomplete, meandering, and poor quality, lacking in facts.[42] The kinds of knowledge that were produced by open-ended narratives could not be easily processed by a commission that had defined its mission as fact-finding in the service of truth recovery.

By 1997, the statement protocol for soliciting stories had shifted dramatically toward excavating a "forensic-factual notion of truth." This emphasis on uncovering the facts of the violations, with perpetrators confessing fully in exchange for amnesty, was related to the compromised position of the TRC within the negotiations over the transition to a postapartheid order.[43] The protocol went from being a series of open-ended questions to a highly specific questionnaire that the respondent was expected to answer concisely. This is an example of questions in one version of the protocol: "Briefly describe what happened to you or the person you are telling us about. Please tell us what happened? Who got hurt, killed or kidnapped? When did it happen? Who did it?"[44] The protocol made available forty lines, or one and a half pages, for responses to the questions.[45] At the actual hearings, committee members were assigned to help the testifiers relate their stories. Along with the protocols, the committee members helped shape the narratives from personal descriptions about painful experiences into easily processed data on rights abuses.[46] The stories were stripped of context and history, and the contemporary and ongoing effects of the conflict in people's lives were no longer seen as important.

In their shaping of stories, truth commissions constructed victim typologies. In the Peruvian truth commission, Kimberly Theidon argues that certain victim categories such as "innocent victims" and "sexually vulnerable women" became what she calls narrative capital.[47] Male-directed communal authorities in Peru developed "memory projects" to prepare for the arrival of TRC mobile teams. Communal authorities decided to discuss only the deaths that occurred at the hands of the armed forces, and not those committed by the Sendero Luminoso guerrilla organization. According to Theidon, women were often told to be quiet, leaving the narration of battles up to the men.[48] Although some women were armed and active combatants in the struggles, they were instructed to play the role of innocent victims, to reduce the suspicion that the community might have been guerrilla sympathizers. Similarly, in the Tribunal of Conscience in Guatemala, there was a desire for stories about "good victims" with whom spectators could empathize.[49] Women who collaborated with guerrillas or took up arms did not fit the profile of the good or innocent victim in the context of truth commissions.

Peruvian and Guatemalan women were asked to speak about sexual abuse and rape, rather than focusing on other aspects of gender discrimination or their protagonism in resistance movements. Bravery for women is defined solely on the basis of their willingness to speak openly about rape, and not the range of other ways that they defended themselves and their families during the armed conflict.[50] Women were often reluctant to retell stories of harm because they represented only one aspect of their lives, as was made apparent in the early narratives told in the South African TRC. But these victim categories were seen as the kinds of capital needed to receive monetary compensation or potential redress.

The truth commissions encouraged storylines that emphasized forgiveness and reconciliation. Colvin describes how in South Africa the categories of "healed victims" and "repentant perpetrators" were created through the process of the commissions.[51] The effort to create these kinds of new subjects as emblematic of the hope for reconciliation and forgiveness is well illustrated by the case of the Gugulethu Seven. Castillejo-Cuéllar describes the case of seven young activists who were ambushed and killed by South African security forces in the Gugulethu township in March 1986.[52] He discusses the 2000 film *Long Night's Journey into Day: South Africa's Search for Truth and Reconciliation*, directed by Frances Reid and Deborah Hoffmann, which shows an encounter organized by the TRC between the amnesty applicant Taphelo Mbelo, one of those responsible for the killings, and the mothers of the young activists. Mbelo asked the mothers for forgiveness, stating that "I know that I have done wrong, that I have done evil things." The mothers react negatively, one saying that she did not forgive him. Then, just before the meeting is about to be adjourned, one of the mothers offers a complex statement of forgiveness, invoking principles of Christianity, morality, and kinship.[53] Yet as Castillejo-Cuéllar argues, in the film the scenario is abstracted from historical context and social conditions and condensed into a representation of remorse from the perpetrator and forgiveness from the victim's family; it becomes an icon of reconciliation to be circulated and replicated as the foundations for a new "rainbow nation."[54]

Storylines and victim typologies on talk shows are strongly shaped by the format of the programs. The choice of topics affects who is solicited for the show and what they are able to talk about. Guests are labeled according to their designated role. Tags such as "cheating parents" and "mama's boy" make the guest into his or her problem, and nothing more. As Janice Peck argues: "The effect is to abstract these people and their troubles from the larger social world in which their everyday lives, their struggles, and the structural determinants of these problems exist."[55] The host is responsible for policing the boundaries of the topic by guiding the guests and audience back to certain points. They cut off some speakers while giving the platform to others, whether through humor in the case of Oprah Winfrey or overt guidance and restatement in the case of Sally Jessy Raphael.[56] The use of the topic frame effectively silences an awareness of deeper structures such as class. Peck gives the example of a Winfrey episode entitled "Couples Who Fight about Money." Two white couples, one wealthy and the other working class, and one black couple are set up to discuss how men control their wives by controlling the household finances. Guided by Winfrey and the guest expert, the audience comments address the gender differences between the couples. But by seeing the working-class white woman as being denied the pleasures of life by her husband, the wealthy woman as greedy and irresponsible, and the black woman who is the breadwinner as strong compared to her unemployed husband, the audience fails to see the ways in which gender intersects with race and class to affect the conflicts at play. Peck notes that "The problem perpetually 'unproblematized' in these talk shows is that of social class."[57] Although the shows give the illusion of addressing social issues in a collective audience-driven setting, in reality they work to individualize problems by blaming particular individuals with certain stereotyped traits for creating these issues.

The talk show format is not always able to contain the kinds of conflicts that it unleashes. Laura Grindstaff observes that the shows reflect a struggle between producers and talk show guests, who have their own agendas and desires.[58] This is particularly the case with activists, who may sometimes appear on talk shows to promote their own campaigns. Sometimes, once they have made it through the initial coaching by producers and taping is underway, activists may simply deviate from the scripted performance expected of them and assert their own views.[59] The limitation is that producers can edit the final version, cutting out these alternative views or simply making the activists look foolish, which is why some activists refuse to go on talk shows.[60] But attempts by hosts and producers to control and script talk show discourse are not always entirely successful. Similarly, victim testimonies in truth commissions sometimes broke through limiting protocols to express anger and address structures of power. Klein describes how a tobacco farmer who was tortured under Argentine military rule came to give his testimony at the Argentine Tribunal against Impunity in 1990, and instead of naming the soldiers who had abused him, he pointed out the local and foreign corporations who controlled the politicians: "Ford Motors, Monsanto, Philip Morris."[61]

In addition to truth commissions and talk shows, in the 1980s, courtrooms became another venue for storytelling as domestic violence, anti-rape, and child abuse survivor movements used personal stories as a way of engaging legislators and lawmakers. Like the victim typologies of the truth commissions and talk shows, legal advocacy also relied on and reproduced certain tropes. Feminist activists had won for survivors of domestic violence the right to claim self-defense in cases of homicide. But Francesca Polletta argues that in the courtroom, women who killed their abusers were often limited to stock characters—being either powerless and incapacitated victims or, conversely, unapologetic and provocative.[62] Lawyers tended to emphasize the former as "good victims" and if they departed too much from this stereotype by being angry or aggressive, then they would be penalized for it. But adopting the stereotype of the helpless female may have hampered them from defending their rights in other areas, such as retaining custody of their children.

Similarly, child sexual abuse advocacy groups won the rights for adult survivors to bring civil suits against offenders, in cases where the statutes of limitations prevented criminal cases. But Nancy Whittier argues that in contrast to the empowering identity of "survivor" that the movement had championed, in civil litigation, survivors had to present themselves as "damaged victims."[63] Although the movement produced survivors who spoke without shame and were in control of their own lives, in court, they would have to show that they needed therapy and suffered lasting effects from the abuse. Whittier argues that "the requirements of civil litigation make it almost impossible to maintain an oppositional identity as survivor, but rather require participants to display a pathologized identity."[64] Following Brown's logic of "wounded attachments," victims had to rely on medical discourses of pain and suffering in order to qualify for compensation, rather than as survivors of patriarchal violence. Through the legal process, domestic abuse and child abuse survivors often lost their ability to define themselves on their own terms.

Legal storytelling not only promoted certain stock characters, but it also encouraged specific storylines. James Nolan describes the case of drug courts, where drug offenders were offered the option of court-monitored treatment as an alternative to traditional adjudication.[65] Defendants submit to therapeutic treatments and frequent meetings with a judge, who may dismiss the criminal charges or expunge the defendant's drug arrests if they can demonstrate through their stories to the court that they have successfully completed the treatments. Nolan argues that stories with "happy endings," where the drug court has helped the defendant to turn his or her life around, are the most encouraged storylines. The stories follow a particular script, drawing on therapeutic symbols such as self-esteem, ownership of treatment, and assessment of feelings. Not telling the right story means that the person is in denial.[66] Successful legal storytelling is about learning the right tropes and storylines through which to frame one's narrative—tropes and storylines that resonate with lawmakers, judges, and policymakers.

The rise of these new approaches to storytelling as pioneered in truth commissions, talk shows, and legal advocacy took place in the context of pacified social movements and the global turn toward neoliberal economies. In the new millennium, with the growth of nongovernmental organizations (NGOs) and nonprofits as a privatized form of service delivery and professionalized social action, these refashioned storytelling approaches were to find expression in various kinds of instrumental projects and campaigns designed by governments, political consultants, and grantmakers.

THE NEOLIBERAL REFASHIONING OF STORYTELLING

Storytelling was retooled again toward the beginning of the new millennium, following transformations in the nature of capital and the neoliberal state in Euro-America. Wendy Brown points to a shift within neoliberalism from productive to finance capital and profit rooted in economic rents rather than production.[67] Along with this shift, there has been a marketization of all spheres: "neoliberal rationality disseminates the *model of the market* to all domains and activities—even where money is not at issue—and configures human beings exhaustively as market actors."[68] As political and social realms come to be governed by market principles and the state is further degovernmentalized under conditions of advanced neoliberal rule, Nikolas Rose argues that the responsibilities for resolving issues of order, health, productivity, and security are increasingly devolved to self-regulating communities.[69] The pared-back neoliberal state was justified by reference to empowered communities who could carry out the tasks of social welfare and self-improvement. Under these conditions, storytelling comes to be more closely defined in terms of market principles, stories are valued for the returns they can provide, and storytelling campaigns encourage people to participate in order to resolve their own problems and in service of narrow goals such as mobilizing voters and raising money for political campaigns.

Redefining Stories Within a Market Model

Stories as they were told in truth commissions and talk shows were commodified and packaged to circulate within global humanitarian and media networks. In the new millennium, stories come to be redefined within a business model. Within a reconfigured field of social action where service-oriented nonprofit organizations are dependent on foundation funding, there has been a proliferation of toolkits, philanthropy manuals, and websites that instruct nonprofits in how to compete successfully for funding and "target audiences," and many manuals have been produced on storytelling. Jonah Sachs's *Winning the Story Wars* is one example. Another is Paul VanDeCarr's seventy-two-page manual, *Storytelling and Social Change: A Guide for Activists, Organizations and Social Entrepreneurs*. These guides draw on the financial language of investment, market metrics, and competition in advising organizations how to pursue a storytelling strategy.

The storytelling strategies of international agencies and nonprofits are often shaped by communications consulting firms, which encourage them to behave like firms, to enhance their competitive positioning, attract investors, and increase their rating.[70] In *Storytelling and Social Change*, VanDeCarr advises organizations to use stories to "neutralize the effect of your opposition" and "leverage your active opponent's force in your favor."[71] VanDeCarr interprets the storytelling of gay rights activist Harvey Milk and an activist prank by the group Yes Men within this neoliberal language of neutralizing and leveraging the opposition. In an article called "Making the Case to Invest in Story," the Vice President of Global Communications at the Rockefeller Foundation suggests borrowing story strategies from comparable nonprofit organizations so that your organization can be "as cutting edge as the competition."[72] Storytelling is seen as a "good investment"[73] and a "best practice"[74] that can produce returns if others see the value of a storytelling approach.

In this market model of storytelling, traditional categories of social movement organizing are replaced with new corporate language that connotes consensus building and practical problem solving over confronting power and class conflict. Rather than supporters or allies, people are seen as "stakeholders," who must be invited to participate in storytelling projects.[75] To change the minds of people like legislators and other decision makers, you need their "buy-in."[76] A director of a communications consulting firm speaks about having "buy-in" at the top of your organization and creating "demand for stories" by including stories on a regular basis at staff meetings, in newsletters, and on websites.[77] Grantmakers are encouraged to make storytelling a part of their "portfolio."[78] Social issues are reduced to technical problems that can be resolved by investing in storytelling as best practices.

Storytelling has been touted by grantmakers as an efficient tool for evaluation and measurement of impact. Anthropologist John Gledhill refers to the continuous assessment and demands for evidence of goals being met among development agencies and NGOs as part of an "audit culture."[79] He traces this audit culture to the disciplinary effects of neoliberal regimes that inculcate in people a need to maximize labor market performance through systems of project evaluation rather than measuring their actual impact on the lives of human beings. In a storytelling guide for grantmakers, VanDeCarr argues that story "helps communities assess needs and strengths and evaluate a program throughout its life."[80] The managing director of evaluation for the Rockefeller Foundation says in the guide that storytelling can provide small organizations with a cheap way of managing typical monitoring and evaluation functions required of them by foundations.[81] Storytelling is also promoted as a way to access people's private information and build databases that can be used for targeting people in campaigns, just as corporations do.[82] Storytelling does not just assist with evaluation metrics and outcomes; it comprises them. As grantmaker Gara LaMarche states in the Afterword to the strategy guide, "Demonstrated impact is not a substitute for storytelling—it is the story."[83] A storytelling project by the NGO GlobalGiving suggests that stories can help "stakeholder" voices to be heard by "developing better feedback loops."[84] Between 2010 and 2011, the organization collected 57,220 stories in Kenya and Uganda about when a person in the community tried to change something. Feedback loops are valued above the pursuit of social change itself. GlobalGiving quotes the Vice President of the Center for Global Development who says, "As change-makers, we should not try to design a better world. We should make better feedback loops."[85]

This storytelling strategy draws on marketing language of "targeted audiences," "segmenting" audiences, and "activating" audiences, in order to describe outreach to the public. The language of "audience" itself implies a passive role of consumption. A "target audience" may be high school students' parents or voters. The goal of telling stories is to "activate" this "target audience."[86] You must also "segment," or specify the audiences you want to reach through storytelling. VanDeCarr suggests a technocratic approach of "segmenting" your "audiences" on a 1–5 scale, from active supporters to opponents. Then you can create tailored strategies for each of these groups.[87] Especially in an era of new media users, VanDeCarr argues that your audience can participate by sharing their own stories, whether on LGBTQ youth suicide or mass incarceration.[88] It is not just that this market-oriented language has infiltrated the work of social justice organizing, but that participation is reduced to sharing or commenting on a story on a website or donating to a Kickstarter campaign.

The Paradox of Participation

During the late 1990s and new millennium, "telling one's story" became linked to discourses of participation, empowerment, and social capital. As the facilitating and enabling state is relieved of its obligations to plan from the Center, Rose argues that individuals organized into local groupings must take responsibility for meeting their own needs in what he refers to as "governing through community."[89] Efforts to govern through community are premised on building social capital and encouraging participation, as a way to develop the kinds of local-level networks that can promote economic growth and alleviate poverty. In their storytelling campaigns, organizations and political consultants use the discourses of participation and empowerment to motivate people while proposing limited solutions to the problems raised. In her study of postdictatorship Chile, Julia Paley refers to this as the "paradox of participation" whereby "participation offered a sense of meaning to citizens at the same time as it limited avenues through which citizens could act."[90] Using the language of empowerment and participation, people are directed to tell their stories in order to bolster election campaigns, mobilize voters, raise money for organizations, and engage in legislative advocacy—confining their range of action within a narrow set of alternatives.

We can see the paradox of participation in the Camp Obama experience, spearheaded by strategist Marshall Ganz. Ganz is a Harvard lecturer who had spent many decades as an organizer in the civil rights movement in the South and the farm workers struggle in California. After Barack Obama declared his candidacy, Ganz used his Kennedy School connections to broker a meeting with Obama and his political consultant David Axelrod in April 2007, and he was invited to the campaign headquarters in Chicago the next month. In June, Ganz was given the task of setting up a series of workshops known as Camp Obama, where young people would be coached in various election campaign strategies, including how to tell their story of conversion to Obama's message.[91] In his recapitulation of the campaign, Ganz argues that he wanted to move away from the conventional approach to campaigns, which was based on marketing. Rather than employ political marketers who sell candidates by appealing to people as consumers, Ganz proposed "the development of volunteer leaders, rooted in communities they are trying to organize and on whom the vitality of the movement rests."[92] At the core of Ganz's approach was the idea that stories appeal much more effectively to people than "traditional scripts, talking points, or messaging."[93] People were encouraged to tell their stories at volunteer trainings, house meetings, and when speaking to voters.[94]

Ganz employed the rhetoric of participation and empowerment, encouraging people to participate by telling their stories in pursuit of narrowly defined goals. Volunteers did not come up with a collective agenda based on the expectations of their members—the candidate is the one who comes up with the agenda. They do not form relationships with voters. Given the scale of the operation, they are just required to bring people out to vote. These narrow goals are reflected in the kinds of organizing strategies that Ganz focused on in the Camp Obama workshops. Whereas civil rights and farm worker organizing relied on a range of strategies, the Camp Obama trainings focused mostly on storytelling, while dropping most of the other organizing skills. According to Aaron Schutz and Marie Sandy, the Obama election campaign resembled more an evangelical effort of conversion than an organizing campaign.[95] The social networks and infrastructure created through the 2008 and 2012 elections campaigns, referred to by Ganz as "civic capital," were the basis of the Organizing for Action (OFA) group. On the barackobama.com website, OFA is described as "the grassroots movement built by millions of Americans to pass the agenda we voted for in 2012."[96] But OFA was not an independent, mass-based movement equipped with the ability to put pressure on the administration. It was rather a network of volunteers who were assembled to support the proposed policy reforms of the Obama administration. As one participant in the Camp Obama workshops noted, "The focus is on motivating involvement through the emotional pull of storytelling, not inculcating the conceptual and practical tools of democratic mobilization."[97] It is not surprising then that the OFA group demobilized, its urgent task of voter conversion completed.

Observers of the Obama campaign have noted that there was a concerted effort not to engage young people who were already organized into networks, which would require a higher degree of accountability from the president once in office.[98] Rather, the Obama campaign drew constituents of young people, migrants, hip-hop activists, and African Americans away from other kinds of independent organizing and into the electoral campaign.[99] Because they were not organized outside of electoral campaign networks, these volunteers were disempowered once the campaign was over, with few channels to press their concerns before an established administration.

Emotions and Values in a Neoliberal Era

The utilitarian deployment of stories and storytelling in electoral campaigns and advocacy projects enabled a valorization of the individual, an emphasis on values over ideas, and feelings over political analysis. What is most compelling about stories is the emotional connections they can make with the audience. Stories convince not through logical arguments but rather through the visceral power of personal experience. That emotional bond can be usefully harnessed in order to couch political critique; feeling and thinking can be parallel and mutually interactive processes.[100] But the contemporary approach to storytelling by political strategists and consultants is one that privileges feeling and emotions, tying them to an amorphous notion of values that discounts a critique of macro structures and political analysis.

During the Camp Obama trainings, Ganz argued that the strength of storytelling lay in its ability to promote "values" rather than "ideas." He contrasted the typical approach by Democratic party candidates of focusing on the "means" of public action that include policies or programs, with Obama's strategy of focusing on the "ends" of public action—these being values and moral reform.[101] Ganz contrasted what he refers to as "values-based organizing" with "issue-based organizing," arguing that because values are experienced emotionally, they can be a source of moral energy.[102] Camp Obama volunteers were explicitly instructed to resist from engaging voters in questions of policy; instead, they were asked to refer people to Obama's website.[103] Two volunteers in the trainings, Hahrie Han and Elizabeth McKenna, say that the emphasis on values rather than policy positions such as healthcare, the war in Iraq, or the economy helped to win over conservative voters in battleground states who may not have shared their political positions but could relate to people's personal reasons for supporting Obama.[104] But this focus on values rather than policy depends on removing controversial issues from the table. By valorizing values and emotions over practical policy decisions about key issues, the campaign further contributed to a binary of emotions and analysis.

In a Camp Obama training excerpted on YouTube, the trainer Joy Cushman emphasized to volunteers the importance of reaching out to voters through the concept of values rather than strategy or analysis.[105] She said to them, "Stories connect to our values, and we don't *think* our values, we *feel* our values." The values that were promoted through the Camp Obama trainings were often those of the nation, the family, and faith. The nationalist narrative is embodied in Obama's speech to the Democratic National Convention in 2004, which is a staple of the Camp Obama toolkit and Ganz's Harvard course in Public Narrative. During the Camp Obama training, a group of young, racially diverse organizers watches an excerpt from the speech. The excerpt begins with Obama's story of his father growing up in a small village in Kenya. Obama immediately ties the personal story of his father to a nationalist discourse about America, as "a beacon of freedom and opportunity" where his father got a scholarship. Weaving in the story of his white mother who was born in Kansas City, Obama frequently connects his own story as part of a "larger American story." He presents his vision of a tolerant and generous America as embodied in his own experiences as the child of an African immigrant who could one day run for president, although there is a constant slippage between the ideal meritocratic America that Obama envisions and the one that already exists, the one that he argues has made his story possible.

After playing the excerpt, Cushman directs the volunteers to comment on the choices that Obama and others made in this story. The training materials emphasize that the choice made by individuals at a key moment is both a crucial element of plot in storytelling and a model for the kinds of conversion stories that these volunteers will tell about why they decided to follow Obama. One African American male volunteer says, "One story that I heard is that he refused to be a victim of circumstance despite the cards that life dealt them." Cushman agrees that Obama's parents chose not to be victims, and one way they did this was by naming him Barack. She ends by saying that "The story of self is all about choice." The conversation valorizes the neoliberal discourse of individual choice over the macro structures that shape people's life chances.

The campaign organizers needed a simple way to convince people to vote for Obama, and this is what Ganz gave them. The actual complexity of people's life histories and stories was not necessary for the campaign. In all of his materials, Ganz emphasizes the idea of the "two-minute story." Volunteers should practice telling their story in two minutes or less. The story-crafting sessions actually began with an extended discussion and sharing of personal experiences. One participant in the August 2007 Camp Obama training in Atlanta recounts how the seven volunteers in his group shared meaningful and rich stories: Ben, who grew up on an Alabama farm as one of fifteen children, lost his father at age ten. Lavell lost his mother to breast cancer as a child growing up in a poor neighborhood of Queens, and Tryshanda came from a failing school system and was told that black girls couldn't enter the field of astrophysics where she wanted to study.[106] But having shared these intensely personal stories, the volunteers were asked to rewrite their stories to emphasize how they made the decision to work for the election of Obama. One of these stories was that of volunteer Susan Christopher, from the Camp Obama training session held in Burbank, California, in July 2007. The story was uploaded to YouTube, where it has over 6,000 views to date.[107] In two minutes and twenty seconds, Christopher relates how she felt when she hesitantly attended a training session and she heard Ganz talking about how Obama was a return of the hope embodied by the Mississippi marches and Cesar Chavez. She describes her reaction in emotive terms: "I felt my heart softening again, I felt myself able to give a little bit more of me to this process." Christopher doesn't talk about her intellectual reaction to Obama's policies but her visceral and bodily reaction to hearing the public narrative of Obama as framed by Ganz. There is an evangelical sense of rebirth that drives these kinds of narratives, which is not surprising given the religious underpinnings of Ganz's approach.

Despite references to Mississippi marches and civil rights during the training sessions, in separating emotions from analysis, the Obama campaign was vastly different from these earlier campaigns. In their book *Passionate Politics*, Francesca Polletta, James Jasper, and Jeff Goodwin describe how contentious movements like the Black Power movement and the women's movement in the 1960s and 1970s drew on a "politics of rage" and "outlaw emotions" as the basis of powerful political challenges.[108] According to the authors, "emotions can be strategically used by activists *and* be the basis for strategic thought."[109] By contrast, the separation of feeling from thought and values from politics by the Obama campaign were related to its goals, which were not to challenge broader structures of patriarchy and racism like the earlier civil rights movements, but rather to elect a president.

The shift away from political analysis and toward an amorphous notion of values is often framed in terms of collectivities, envisaged as natural and organic. In his "Telling Your Public Story" worksheet, Ganz states that personal stories should be linked to a Story of Us, which refers to shared identities based on family, faith, communities, and nations in which we participate. He says, "Your challenge will be to define an 'us' upon whom you will call to join you in action motivated by shared values, values you bring alive through storytelling." On the basis of shared values such as religion, or more vaguely, hope, individuals come together in a culture of consensus to support a candidate or heal a nation. Christopher finishes her two-minute story by alluding to Obama as a candidate who can heal the racial divisions of the country: "It's the beginning of a healing for our nation, and a healing of generations." Rather than connecting the Story of Us to a particular class or race-based group struggling for its rights, the Camp Obama trainings present the "Us" as the family, professional association, or religious group who needs to be mobilized to vote, or the divided nation that must be reconciled.

The Camp Obama storytelling model was widely disseminated once Obama came into office. The Camp Obama worksheets and workbooks were circulated through trainings by Ganz's National Organizing Institute

(NOI) and many other organizations including the Sierra Club and MoveOn, as well as the websites of prominent journalists like Bill Moyers. Camp Obama trainers like Cushman came to play an important role in subsequent trainings with immigrant rights groups and Dreamers. Together with the other training materials devised by development agencies, nonprofits, and NGOs, Ganz's materials comprised an "organizing toolbox" that was applied to the immigrant rights movement, workers movements, and used by foundations in the Obama era.

The social movements of the 1960s and 1970s used confrontational tactics such as strikes, marches, boycotts, guerrilla warfare, and occupations to create a new terrain of the possible. It was in this context of revolutionary mobilization that social movements developed interrelational models of storytelling, based in consciousness raising, one-on-one organizing, and *testimonio*, as a way of working through more deeply their analysis of power relations, communicating to wider audiences, and building their organizations. But alongside a period of repression and professionalization of social movements globally, there was the establishment of neoliberal orders in need of legitimation. It was these very storytelling tactics pioneered by social movements themselves that—stripped of history and context, divorced from political analysis, and employed in isolation from more adversarial methods—were adopted and refashioned by truth commissions, talk shows, and legal advocacy groups to lay the groundwork for more transactional modes of political engagement that promoted reconciliation over class-based antagonism. In the new millennium, with the shift to financial capital and a spread of the market model to noneconomic domains and conduct, storytelling came to be construed in terms of competitive positioning and market metrics. It also dovetailed with other discourses such as participation and empowerment that encouraged people to take responsibility for their conditions while limiting the avenues by which they could act.

What is it about stories that made them such an ideal candidate for this juncture? My answer is that stories on their own, disembedded from their contexts and as the relating of isolated personal experiences, facilitated an individualizing of collective struggles. Stories valorized experience above structure, falling prey to a relativist dogma that each person's truth is as valid as another. They promoted emotional response and feeling over thinking, creating a binary that was never present in earlier iterations. And storytelling encouraged the idea that individual redress or compensation, such as court judgments in favor of battered women, would provide the solution to deeply entrenched systems of poverty and patriarchy. Throughout the process, the illusion that highly curated and scripted stories were real and authentic was necessary to their success. Talk shows emphasized "real people telling real stories," and truth commission officials insisted on the mythic origins of storytelling practices in traditional cultures. The spectacle of stories as cathartic for individuals and for divided nations has been crucial in giving legitimacy to orders ranging from postapartheid South Africa to post-Bush America. This is the backdrop for the storytelling projects that animate the pages of this book, from US-sponsored projects in Afghanistan, to advocacy campaigns by undocumented migrants in the United States, and story workshops in Venezuela.

CHAPTER 3

Stories and Statecraft

Why Counting on Apathy Might Not Be Enough

Afghan women could serve as ideal messengers in humanizing the ISAF [International Security Assistance Force] role in combating the Taliban because of women's ability to speak personally and credibly about their experiences under the Taliban, their aspirations for the future, and their fears of a Taliban victory. Outreach initiatives that create media opportunities for Afghan women to share their stories with French, German, and other European women could help to overcome pervasive skepticism among women in Western Europe toward the ISAF mission.

CIA Red Cell Special Memorandum, March 11, 2010

In March 2010, with the Dutch government pulling out troops from the US-led war in Afghanistan, the CIA released a confidential memo calling for targeted manipulation of public opinion using stories by Afghan women.[1] The subheading of the memo, "Why Counting on Apathy Might Not Be Enough," refers to the indifference among the public in Germany and France that allowed these countries to send more troops, a strategy that might not be sustainable if there were more Afghan civilian casualties or public debates. The memo calls for the circulation of stories by Afghan women to humanize the military intervention and build support among Western European women for the war effort.

The CIA memo points to the uses of storytelling in statecraft, with geopolitical strategy and intervention pursued not just through military aggression and economic pressure but justified by emotional accounts of oppressed Afghan women victimized by the Taliban. In May of the previous year, Masha Hamilton had set up the Afghan Women's Writing Project (AWWP), a series of online creative writing workshops conducted by US-based mentors with Afghan women in English. The stories composed in the workshops are edited and published on the AWWP website and, judging by the comments sections, are read mostly by women in the United States and other Western countries. The project was partly funded by the US State Department, which is not surprising given its resonances with the memo. The support for these initiatives reflects an embrace of "soft power" strategies of storytelling within US foreign policy as articulated by the political strategist Joseph Nye: "In today's information age, success is the result not merely of whose army wins but also of whose story wins."[2] The rhetorical guise of women's emancipation in soft power strategies is not new. During colonial wars such as Algeria in the 1950s, the French sought to use mobile sociomedical teams of military women to make contact with Algerian women and promote a message of women's emancipation to be achieved through French victory over the guerrilla forces.[3] This was replicated in such projects as the "Human Terrain System," which sent anthropologists to Afghanistan and Iraq to gather cultural data with the goal of using empathy as a weapon.[4]

The entanglements between the US State Department and a women's storytelling project in Afghanistan is part of a history of alignments between imperialist interventions and the language of feminism that scholars have referred to as colonial feminism.[5] Leila Ahmed defines colonial feminism as the use of feminist ideas and the notion of men oppressing women in the service of colonialism to "render morally justifiable its project of undermining or eradicating the cultures of colonized peoples."[6] Drawing on Edward Said's account of Orientalism as the ways in which European culture produced notions of its others as backward and traditional,[7] feminist scholars argue for an analysis of gendered Orientalism, marking an awareness of the complicity between "Orientalism's imperialist operations" and certain representations by Western feminists of the Orient and its women.[8] Combined with other key writings such as Chandra Talpade Mohanty's "Under Western Eyes,"[9] which she updated in 2003, these interventions powerfully challenged depictions of non-Western women as tradition-bound and victimized as compared to their educated, modern, and free-willed Western counterparts.

From the 1990s onward, partly as a result of the impact of feminist writings on Orientalism, monological discourses on the "oppression" of non-Western women gave way to new tropes of agency and empowerment. As Meyda Yeğenoğlu argues, "what the Western audience desires to hear is the native's own voice, the true and authentic story of the situation of women in Muslim societies, as opposed to the negative Orientalist stereotypes."[10] This desire can help account for the emergence of pulp nonfiction genres of autobiographical writing by Muslim women who escape their situations of abuse[11] and the popularity of TED talks featuring stories of Afghan women who have overcome oppression through education. It can also explain the resonance of projects such as AWWP, which seek to give voice to Afghan women to tell their own stories directly to Western audiences. But despite the new emphasis on Afghan women speaking for themselves and becoming self-determining agents, a "positional superiority" continues to inform these projects.[12]

Positional superiority refers to the idea of the West as a site of progressive gender equality, even though, as Amy Farrell and Patrice McDermott argue, since the late 1970s the women's movement in the United States had been facing a backlash from conservative forces around entrenched gender-based issues of workplace discrimination, poverty, and violence.[13] Farrell and McDermott describe how, after the events of September 11, 2001 and the onset of the US-led war on terror, liberal feminist groups like the Feminist Majority were able to gain renewed relevance, resources, and legitimacy by focusing on Afghan women oppressed by the Taliban, a focus that deflected attention from domestic issues like the abuses of women in prison and the military in the United States. While acknowledging the good intentions of these feminist organizations, I argue, following Laura Nader, that positional superiority functions as a means to assert authority over Afghan women, but it is also a way of diverting the attention of women in the West from the inequalities they continue to face at home.[14]

This chapter is focused on the uses of storytelling in imperial statecraft as a soft power strategy that produces Afghan women as upwardly mobile and entrepreneurial subjects while defusing opposition in Afghanistan and in Western countries to the US-led war and occupation. The directors and mentors of the AWWP are genuinely motivated by a desire to share the stories of Afghan women widely and to make visible the abuses they suffer, but the framing of the project encourages responses and outcomes that often reproduce structural conditions of subjection rather than challenging them. What does it mean for Afghan women to tell their own stories? How does storytelling become implicated in the formation of new kinds of neoliberal subjectivity that accord with Western modes of domination? What do these stories by Afghan women tell us about the anxieties and desires of Western women? What can they tell us about the anxieties and desires of Afghan women themselves? How, at the same time, might these stories make available the possibility for alternative perspectives? Rather than seeing the narratives that circulate within humanitarian and digital media circuits as telling the truth about subaltern lives, this chapter explores how stories can be drawn into strategies of imperial statecraft, can help to construct modes of Western liberal and neoliberal subjectivity, and, conversely, may contain strategically placed critiques of imperialist projects.

CAN THE AFGHAN WOMAN SPEAK? STORIES AS MEDIATED TEXTS

The idea of Afghan women speaking for themselves and telling their stories without mediation is central to the agenda of the AWWP. In the history and mission statement on the website, AWWP founder Masha Hamilton says that in trying to learn about Afghanistan, she found that "the voices of women were primarily available only through the media or their men; we heard little from them directly."[15] The project is aimed at "allowing Afghan women to have a direct voice in the world, not filtered through male relatives or members of the media."[16] At a reading of Afghan women's poetry in Los Angeles in May 2014, Executive Director of AWWP Lori Noack emphasized the unmediated nature of the stories: "It doesn't go through the media, it doesn't go through an approved 'something' that their husband might have said." The stories go through the channels of AWWP and are published on the website, where people around the world can read them and, says Noack, "you know right then that's what the women in Afghanistan are really thinking." This discourse of authenticity—that these are true stories by real Afghan women—is central to the project. But such language conceals the ways in which the "voice" of Afghan women presented is strongly mediated through the framing of the workshops, the selection of writers, the requirements of funding bodies, and the structure of the workshops.

There is a story on the AWWP website by a woman named Roya, called "Feathers of Freedom, Washed Away."[17] Roya narrates the story of a woman called Freshta, a young and intelligent woman who married young and had six children to a man who mistreated her. She started having problems with her children, especially her aggressive and angry oldest son, who one day killed her. Roya relates that the son was put in jail, but then he was released and on the official documents it was said that Freshta was mad. At the end of the story, Roya says that "They wrote with a red pen in the history book of her life: She was insane. She committed suicide." Roya expresses here the ways in which others have sought to speak on behalf of Afghan women, to write their lives for them. Her story compels us to ask whether Afghan women can speak for themselves and tell their own stories. Caught between patriarchy and imperialism,[18] can the Afghan woman speak?

In the mission statement, Hamilton frames Afghan women as silenced and voiceless. Hamilton relates that she became interested in the plight of Afghan women after seeing a video of an Afghan woman named Zarmeena being executed by the Taliban for allegedly killing her husband. The execution occurred in November 1999. It was secretly recorded by a member of the Revolutionary Association of the Women of Afghanistan (RAWA), and the organization smuggled the video out of Afghanistan. But it was not seen widely until the events of September 11, 2001, focused attention on a military intervention to defeat the Taliban, and then the video was broadcast repeatedly by CNN. RAWA was critical of the ways the video was ignored at first and then harnessed in support of an ideological agenda.[19] Women like Zarmeena become visible only when it is convenient for American foreign policy. Like the American media establishment, Hamilton also uses the case of Zarmeena to create the myth of the voiceless Afghan woman:

> I knew far too little about this woman to be party to such a stark and intimate moment. Zarmeena: her name. Seven: the number of children she had. And her alleged crime: beating her husband to death with a hammer as he slept. It all amounted to a scattered detail or two, not a life story. This absence of narrative, in fact, was true for virtually all women in Taliban-held Afghanistan. They were gagged as well as hidden, I understood then.[20]

Hamilton further interprets the video to show that Afghan women were "hidden beneath burkhas" and "their stories were silenced." The idea that all Afghan women are silent was also articulated by Noack, who referred to Afghanistan as "a nation of muzzled women."[21]

The AWWP presents itself as giving a voice to silent Afghan women. Margaret Mills has suggested that the idea of Afghan women as passive and voiceless is an Orientalist construction.[22] Change cannot be generated from within Afghan society; rather, it must be brought through Western intervention.[23] This Orientalist perspective ignores the struggles of Afghan women who persisted through years of war and conflict. Elaheh Rostami-Povey recounts how during the Taliban era women risked their lives to teach in secret schools, they distributed printed materials for education, and they fashioned strategies of mobility through the use of the full veil burkha and masculine escorts known as *mahram*, who accompanied them to secret schools and meetings.[24] When Afghan women are presented as passive and silent victims, this history of struggle and resistance is erased.

The AWWP website flags its inclusion of all Afghan women from different political backgrounds and perspectives. However, given the affiliations of its staff and board members with the US government, most of the Afghan writers they have included in the project are supportive of the US presence in Afghanistan. Hamilton worked for the US embassy in Kabul for sixteen months after founding and then resigning from the project. Other board members worked as communications staff in the US embassy in Kabul and for USAID (US Agency for International Development). The AWWP subsisted partly on grants from the State Department, and about 75% of this funding was cut after the United States withdrew from Afghanistan at the end of 2014.

It has also received grants from foundations, individuals, and nonprofits such as the Fetzer Institute.

Since most of the workshops are conducted in English, they are available only to a very small pool of urban, literate, English-speaking Afghan women. Only about 17% of Afghan women are literate, with that rate dropping to as low as 1.6% in the southern provinces.[25] A much smaller percentage of these women speak English. The AWWP participants are generally middle-class Afghan women working in nongovernmental organizations (NGOs) or nonprofits with ties to the US government. For instance, the Teenage Writers Workshop draws its participants entirely from the School of Leadership Afghanistan, a "small, highly selective and privately funded organization" set up by an American entrepreneur and an Afghan woman who was sponsored by the State Department to study in Wisconsin.[26] Noack says that the women come to them via referral or word of mouth and they are then "vetted."[27] The AWWP does sponsor one workshop in Dari, but most of the writing for the project is done in English. There are also oral history workshops, and the participating women writers often collect stories from others; both of these aspects involve an extra level of mediation and translation.

What is clearly missing from the project are the voices of those women who are openly critical of the US-led military intervention and the US-supported administrations. Contrary to claims that Afghan women are silenced and muzzled, there are a number of literary societies across the country such as the Mirman Baheer literary society with a few hundred members in Afghan cities, and the Kapisa Writers and Poets Society in an area north of Kabul. Some of these writers speak openly about the war economy of private armies generated by US military funding. As one poet, Dr. Masouda, wrote, "Oh my God, all the warlords testing their weapons again and earning a lot of money out of war." Masouda was threatened by local commanders for her poetry.[28] In their social media outreach, the AWWP frequently champions the education rights activist and Nobel Prize laureate Malala Yousafzai, who survived being shot in the head by the Taliban in Pakistan, but they don't mention her opposition to the US-led war in Afghanistan. AWWP does not mention the outspoken women of RAWA or another activist, Malalai Joya, who has been critical of US military intervention in global forums and has survived multiple assassination attempts for opposing US-backed warlords in the Afghan parliament. This range of critical voices is notably absent from the project. Presenting Afghan women as voiceless and muzzled actually serves to silence the more critical perspectives and highlights the voices of those who participate in the project. The George Bush Institute articulates the mission of the AWWP as "amplifying the voices of Afghan women."[29] In actually, however, it is amplifying the voices of those whom Hamilton refers to as more moderate against those who might challenge US influence.

Finally, the structure of the workshops also shapes the kinds of stories and voices that emerge. The workshops take place online, with Afghan women being mentored by mostly white, middle-class Western women. Each mentor is assigned to a group of women. The mentors receive training packets with information on how to edit the writing and provide constructive feedback. Each week the mentors come up with a writing prompt. The stories don't always follow the prompts, but some of the prompts such as "narrow escapes" and "taking chances"[30] play a role in directing women to write about certain elements of their experience and not others, in this case, experiences of crisis and persecution.

The final stories are published on the AWWP website, where they are read and commented on by mostly Western women. There is not much information available about the demographic makeup of these readers, other than their names and sometimes countries. The Afghan women address their stories to Western readers. The mentors and readers generally assume that the stories are the authentic voices of Afghan women. As one of the mentors, Janice Owens, says, "Here was a golden opportunity to reach across culture and half a globe to help give an Afghan sister a voice in this world; an authentic, woman's voice, from a culture where women's voices are not so often heard."[31] It is assumed that both sets of women hold the same perspectives, allowing a purer form of true communication. Another mentor, Maxinne Rhea Leighton, refers in essentialist terms to the commonality shared by women because of their gender: "there exists at a core level, an inexorable place of understanding between women, and their stories, that transcends a common language or place of origin."[32] She also draws on the idea of an "authentic voice" that can help to bypass distinctions of power and position: "the immediacy of both the writing and the exchanges between 'student' and 'teacher' produced work and 'conversations' between us that bypassed the intellect and went straight to the authentic voice." One of the other mentors, Susannah Simpson, said,

> I am stunned by the immediacy and power of writing to one another some 6,731.43 miles away. Given the stumbling blocks of distance, politics, and culture, in what other fashion could I read the intimate thoughts and feelings of my sister writers in Afghanistan? In a matter of minutes, our messages reach around the planet and weave bonds of recognition and sameness.[33]

The belief that the Internet and digital technology can create an immediate connection across the boundaries of class, nation, and ethnicity ignores the relations of power and privilege that structure the interactions between the mentors and students. As Srimati Basu has argued, "imagining same-ness in perspective between women is itself thus an exotic fetish that allows one to speak without interrogating the relations of power within which one does so."[34] In the sections that follow I examine the results of this exercise in translating Afghan women's voices for a Western audience. How can we read their stories, taking into consideration the ways they are framed and mediated? Is there a way for women to communicate across lines of nation and ethnicity that does not assume sameness in perspective?

There is a performative dimension to the texts that contains some simi-larities to the expressive genres of life stories that exist in everyday rituals and events of Afghan society. Benedicte Grima has looked at how personal narratives of suffering, endurance, and hardship are part of a defined genre that is performed by Pashtun women within the social context of weddings, births, illnesses, and deaths.[35] In their recounting of abuse and hardship, the online stories may be considered cultural performances of Afghan wom-anhood.[36] The Afghan writers also sometimes engage what Mills refers to in her studies of Afghan women's memoirs as "double voicings."[37] This involves "saying one sort of thing to a mass audience that derives most or all of its understanding of the circumstances from ambient Western social opinion, and something else to another audience with more access to Afghan viewpoints and experiences, an alternative context of interpreta-tion." Sometimes, the ambiguity in stories means that they can be read dif-ferently by English-speaking Afghans in Afghanistan than they are read by Western audiences.

WRITING WOMEN'S LIVES: STORIES FROM THE AWWP WEBSITE

To date, the AWWP website contains some five hundred stories and poems. I examined three hundred stories, which were all of the stories that had been published on the site from when it was founded in May 2009 until February 2014. I also attended events organized by the AWWP in New York City. The stories and comments that I present here are fairly reflective of the material on the site as a whole. The stories are fairly short, mostly between 500 to 2,000 words each. They are posted in categories that include the Oral History Project and the Teenage Writers Workshop. The pieces con-sist of personal stories told in the first person, stories told in the third per-son, opinion pieces, and poetry. For this chapter, I have mostly focused on the personal and third-person stories, with some inclusion of the opinion pieces. The stories also contain responses from mostly Western readers. In the following sections, I analyze the stories and the responses, trying to understand what the stories do, how they are consumed and responded to, and how we might read them through the discourses and tropes that structure the narratives.

Blaming Culture for Women's Status

Many of the stories on the AWWP website speak about the suffering of Afghan women at the hands of family members or male relatives. The writers often end by calling for Afghan men and women to take a stand and stop these abuses. But there is very little context or history given in the stories; they are personal and immediate recountings of abuses such as rape, murder, child marriage, and beating. In speaking about the personal stories of Muslim women recounted in mass-market paperbacks, Lila Abu-Lughod says that the lack of contextual information leads us to attribute abuses to the culture at large.[38] Similarly, the AWWP stories point to Afghan culture, conceived as static and traditional, as responsible for abuses against women and girls. The stories emphasize the need for change in the home and in the family, without addressing the broader factors of foreign invasions and civil wars that restructured gender relations, the political economy of war and occupation, or the long-standing issues of poverty and class that shape women's lives.[39] Partly, this is a question of genre, of the personal mode in which these stories are narrated. The Afghan women's stories remain mostly on the level of the personal, which leads them to offer individual explanations and solutions to problems posed. Why the stories don't approach the level of the political and collective may be related to the issues raised earlier, to the political framing already being given in advance by the AWWP, and perhaps to an unwillingness by Afghan women to suggest alternative explanations that may put them at odds with the project.

In several stories, Afghan writers act as cultural brokers, recounting and translating the experiences of others. They give their own framing and analysis to the stories, and these often involve judgments about the ignorance of mostly rural people and a critique of their cultural traditions. Take the story "Eight Daughters for Sale, the Oldest First," by Leeda.[40] Leeda recounts the story of fifteen-year-old Fershta, who was told by her father that he planned to sell her and her seven younger sisters in marriage to earn some money to escape poverty. In the story, Fershta is married to Maroof, a man without education or a job. She is beaten by her husband and mother-in-law, and loses a pregnancy due to the beatings. When Fershta returns to her home to recover, Maroof appears and attacks Fershta's parents with a knife and then kills her seven-year-old brother Reza. In the telling of this story, without context, Leeda says that Fershta's suffering is due to her "father's bad behavior," "her terrible husband," and the actions of her in-laws. But what kinds of desperation might drive the father to pull his daughters out of school and marry them off? Did he see it as a way of protecting them? Was it easier to bear his daughter suffering beatings by her in-laws than to see her starve at home?

In a series called "Exchange for a Cow," Marzila recounts the story of Wazira, a ten-year-old girl who is married off for a cow.[41] Marzila attends the wedding, and her negative descriptions of the parents convey her belief that they are responsible for their daughter's situation. When Marzila confronts the mother, asking how her young daughter will manage in a new household, she describes the mother's response as such: "She laughed typically, as careless women do." Later the mother is described as crying bitterly when her daughter must leave. When the girl will not go, a relative asks for an uncle to come and "take this slut to the car." The uncle comes, verbally abuses the girl, and removes her with brute force. The actions of the family members, and the terms used by the author to describe them, reinforce the idea of a dysfunctional culture and delinquent parents as to blame for the girl's treatment. But again, might the mother's irrational response of laughing be a way of coping with her grief at losing her daughter so young? What kinds of economic pressures must the family be facing that they should have to sell off their daughter in exchange for a cow?

The images accompanying the stories on the website also help to reinforce ideas about conservative traditions and Afghan men as the cause of women's problems. Most of the images on the website consist of women in burkhas and bearded Taliban men carrying rifles. As Basu has argued, the imprisoning enemy is imagined as a bearded man, and such images lead to the dehumanization of brown men.[42] Afghan men are depicted with raised hands, shouting and angry faces, sometimes with smoke or flames in the background, a typical depiction of Muslim extremists. They ride atop vehicles carrying guns. By contrast, there are no photos of US military personnel in threatening positions. As is typical with representations of the burkha, the photography is high quality and high contrast, emphasizing the burkha as an icon.[43] Accompanying the story "A Pretty Toy in My Family's Hands" is a photograph with the silhouette of a woman in a black burkha, framed by brightly colored walls. There are shots of women in the mandatory cobalt blue burkha set in stark relief against mountains and valleys. In a story called "The Taliban Takeover, Part 1," a man in a turban raises a stick as he herds groups of burkha-clad women. A story called "Dialogue about Sexism" is accompanied by a picture of two men in a store with racks of cobalt blue burkhas, and they hold up one between them. The burkha-clad woman is usually depicted with her head tilted downward submissively, whereas women without burkhas appear happy and smiling. Marzia N.'s story "A Woman of Ambition" begins, "I am a woman who wants freedom." The story is accompanied by a full-screen image of the mesh frame of the burkha used as an eyehole. By focusing in on the eyes, the image conveys all of the stereotypes about the burkha as cage, and women as trapped inside it. The effect of these images, which shape the ways in which the stories are read, is to show Afghan men as aggressive militants and Afghan women as their prisoners, held captive within burkhas.

The view of traditional culture as the source of women's problems is also repeated in opinion pieces. In a piece called "Afghan Women's Rights: Will History Repeat Itself?," Marzia argues that "for generations the people of Afghanistan, especially men and elders of the families, have taken away rights from women by following their own way of tradition and local culture."[44] Zainab makes similar arguments in a piece entitled, "Teach the Children."[45] She places the blame for violence against women with Afghan mothers who themselves experience violence and allow it to be perpetuated: "If a society has fundamental flaws, we should search for the solution in the behavior of mothers." She says that "In Afghanistan I see many mothers who themselves are the barrier to their daughters' rights as a woman. The problem is in our culture." But this reified notion of unchanging traditional culture prevents us from seeing how gender relations in Afghanistan have been profoundly shaped by factors of war, occupation, and conflict. Afghanistan has historically been used as a pawn by rival colonial and imperial powers. During the Soviet occupation of Afghanistan in the 1980s, the CIA gave billions of dollars in aid money to *mujahidin* fighters commanded by regional Afghan warlords to fight a proxy war. A few years after the Soviets withdrew in 1989, the *mujahidin* engaged in a brutal civil war, with millions of people killed and displaced. The Taliban came to power in 1996 and sought to restore law and order through imposing a strict version of Islamic law that was welcomed in some cases given the excesses of the civil war. Deniz Kandiyoti argues that the war economy profoundly altered social relations. The Taliban imposed a virtual curfew on Afghan women and mandatory use of the burkha, removing urban women from most of public life and education.[46] But rather than being synonymous with traditional forms of social control, the Taliban rule represented a new gender regime that undermined traditional tribal elders and rejected customary law. Rather than seeing gender-based violence such as rape and murder as resulting from "tradition," Kandiyoti argues, we must distinguish between privatized violence exercised to ensure honor, sexual violence as a tool of war, and public performances of violence as a means of social control.

Some of the stories on the AWWP website present these more complex and subtle views of Afghan culture and gender relations. A few of the writers discuss what the burkha and hijab mean for them, in contrast to the framing of these in the AWWP project materials as Taliban-imposed restrictions that keep them hidden from society. In a piece about the hijab, a headscarf that keeps the face visible, Emaan contests the Western idea of Muslim women as silent and passive by saying that "Wearing a hijab doesn't make a woman passive because scarves cover the heads, not the minds, of Muslim women."[47] She makes the arguments that the hijab provides women with a degree of freedom from scrutiny over their physical appearance, removing "their beauty, or perhaps lack of it . . . from the realm of what can be legitimately discussed." Emaan states that restrictions on women don't come from Islam, but rather from cultural customs wrongly justified under an Islamic banner.

Writers talk about how cultural practices such as arranged marriage could be a haven from forced marriage to warlords or Taliban fighters. In her story "Forced Marriage—Shame of Divorce," Safia describes how she was engaged to her cousin Javid since she was two years old, and how they fell in love through their phone conversations, even though they had never met.[48] But after the US-backed interim government came to power in 2001, one of Safia's uncles, Wal Khan, who was a warlord, became a political leader and wanted to take Safia as his second wife. After initially resisting, Safia's parents agreed to marry her to her uncle in exchange for providing employment opportunities to all of the men in their tribe. Safia was inconsolable, thinking of Javid: "I cried for being away from Javid . . . I searched for Allah-Pak to beg him for Javid, whom I loved so much." In contrast to a Western perspective, which would see both forms of marriage as coerced, for Safia it is the marriage to the warlord that is a "forced marriage," whereas the arranged marriage is one of consent.

Other writers also provide explanations for why some cultural practices may be a response to the vulnerability produced by situations of war, rather than related to a timeless traditional culture. In a piece on early marriage, Fatima F. argues that poverty and the need for protection are two reasons why families may marry off their daughters early.[49] Some families cannot afford the expense of having a daughter at home. And some see marriage as a form of security; this was especially true during the time of the *mujahidin*, when families married off their daughters to save them from being murdered or raped in the war. But despite these acknowledgments of the societal causes of early marriage, Fatima F. ends by placing the responsibility on parents, who must educate their children correctly and help them learn social skills. She closes her piece by saying: "Fathers! Mothers! I beg you to please stop early marriage!"

One of the exceptions to the individual focus of many of the pieces is a powerful account by Roya called "1 + 1 = 1."[50] It is a story about her struggle to get an education, but instead of the uplift through education narrative that dominates most of the stories, Roya outlines systematically the ways that she has been prevented from getting an education because of war and occupation. She narrates her educational life with reference to the war going on around her. Although she loved going to school, her school was closed in fourth grade because of war and rockets. Throughout fifth and sixth grade "rockets fell like rain from the sky." In seventh grade the Taliban came into power and she stayed home. The students didn't have chairs to sit on, boards to write on, or books to study with. The teachers were not paid and most did not even have college degrees. Roya identifies war as the root cause of this situation:

> It was not the fault of our teachers; with all these problems they were trying to be kind and teach the best they could. The cause was that our country was born in war. The cause is war, always war . . .

Roya moves away from individual blame or calls for responsibility toward recognition of the broader structural causes for hardship. She combines the telling of her individual story with a sense of political context that shows how people are not simply free to change their behavior but are subject to larger forces that shape their lives.

Subject-Making Through Storytelling

In contrast to the patriarchal Muslim cultures depicted in AWWP sto- ries, Afghan girls are encouraged to aspire to Western capitalist modes of desire and being that represent progress in the Orientalist framework. In the AWWP mission statement, Hamilton explicitly declares this project of subject-making as being one of its goals:

> But why should we care about an essay by a woman from Kandahar, or a poem by a woman from Logar? Because in telling their own stories, we've seen these women gather strength, courage, and self-confidence. They become empowered to make change within their homes, their communities, and eventually their country. They also gain computer literacy and skills of language and critical thinking, which increases their job-related skills. . . . They have become lawyers, journalists, parliament members.[51]

The ideal Afghan female subject is one who is self-reliant, self-determining, modern, and entrepreneurial. While Afghanistan is generally stigmatized as a failed state dependent on foreign aid, the NATO intervention and its attendant self-help projects are presented as creating self-actualizing sub- jects who can participate in a modern world of commerce and democracy.

Computer literacy and job-related skills geared to a Western capitalist economy are seen as key to integrating these women into a broader global system. The use of English in the project is justified by it being the "international language of commerce and diplomacy."[52] Mills asks whether, in order to escape the Orientalist stereotype of the silenced victim, Afghan women must "ventriloquate the sovereign individual subjecthood of Western liberal ideology."[53] Through narrating their stories, Afghan women shape their desires and participate in processes of self-making that are compatible with a Western capitalist project.

Creative writing workshops have been used historically to foster Western liberal forms of subjectivity. In his book *Workshops of Empire*, Eric Bennett outlines how creative writing graduate programs beginning with the renowned Iowa Writer's Workshop at the University of Iowa were nurtured by the State Department in the post–World War II period as a way of venerating the liberal democratic subject as an antidote to the growing global influence of communism.[54] Foundations, including the Rockefeller Foundation, Ford, and Carnegie, also expanded their philanthropic activities into graduate writing programs during the Cold War era as a way of engendering a climate conducive to stable markets. Workshop directors such as Paul Engle collaborated with the State Department, foundations, and the CIA to set up international writing programs that recruited foreign students from countries such as China, where writers were perceived to be under the cultural influence of the Soviet Union. The contemporary uses of storytelling as a form of soft power are situated within this history of cultural diplomacy and its goals of subject formation.

The online writing workshops of the AWWP are also set within a whole range of practices in the post-2001 period that seek to draw Afghan women into transnational humanitarian and consumer networks. In her ethnography of Afghan women's NGOs, Julie Billaud describes how in urban areas such as Kabul, Afghan women interact with transnational humanitarian organizations, reconstruction experts, and Western feminists, learning the technocratic neoliberal language of "gender training" and "empowerment" in order to access resources and opportunities such as fellowships and conference invitations, and to leverage positions in international organizations.[55] These trainings give certain Afghan women the feeling of belonging to a cosmopolitan elite and the promise of social mobility. Within these cosmopolitan networks, Afghan girls and women are also exposed to American consumer culture through Hollywood films such as *Titanic*, student exchanges, and their interactions with foreign colleagues.[56]

The AWWP represents Afghan women as desiring the same consumer freedoms and romantic arrangements that Western women have. As Abu-Lughod says, the idea is that we would "free Afghan women to be 'like us.'"[57]

Afghan women are portrayed as wanting the things that Western women want—love, choice, and sexual freedom.[58] In the stories, Afghan women talk about wanting to eat ice cream, ride bicycles, and go to a prom. In "The Evening I Will Never Forget," the author Fattemeh talks about going to a prom while in the United States on an exchange program.[59] She talks about it as a rite that all girls must experience: "This was my high school prom." She describes buying her prom dress and shoes, having her nails and hair done, and taking photos before the event. In the comments section, people refer to her experience as an "American rite of passage" and a "fairy tale evening." Freedom, in the case of the prom, is identified with a heterosexual institution that is key to producing the gendered subjectivity of modern American girls as consumers and one that can be available to Afghan girls, too.

Some of the stories address the romantic mythologies of Western white weddings as another aspiration for Afghan women. In Seeta's story "The Burqa Bride," Seeta observes going to the wedding of one of her students in Farah Province.[60] Seeta describes waiting to see the bride:

> I asked a woman beside me, "Auntie, can you tell me when the bride came out, because I did not see her. I saw no bride in a beautiful white dress. Did you see her?"
>
> The woman laughed. "My daughter, we are from the villages. We do not like to dress our brides in these long dresses with no sleeves."
>
> "Okay, Auntie, but I did not see any woman who looked at all like a bride."
>
> "My daughter," she said. "Come with me. I will show you where she is now."
>
> I went outside with her and saw a car decorated with a few flowers, and then I saw a man who held the arm of a woman under a burqa. They both got into the car.
>
> "Did you see the bride now, or not?" the woman asked me.
>
> I still did not see my student, my bride. "No. Where is she?"
>
> "Look at those two—the man and the woman together."
>
> "Oh, I see," I said. "But why should she be under a burqa today? She has only this day to start her life with happiness. Why should she be hidden under a burqa even on her wedding day?"

Seeta's wish to see a bride in a beautiful white dress and her idea that happiness is associated with an uncovered bride reveals similar assumptions to Fattemeh of Western rituals of proms and white weddings as something to be emulated by modern Afghan women. At the end of her story, Seeta refers to the veiled woman as "invisible," meaning that she is not legible within Western, heteronormative accounts of the ideal bride. This trope of the "invisible bride" is taken up in the comments section. One woman named Silvia wishes for the bride to be happy by having "a day without a burkha."

One of the Afghan writers, Mariam, responds in this comments section to say that she is sorry to see the burkha being made into a symbol of imprisonment, which is partly due to the way it was imposed under the Taliban. She reclaims the burkha for herself, saying, "I would be proud to wear it at my wedding in public." Mariam redefines freedom as "the freedom to veil my figure from anyone I choose, and I feel safer knowing that I am not being evaluated by my sex appeal or my appearance but by my conversation and my personality." Mariam's words are validated by the workshop director. But then there is another comment by someone called Jeanne who responds directly to Mariam, saying that it is one thing if the burkha is a choice, but otherwise it infringes on a woman's rights as a person. Jeanne refers to the 1920s when it was a scandal for women to show knees or ankles. The commenters often compare Afghanistan today to the last century for women in the West, thereby encouraging a narrative of progress that one day Afghan women will emulate their Western counterparts.

Some of the stories refer to the expression of emotion in Afghan culture, and particularly the ability of women to express laughter, especially in front of men. In her piece, "To Laugh," Sabira talks about how in Afghanistan women are taught not to laugh, that it will bring disrespect upon their families, and will make them seem uncontrolled.[61] She also says that women in Afghanistan do not have much reason to laugh, as they are affected by wars, have lost family members, have faced danger, and are afraid for their future. This is an example of Mills's double voicing: while Sabira's story feeds into Western expectations about patriarchal suppression of Afghan women's impulses, she also gives the reasons why women in a conflict situation might not wish to laugh. Most of the responses to the piece predictably ignore this latter point and focus on laughter as an expression of freedom. One person says, "We take laughter and smiling for granted here." Another, Kathleen D., says, "I hope that one day you and other women inside Afghanistan are able to freely express your emotions, rather than having to bottle them up inside." The free Afghan woman is seen as one who is able to express her emotions without inhibition. In another piece, "The Mirror," Shogofa talks about how it is difficult to laugh with men and in front of men, but when women get together they can laugh a lot.[62] The piece has a very large number of comments, and several of the responses lament the inability of women to laugh in front of men. One woman, identified only as K, states that she is fortunate to be able to laugh with her fiancé, and she hopes that one day Afghan men will learn to laugh with women. Another comment by Emma says that the "obstacle" of not being able to laugh in front of men will be overcome in a "growing society." Although the writers themselves are not saying they are desirous of these culturally specific forms of interaction with males, they are interpreted by Western readers as less free and intimate with males than Western women.

The free expression of emotion is linked to other modes of individual empowerment such as self-image and self-esteem. Mimi Nguyen refers to this as a form of neoliberal governmentality as women become legible to a state power by learning to esteem the self.[63] One of the writers, Shakila, in her piece "The Different Daughter" refers to her life under Soviet occupation and then as a refugee in Iran as one of conformity, monotony, and dependence.[64] Even as a young woman of twenty, she infantilizes herself as "a child, afraid to speak my mind" and "skinny and unsure." One day, during a "boring, repetitive day" in the "oppressive" library, she comes across a book titled *The Psychology of Self-Esteem*. Shakila talks about how the book changed her life. It made her think about self-esteem, to think independently, and helped her escape traditional beliefs in a society where the power of traditions determined everything about a woman's life. In the story, self-esteem is celebrated as a liberal form of empowerment and freedom based on individualism. Nguyen sees the celebration of self-esteem as part of a broader set of discourses about women's freedom that elides the structural violence of geopolitics.[65] Not surprisingly, the story had a tremendous response from readers, with twenty-nine responses to date. One response celebrates Afghan women for "coming out of their cocoons," others encourage them to stand up for themselves and become self-reliant, and some suggest that individuality and difference should be cultivated. By remaking themselves as ideal modern subjects who value self-esteem, Afghan women are prepared as subjects who can enter into a market democracy, which is proposed as the solution to Afghanistan's entrenched problems of war and militarization.

Narratives of Military Engagement

The AWWP stories reflect and often reproduce official American narratives of military engagement. In their internal communications, the CIA and US State Department have tried to claim that Afghan women support the US presence in Afghanistan. In a 2009 cable entitled "Inverting the International Interference Paradigm: Afghan Women Seek Support," former US ambassador Karl Eikenberry refers to a series of meetings held with women in Kabul that showed they were in favor of the US presence.[66] He contrasts this with Malalai Joya, who was touring the United States and calling for the removal of US and NATO troops from Afghanistan. Although the stories in the AWWP show some ambivalence about the war and US presence, many reinforce the dominant American narrative to be found in most reports, speeches, and official statements. The official narrative claims that the oppression of women in Afghanistan was due to the Soviet invasion, civil war, and Taliban rule. There is no reference made to the American arming of the *mujahidin* fighters during the Soviet occupation or the ongoing brutalities committed by the *mujahidin* warlords who have occupied key positions in the Afghan parliament since 2001. According to the official US narrative, the United States liberated Afghanistan from the Taliban in 2001, and since then women have made remarkable gains, with life expectancy increased significantly, the number of girls in school growing, and women elected to parliament and other offices.[67]

Many scholars and journalists have contested this account of the liberation of Afghanistan. The American bombing campaign in October 2001 led to the killing of over 400 civilians, with a further 4,000 killed and 2.2 million displaced over the next three months. The Taliban and Al-Qaeda forces escaped to the Tora Bora mountains near Pakistan, where they were defeated by US air strikes.[68] However, the journalist Anand Gopal has provided a compelling account of how the United States revived the civil war, even after defeating the Taliban.[69] Without a clear adversary by April 2002, the US army and Western corporations, in the business of war and weapons manufacture, created enemies where there were none and packaged personal feuds as "counterterrorism." They fostered a strong network of former *mujahidin* warlords, accountable only to the governors and US Special Forces. The unchecked power and brutality of US-funded warlords led to a countermovement of young men along with former Talibs reviving the defunct grouping to make the Taliban a formidable force again. In her autobiography entitled *A Woman among Warlords*, Joya argues that women have borne the brunt of this renewed civil conflict.[70] She says, "You may have been led to believe that once the Taliban was driven from power, justice returned to my country. Afghan women like me, voting and running for office, have been held up as proof that the US military has brought democracy and women's rights to Afghanistan." But she goes on to recount that she was threatened with death for speaking against the warlords in the US-backed Hamid Karzai government. "We remain caged in our country," she says, "without access to justice and still ruled by woman-hating criminals."[71] Rostami-Povey argues that since the US invasion, poverty has worsened and women have been forced to turn to begging and sex work in large numbers.[72] Many parents don't send their daughters to school in fear for their safety, and schools lack basic supplies. While gender equality is talked about in formal terms, there is no attention to problems of poverty and insecurity that impact most women's lives.

The United States and the United Nations invested large amounts of money in three presidential elections in order to provide the façade of a democratic order in post-Taliban Afghanistan. Given the wide skepticism over the 2014 elections, which were seen to be driven by US strategic interests, plagued by corruption, and dominated by warlords, US agencies tried to enlist the support of cultural projects like AWWP to legitimize the elections. The AWWP ran a series called the "2014 Afghan Elections Project" in partnership with the nonprofit International Foundation for Electoral Systems and with funding from USAID. The introductory narrative to the stories explains that AWWP writers from seven provinces in Afghanistan were asked to share their hopes and fears about the "democratic process," which was unfolding for the third time "since the ouster of the Taliban and the formation of a new government." Of the twenty-five pieces run in the series, most are fairly optimistic about the elections as vehicles for democratic change. Marzia speaks about voting as being the "greatest moment of my life . . . For the first time in my life I tasted the sweet taste of democracy."[73] Nasima talks about voting as "our national duty and responsibility."[74] In another piece she talks about how voting will lead to freedom and an end to violence against women.[75] Several of the authors recount tales of women defying their husbands and fathers to go to the voting booths.

Others are concerned because they see most of the political candidates up for election as warlords.[76] Sitara B. says that when she sees the faces of those running for office she sees those who ruined Kabul, killed thousands of people, and are antiwoman and conservative. However, she ends by claiming that the presidential candidate Ashraf Ghani, himself a strongman with ties to warlords, is the only candidate without such a negative history.[77] The dominant narrative running through the election stories is that the Afghan people will be engaging in a democratic process and that women need to defy their husbands and banish their fears in order to vote so that change can be brought about. Only a few of the pieces refer to the control by warlords and the United States over the process, and the impossibility for a warlord-dominated parliament to bring about any changes, regardless of whether women vote or not.

One of the frequent tropes used in the workshop materials and in the stories is that of the monstrous Taliban who are oppressing women and denying them their rights. Although the US intervention broke the power of the Taliban, replacing them with the equally brutal warlords, as Gopal argues, the US Special Forces were still on Afghan soil with the mandate to fight terrorism and defeat the Taliban.[78] The label of Taliban was used strategically by warlords, Afghans, and the US military to denounce anyone who posed a threat. For instance, in her story "Forced Marriage," the writer

Safia recounts that when her cousin Javid wanted to protect her from the warlord who wanted to marry her, the warlord "threatened to accuse him of being Taliban or Osama Bin Laden's spy."[79] This has been a typical way to eliminate those identified as enemies.

When reading the stories by Afghan women, we should therefore be mindful of the ways that they may invoke the specter of the Taliban because of their fear to indict warlords or other US-backed criminals or in order to gain foreign support for their case. In a different context to the AWWP, Gopal gives the case of Heela, an educated woman from Kabul who had married Musqinyar, a communist and supporter of women's rights during the time of Soviet rule.[80] At the time of the civil war, they were forced to flee the city for Musqinyar's ancestral rural home of Uruzgan, where Heela had to wear a burkha and be confined to the home. During the 2009 parliamentary elections, Musqinyar and Heela worked with the United Nations and the Americans. After the elections were over, Musqinyar came across local police officers trying to charge people in the villages fees for not voting, and Musqinyar went to the office of the district governor to complain, discovering that the governor himself was complicit in the scam. Musqinyar and the governor entered into a fight, with Musqinyar threatening to report the governor to the United Nations, and Musqinyar was later shot and killed by the governor's police. Heela took her children, fled her home and sought out the American base. She knew that the Americans would not be sympathetic to her story. As Gopal says, "She had to speak a language that they would understand. She said, 'The Taliban killed my husband. I need your help.'"[81] The soldiers took her and her children in a helicopter to the safety of Kabul. Given both the strategic mandate of the US army, but also the broader international condemnation of the Taliban, it can be easier for women like Heela to frame their stories in terms of conflict with the Taliban, thereby being assured a sympathetic audience.

Afghan refugees also sometimes invent stories about the Taliban to win a sympathetic hearing for their asylum cases. Billaud gives the example of one woman in her ethnography, Massoma, whose brother was smuggled to Europe and was being held in a detention center in France, awaiting his asylum case review.[82] Massoma's brother Farid told the French authorities that his family members were Taliban supporters who were pressuring him to take part in terrorist activities, a difficult thing to prove since he was of Hazara ethnicity, a group frequently repressed by the Taliban. So Farid had asked Massoma's help to send a picture of the family dressed up as Taliban terrorists. Billaud relates how the boys applied black kohl under their eyes to look "scary" and they had to borrow a blue burkha from the neighbors for Farid's mother as she didn't have one. These elaborate stagings of Taliban oppression are performed for the benefit of foreigners who can only read persecution through this lens. It is important to be aware that the stories in the AWWP may also sometimes utilize the language of the brutal Taliban that their audience can understand, rather than the truth about the perpetrators of atrocities committed against women.

Although the directors of the AWWP claim that the project is neutral and not tied to any one side of the conflict, some of the pieces resist this claim. One of the poets, Tabasom Halal, who was killed in 2011, has a memorial on the AWWP page.[83] The memorial page contains the emails that Tabasom sent to the AWWP editors, including one on June 7, 2010, where she vents her anger at the US occupation:

> We tolerate the suicide attacks that kill innocents in the street, we tolerate when we sleep hungry at night, we tolerate when we lose our family members in war, we tolerate the president and the government you, you, you people selected for us, but we can't tolerate if you come here and take our religion.
>
> We are Muslims, yes, but I am ashamed to call myself a Muslim. I don't know Islam, I don't know the reality of Islam that is peace . . . I know Islam from you, from books printed by you, from your money, from your media. . . .
>
> You brought Taliban in our country, the world treated Talibs and al Qaeda to show that Islam is the religion of Terror. . .
>
> You took everything from us, you kill our families, you threat and bring up the Taliban and then you announce "we help Afghanistan!" You are lying. You are lying.

The editors frame Tabasom's message with a note that she was angry upon hearing reports about nonprofit groups converting Afghans to Christianity, but editors assured her that AWWP has no religious motive and "the intent of the project was to give writers a place to freely tell their stories and opinions to the world." There is no engagement with the more difficult arguments that Tabasom is making about American complicity in Afghanistan's problems, from arming the *mujahidin* that would give rise to the Taliban, putting those former *mujahidin* into parliamentary offices, and then claiming to help Afghanistan.

The practice of editorial comments accompanying pieces occurs mostly when there is a criticism of the US military role. Freshta's story "American Soldiers: Here to Protect or Violate?" is about a woman from the southern province of Ghaznai whose husband Hamdullah is killed during a night raid by American soldiers.[84] In search of Habib-u-Rahman, a computer programmer whom they accused of being an Al Qaeda member, the soldiers entered Hamdullah's compound. They blew up the front gate of his house with explosives, and they shot and killed Hamdullah and another neighbor before finding Rahman and taking him away. A fifteen-year-old boy who was detained and then released said that the American troops stole money, jewelry, mobiles, and laptops from the families. Freshta cites a neighbor who says that such reports have created disgust about the American troops. There are many such incidents, she says, and their "stories remain buried in the dust." The editor has framed the piece with a note saying that while night raids are a frequent practice, "the American administration is now calling for restrictions on this practice to prevent further unnecessary loss of life." Freshta herself also ends with a note, saying that these are only the facts and not her opinion. She then shifts register from a personal recounting of the neighbors' experiences of violent assault to the political mode, arguing that the incident does not change her mind about the American troops, who should not yet leave Afghanistan because before they came there was no peace. This shift in narrative mode is a way for Freshta to protect herself from accusations of being too critical or anti-American.

Another indication of the military ties of the project is that it is read by US soldiers who comment on some of the posts. In a story by Shafiqa called "Ocean of Disappointment," a friend of the writer is working in a private organization abroad while waiting to do a master's degree.[85] Her father calls from Afghanistan and orders that she return home. The girl is devastated and describes her life as being "tied with cultural chains." One of the comments on the website is from a US soldier called Carlon Addison, who says that he is a father who encourages his daughter to do well and how the stories posted on the web help him to understand why they are in Afghanistan to help people like this girl achieve their freedom. One of the AWWP editors responded to Carlon to thank him as a father for writing a comment. She adds, "It makes it all the more special that it comes from one of our members of the Armed Forces." Despite the cited neutrality of the project, the editorial notes, framings, and comments to US soldiers show their affinities with US military interests.

There are a few critical stories in the project that are not framed by editorial comments or a reaffirmation by writers of the need for an American presence. In her piece "Dear President Obama," Shogofa expresses her critiques of American foreign policy.[86] She says that people had hopes that after Barack Obama was elected things would get better in Afghanistan. But she says things are now worse. She asks: "Why doesn't an Afghan life have value? What did we do that we are the victims of first the Taliban, and now the US?" In another similar piece called "When Can I See?" Shogofa makes an implicit critique of the idea that telling stories can bring about change: "I wish that we could solve our problems just by talking or writing. But talking gets us nowhere."[87] Another writer, Sitara, argues in a piece called "How to Change Afghanistan" that if the United States really wanted to bring about change in Afghanistan it would not support the warlords. She says, "I think the international community should drag the warlords into an international trial for corruption. Instead, the U.S. supports them and makes them more powerful."[88] These writings are mostly opinion pieces that exceed the bounds of the workshop framings and editorials to make more critical statements about the narrative of US military intervention and what it brings for ordinary Afghans. The presence of these more subversive narratives shows that the production of subjects and stories through framing narratives and vetting procedures is a partial and contested process. As a project that encourages Afghan women to express themselves openly, the editors are somewhat bound to include even those stories that might contest the dominant framing given to the project.

AFGHAN WOMEN'S STORIES AND THE PROJECT OF US FEMINISM

Given the fraught nature of the AWWP stories, rendered in the idioms and tropes of Western discourse about Afghanistan, what we learn of Afghan women's lives is available only in glimpses and fragments. Rather, I contend that the AWWP is a mirror held to the anxieties and desires of its Western women readers, at a moment when the gains of the feminist movement are being rolled back. By constructing Afghan society as primitive and patriarchal, and Western freedoms as something for Afghan girls to aspire to, Western women who participate as mentors and readers create their own notion of themselves as living in a postfeminist society.

In the comments sections of the AWWP stories, there are many responses that posit the freedom of Western women with reference to the lack of rights available to Afghan women. As Abu-Lughod argues, "The fiction that any of us can 'choose freely' is maintained by conjuring up those in distant lands who live in bondage with no rights, agency, or ability to refuse or escape sex or violence."[89] Several comments on the website from American women specifically refer to themselves as lucky to be in a country that recognizes women's rights. A woman named Jessica Spinnler comments on a story by Fatima H. that describes her fears about the Taliban and what will happen when the American soldiers leave:

> I cannot even begin to imagine what it is like to be a woman in your position. I feel very blessed to have been raised in America. I take things like going shopping, wearing make up and clothes, and even getting an education for granted every day. . . . I will never understand how a group of people feel it is ok to oppress an entire group of people, based on sex, color or religion. History has proven that this type of behavior will not be

tolerated. I hope that things change for the women in your country sooner than later. May peace be with you![90]

The fiction that Spinnler lives in a free country where she is able to dress and consume as she wishes is expressed through her construction of Afghan women as completely lacking in the rights that she has. Wendy Brown suggests that it is a folly to compare women's lack of freedom across cultures rather than to see freedom and equality "in terms of parameters, textures, and relation to the powers constructing, organizing, and positioning subjects."[91] We should instead see both Western fashions and the burkha as a negotiation of women's status in male-dominated orders. Brown argues that in one case sexuality is hidden from public view and in another it is orchestrated through expensive cosmetics and revealing fashions, but in both cases women are bearers of culture in a way that men are not.

Mentors and commenters on the site frequently refer to themselves as lucky to be born in the West with the freedoms it offers. The mentor Lisa Takeuchi Cullen says, "I was born free. Thus, I write. I must write. The women I worked with have no such privilege."[92] Another mentor, Season Harper-Fox, says, "In the U.S. and many other countries, we take our rights for granted. So many of us don't understand how fortunate we are to speak the words we want to speak, to freely write our views, to know that our lives aren't endangered because we express our own opinions."[93] It is with reference to what they imagine to be the lives of Afghan women that Western women are able to construct their freedom.

Commenters on the stories also echo these ideas about being lucky to be from the West. An Italian woman, Francesca, comments on a story by Roya about her friend Freshta who is killed by her eldest son.[94] Francesca comments that if this had happened in Italy the police would investigate and not just believe the relatives of the victim. Francesca states, "I was lucky because I was born in a State, where men and women have (almost) equal rights. What can we lucky 'Western' women do, in order to help you?" Safia's story, "Forced Marriage," has some forty-two comments, most of which anglicize her name to Sofia.[95] Many of the comments thank her for telling her horrific story as it has helped them to realize the rights that they have and has inspired them to work toward their goals. Taryn from New Zealand says, "I take for granted all I have available to me in my world and sometimes feel trapped and lost in my life but you inspire me to do all I can to be happy and work toward my goals." Jennifer says that "As an American woman, it is easy to forget that there are still situations like this in the world." And Amanda comments, "Thank you for inspiring me to be a better woman and realize the rights that I have as well!" It is assumed that the West is the site of freedom, which is defined more clearly in relation to Afghan women's unfreedom. Such positional superiority functions as a means of social control, deflecting the attention of readers from entrenched gender-based issues in Western countries such as ongoing workplace discrimination, poverty, and violence.

Many of the readers assume an Orientalist divide between an enlightened and progressive West and a patriarchal, repressive Islamic society like Afghanistan. They construct a teleology from primitive patriarchal society to modern progressive society that the West has undergone and that Afghanistan must experience as well. One of the comments on Marzila's story, "Exchange for a Cow, Part II" about child marriage explicitly compares Afghanistan to the Dark Ages in England and continental Europe.[96] Another comment by a woman called Arlene on a story by Sabira about Afghan women's rights states that American women have had to struggle through a series of obstacles to reach where they are today: "Over the last 200 years our citizens had to struggle through many obstacles including slavery, civil war, women's rights, racial segregation."[97] Patriarchy is seen as something that happened in the past for Western women. In response to Sitara's story about the United States supporting warlords and corrupt women's organizations that don't help Afghan women, one reader Pat Collins comments that, "We in the West often forget the past struggles of our former sisters who suffered themselves under the yoke of male domination."[98] Readers assume that the enlightened West has solved issues of inequality and patriarchy, and it must now impart these lessons to others. Such a teleology also ignores the complex history of women's rights in Afghanistan. Urban women did experience modernizing top-down social reforms in the 1920s and 1970s, which failed to take root for their lack of sensitivity to the family and kinship networks that structured women's lives, particularly in rural communities.[99]

Another area where we can see the engagement with and responses of Americans, mostly women, to the AWWP stories is in the readings and other events held in the United States. These events usually involve volunteers reading the stories of the women, with the idea being to "give voice to Afghan women writers."[100] This is similar to what Basu has described in the case of the inclusion of a veiled woman in Eve Ensler's *Vagina Monologues*.[101] Basu argues that "performers project, render experiences, and speak 'for' women assumed to be invisible and silent, thereby foregrounding the cultural assumptions and political imperatives of the writers' and performers' locations."[102] She refers to this as ventriloquism.

We can see this dynamic at play in two events organized by the AWWP. One was a Night of Poetry and Song organized by the AWWP together with Forte Poesy Music in Los Angeles.[103] It brought together twenty-three teenage girls, mostly white, to perform the Afghan women's poems and writings as songs. The event was introduced by Noack, who contrasted the empowerment of the American girls with the subjugation of the Afghan girls:

> At the Afghan Women's Writing Project we believe that it is a human right to be able to voice your own story. For 99% of us who are here tonight that's a very hard and difficult concept to internalize because all we've heard most likely since we were children is "Speak your mind." "Say what you want." "Be empowered." "You can do whatever you want."

Noack compares Afghan girls who have no rights to the young, white, and presumably privileged girls from the event, in order to celebrate the empowerment of young girls in America. Empowerment is defined in terms of wearing what you want, including revealing clothing; eating what you want to have for dinner; and talking to whomever you want. By singing songs written by girls who have none of the rights that they do, the assumption is that these American girls are becoming aware of their own power. Noack says, "When one of these girls write these songs you can see in their faces this glorious power that they're finding in their ability to write music—to sing it and share it and the empowerment of that voice." Although Noack mentions that the Afghan girls find power in writing, too, it is clear that this event is not really about the Afghan girls, but is about redefining empowerment for young white girls. Rather than engaging in a movement to challenge the sexual discrimination that confines them within narrow sex roles, subjects them to high rates of rape and sexual violence on campuses and in their families, with lower rates of pay and advancement in the workforce than males, the discourse of empowerment asks American girls instead to celebrate being female in America.

Another event, which I attended in person, was titled "Readings from the Afghan Women's Writing Project," held in a small room in the Church of St Luke in the Fields in New York City on October 20, 2014. Compared to the mostly young white girls of the Los Angeles event, this event in New York had fairly diverse participants, both racially and politically. Among those who read the women's stories, there was a pro-Palestine activist wearing a kaffiyeh, a transgender woman, and a young black man. The reading also had one Afghan woman writer in attendance, Marzia, whose stories I discussed earlier. Marzia had worked as an intern at a range of women's nonprofits, including the Feminist Majority. Marzia introduced the event, read, and answered questions. She said that Afghan people were happy about the new president, Ghani, who wants to support women. She said that girls are going to school and getting an education, and there are signs of improvement like young people rejecting arranged marriages. She feels that the situation in Afghanistan can be improved further by creating more exposure for Afghan men to America through Fulbright exchange programs so that they can see how things can be done in a more progressive way.

While Marzia made these statements about the US intervention improving Afghan women's lives, she also read a poem called "War," which she had written herself. In contrast to the optimism of her framing narratives, the poem spoke about the realities of the experience of war:

> War means poverty. People kill for food.
> Parents sell their children. Children sell opium.
> Girls marry old men. Teenagers take responsibilities
> that are too big. They feel old, begin to be cruel,
> see things they shouldn't—do things they shouldn't . . .
> War makes the warlord thirstier and thirstier.
> He cares only about himself, seeks to drink power,
> becomes blind, deaf, a liar. With no laws, no rules,
> you make no goals anymore for your unknown future.
> You become cheap, worthless.

While reading the poem, Marzia became visibly emotional. There was a strong disconnect between her discourse of women's improved lives and her poetic account of how the war is leading to violence and poverty, and contributing to the power of warlords. I see this as another example of double voicing—Marzia's framing appeals to Western hegemonic ideas about progress in Afghanistan, while her poem speaks to those who have some understanding of what is actually taking place on the ground. Few of the latter were present in the audience, though, and most of the questions focused on how to change men's attitudes in Afghanistan, why mothers need to be educated in order to educate their sons, and how to get more women in government. Despite the possibilities for some interesting connections to be made between the diverse range of participants and the stories they were reading, by hewing to the framing narrative given by Marzia, these participants did not enter a deeper discussion of the issues raised by her poem.

There are indications that some of the writers and readers are aware of the ways in which the Afghan women's stories are being used to bolster US foreign policy goals. In her piece "A Tale of Two Teenagers: Malala and Anisa," Sitara compares the story of Malala Yousufzai with that of Anisa, a health services volunteer in northeast Afghanistan who was shot in the stomach and killed by the insurgents.[104] Sitara describes how Malala's shooting attracted the attention of the world. She was flown to the United

Kingdom for surgery. Karzai announced that children in schools would pray for her. And, she says, "The United States, many European countries, feminist networks, and human rights organizations, including writers of the Afghan Women's Writing Project, wrote about her bravery." Meanwhile, she says, "And Anisa? We don't even know her last name . . . Where are the feminist groups that always pledge to fight for women's rights around the world? They barely mention Anisa's name." Sitara ponders the reasons for this, that maybe it is because Anisa is not from the majority Pashtun tribe like President Karzai, or because the United States has a closer relationship with Pakistan. Most of the comments on the site miss the broader critique of her story, saying that the media needs to include stories like that of Anisa as well. But one reader, Johanna, states that "It is easier for the West to tell stories of triumph than of death. Malala survives and fits our idea of a hero. We are not used to heroes who die as Anisa did. I think it makes us uncomfortable." To add to this insight, Malala's story is one of uplift through education, which is a crucial trope of empowerment within Western discourses about women's status in places like Afghanistan.

Among all of the comments on the site, there are a handful of more critical comments like Johanna's. In response to Marzila's story about child marriage, "Exchange for a Cow," Therese says that in "enlightened societies," this would be seen as "child rape, pedophilia, and enslavement."[105] A woman called Noela comments to Therese that she does not feel it is helpful to divide societies into enlightened and nonenlightened. Another woman, Sarah, then builds from Noela's comment to make a series of points about how the stories from the project are read:

> Noela's comment brings up an important point about how we read stories such as Marzila's on this website. While Marzila is right to condemn this abuse of a child, and I am grateful to read her story in her own words, rather than told by someone who is only visiting the situation, I am aware of the limitations of my own perspective as a reader. I do not know much about Afghan women's lives, especially as refugees in Pakistan, about the school described in the story, the region, or the family in question and how they came to think and make choices as they did. It is easy for me to read this story through my own titillation, fascination, pity and smugness, and imagine that anyone who does not vocally condemn the abuse of women and girls is just a backwards collaborator. But perhaps all people, like me, make the best choices they can from the options available to them—even when the options are not good.
>
> What I do know about Afghanistan is that things have not always been this way for women, and that things are different for different women, depending on whether they live in urban, rural or remote regions, on their class, and on how much control the Taliban has over where they live. The Taliban's control over some people and some parts of Afghanistan was not ended by the US/Canadian invasion—rather it is

a product of nationalist sentiment that developed in response to decades of colonial invasions, economic coercion and military threats, from the USSR, the US and other nations where we think of ourselves as "enlightened." It is ahistorical to pretend that "progress" brings women's rights, or that Afghanistan is a throwback to humanity's past that just needs to catch up with those of us who are "enlightened." Afghan women live very much in the present, and their experiences are products of local and global political economy.

In short, those of us who read this story and believe we are "enlightened" are implicated in these events, as people who benefit from the global economic imperialism that has rolled back women's rights in Afghanistan (among other places) since the 1970s.

I have reproduced Sarah's comments in full because I think that they get to the heart of what is problematic about the idea of Western readers connecting with the authentic lives of Afghan women by reading their online stories. For the most part, the comments on the site reveal a level of miscommunication and misrecognition—with readers anglicizing the names of the Afghan women, and interpreting their already mediated stories through the lens of their own assumptions and political beliefs. Western women readers use the stories to construct a notion of their own freedom in a contemporary moment of persistent gender inequalities in the West.

Following on from these few critical interventions found in the AWWP, is it possible to think of forms of dialogue, storytelling, and cross-cultural engagement that are not colonizing or Orientalist? How might we conceive of nonimperialist Western feminisms? Various scholars have proposed alternative feminist solidarity work that includes contextualized anti-imperialist projects,[106] feminist internationalism that takes into account the ways in which gendered subjects are produced and that includes solidarity with refugee women in the metropolis,[107] and feminist projects that are conscious of their own historical and political situatedness.[108] There is a space for storytelling projects that build on the work of existing Afghan women's literary societies and antiwar activist groups such as RAWA and Code Pink. The pain and suffering endured by Afghan women and men deserves to be heard, but we need a critical, complex, and contextualized storytelling that interrogates its material and historical conditions.

CONCLUSION

In the AWWP storytelling project, the silent and captive Afghan woman in a burkha functions as a site for Western women readers to project an image of themselves as living in an enlightened and progressive postfeminist society, at a time when feminist gains are being rolled back in a number of arenas. The fantasy of Western readers connecting with the authentic lives of Afghan women by reading their online stories is tied to strategies of imperial statecraft. The presentation of the stories, with their horrific and painful recounting of abuse upon abuse, with little context to understand why this might be happening, encourages responses of rescue by outsiders rather than a more critical analysis of US military and imperial power. Solutions are presented as possible mainly through individual empowerment, self-esteem, and uplift through education.

This chapter has looked at the uses of storytelling in imperial statecraft. Telling and publishing stories by Afghan women is a way to amplify certain moderate voices within Afghanistan at a time when the United States faces growing resistance to its role in interventionist wars. The writing workshops are part of a broader network of State Department–funded exchange programs, leadership schools, Fulbright scholarships, and development agencies that aim to cultivate the subjectivity of a layer of leaders from the upwardly mobile urban elite who will help to lay the groundwork for a neoliberal market democracy. Those Afghan women who oppose US intervention, campaign against the US-supported warlords in the parliament, and seek to promote self-determination and economic independence for Afghanistan are further marginalized politically. A vast number of Afghan women, especially those in the rural areas of Afghanistan, will never access a Fulbright scholarship or exchange program. Rather than experiencing democracy as a new political system that affords them greater opportunities of international travel and exchange, rural Afghan women see it as a ruse that enriches some at the expense of others. As Roya says in her piece, "The Meaning of Democracy:" "I think Democracy knocked on the doors of only some women in Kabul, Mazar, Herat, only a few of Afghanistan's 34 provinces. In most areas, Afghans still don't know this word. Many think it is a word used only by politicians who travel all over the world, live in the tallest buildings and own the latest car models."[109] Where poor women are incorporated into these networks it is as entrepreneurs who are encouraged to develop skills so that they can take responsibility for their families rather than begging in the streets or being dependent on the government.

Yet in the stories that Afghan women tell and in some of the reader's comments, we can find small kernels of an incipient critique that could be the prelude to a deeper understanding of US militarism and the limits of liberal feminism. This critique also points to other kinds of feminisms based less on hierarchies of freedom than, as Brown argues, Western self-scrutiny that can better advance the prospects for women's equality, freedom, and peace globally. Instead of seeing Afghan women as awaiting the modernity and liberation that has already been attained by their Western counterparts, critical feminist perspectives present both as being positioned within orders of patriarchy and gender that limit and regulate women in different ways.[110] This recognition could be the basis for new kinds of storytelling that situate personal narratives within broader structural forces, allowing for more critical forms of solidarity between women on opposite sides of an interventionist war.

Alongside the uses of stories within geopolitical strategies, storytelling was also being deployed in domestic strategies of *trasformismo* in response to the mobilizations of undocumented migrants. In the next two chapters, I look at immigrant-based organizations in the United States and how their use of storytelling to address injustices of cultural recognition came to separate personal narratives from the root causes of the injustices.

CHAPTER 4

Out of the Home, into the House

How Storytelling at the Legislature
Can Narrow Movement Goals

During the 2000s, undocumented migrant workers and students in the United States began telling their stories publicly. Much like the Afghan women I described in the last chapter who were presented as "coming out from behind the veil," undocumented migrants[1] were seen to be "coming out of the shadows" by sharing their stories. In this chapter and the next, I examine in detail two examples of curated storytelling in migrant-based social movements—the campaign for a Domestic Workers Bill of Rights in New York and the undocumented student Dreamer movement. In their campaigns, immigrant rights groups produced brief stories that could be shared at a congressional hearing, legal hearing, or in the media. I will look at the ways that these curated stories bolstered legislative and electoral goals, often at the expense of fostering a deeper critique of inequality. I am also interested in how telling stories helped to produce new kinds of subjectivities among niche groups of women workers and students who presented themselves as upwardly mobile, self-reliant, hard-working immigrants aspiring to the American Dream. Just as storytelling strategies were used within imperial statecraft to humanize military interventions and counter antiwar sentiment, advocacy networks also deployed stories as they engaged with and redirected activism by migrant workers and students.

In the Domestic Workers Bill of Rights campaign in New York, storytelling helped to draw mainstream attention to the plight of predominantly migrant domestic workers but also truncated larger political possibilities. I argue that the narratives used in the campaign drew on long-standing cultural tropes of bad masters, individual victims, and the home as a site of care that have longer genealogies in slavery and colonialism. Various scholars have discussed these cultural logics of meaning that masked the relations of conflict in the plantation household of slavery and intimate spaces of the domestic sphere under colonialism. Slave mistresses presented their actions as benevolent and caring rather than violent.[2] Colonial employers described servants as gentle and nurturing companions who loved their charges as their own.[3] The liberal script of the domestic worker as an individual victim of bad employers also has its genesis in the tropes of the deviant bad master versus the paternalistic, caring master under slavery, the latter who serves to redeem the institution. As earlier myths of domesticity masked labor relations in colonial and slave economies, so too these narratives used by contemporary leaders disguise the racialized and gendered division of labor in a neoliberal globalized economy.

There is a long history of domestic worker organizing in the United States, and the contemporary movement has emerged in a neoliberal climate of cutbacks to publicly funded childcare programs and the use of low-wage migrant women as domestic workers to drive down wages and provide privatized care for individual families. In a moment when service-based organizations come to fill the space left by a downsized neoliberal state, those organizations fighting on behalf of domestic workers are compelled to operate as nonprofit organizations dependent on foundation funding, rather than as labor-based unions or worker-led social movements. Alongside broader shifts to financialized economies, foundations increasingly base their philanthropy on the model of the market,[4] and they require their grantees to pursue strategic and measurable goals such as legislative victories.

During the Bill of Rights campaign, the heavy involvement of advocacy networks and foundations in shaping the strategies and narratives employed by the groups ultimately narrowed the goals of the movement and resulted in limited changes for domestic workers. The campaign came to focus more on the Bill as a symbolic victory, rather than as an instrument for winning deeper structural changes for domestic workers. This shift is similar to what Nancy Fraser describes in her essay "From Redistribution to Recognition," where the "struggle for recognition" has increasingly supplanted class interest and displaced socioeconomic redistribution as the goal of political struggle.[5] Legal advocacy groups focus on "injustices of recognition," including harassment, invisibility, violence, and a "denial of full legal rights and equal protections."[6] But while advocates focus, rightly, on remedying these injustices by creating positive modes of recognition through modes such as storytelling, they do not address the deep structures that generate class disadvantage and the global divisions of exploitable labor that underpin cultural injustices.[7] While symbolic recognition through story-telling has been important in humanizing and making visible the struggles of a mostly undocumented female workforce, this strategy, when based in individuating, liberal tropes and divorced from a larger grassroots and autonomous movement, has been incapable of challenging broader global patterns of gendered inequality. Workers themselves have been calling for complex kinds of storytelling that can more fully portray the depth of their transnational lives and their situatedness in the violence of the global economy.

DEPLOYING STORIES: THE IMMIGRANT RIGHTS MOVEMENT

In dominant representations, undocumented migrants have been portrayed as freeloaders, acting as a drain on public services and taking the jobs of native-born Americans; as lawbreakers, who engage in criminal activity such as drug dealing; and as irreducibly foreign to American values and society.[8] These representations have been crafted and deployed by nativists who demand harsher measures of border security. They have been circulated by some academics such as the late Samuel Huntington, who argued for the incompatibility of immigrants, mostly Mexican immigrants, with America's Anglo-Protestant values.[9] The media uncritically adopts and perpetuates these representations, using the term "illegal" to refer to undocumented migrants.

In addition to facing such negative representations, undocumented migrants confront the constant threat of deportation or arrest if they speak up for their rights, and they have limited economic power in labor markets due to an oversupply of labor and the difficulties of aggregating their numbers due to such practices as subcontracting.[10] Given all of these hurdles, scholars of immigration and labor have argued that there are very few opportunities for undocumented migrants to publicly assert their rights.

But the nationwide mega-marches in 2006 gave a glimpse of one way that undocumented migrants could assert themselves. Over the course of several months, large numbers of undocumented migrants took to the streets to oppose the criminalization and exploitation of migrant labor. Protesters demanded full legalization of all undocumented migrants, and they challenged processes of neoliberalism that generated massive migration from the Global South due to immiseration and the demand for cheap labor in the North.[11] However, the momentum of the movement was lost partly because mainstream organizations, political consultants, and nonprofit leaders channeled the energy of the marches back into narrow legislative and electoral strategies. One of the key tools employed by nonprofit groups in their legislative campaigns was storytelling, including mass trainings of immigrant rights activists across the country in how to tell their stories to legislators and how to use stories to recruit voters.

In their legislative battles, immigrant rights groups focused on fashioning representations of undocumented immigrants that could appeal to mainstream society. A poll by the Center for American Progress, who helped to design the communications strategy of groups like Reform Immigration for America (RIFA), showed that immigration reform would depend on appealing to the sensibility of middle-class, white Americans.[12] Advocacy organizations focused on niche groups such as students and youth who were brought to the country at a young age, and workers in industries such as domestic work and agriculture that rely on a steady supply of immigrant labor.[13] Those who fit the attributes of these niche openings appeal to the strategic qualities of their group that make them deserving of rights. As Walter Nicholls argues, these niche groups must continually stress the qualities and values that make them exceptional, while silencing aspects that may not fit. In portraying themselves as innocent, easily assimilated, and hard-working, immigrants repudiated the harmful representations circulated by the nativists, but they also participated in what Nicholas De Genova calls "reracialization," locating themselves between polarized identities of "black" and "white" in the US racial order, usually by distancing themselves from blackness, associated with criminality and welfare dependence.[14]

Undocumented youth and domestic workers were two of the key niche groups who drew heavily on storytelling strategies in their campaigns for legislative rights. The national campaign for a Development, Relief, and Education for Alien Minors (DREAM) Act presented the case of undocumented minors who had legally attended elementary or high school. But when it came to attending college or finding a job after graduation, they faced the barriers of their undocumented status. Immigrant rights groups argued for the exceptional status of these youth because they were brought at an age when they couldn't understand the legal ramifications of what they were doing; therefore, they could not be held responsible. Likewise, in the New York Domestic Workers Bill of Rights campaign, legal advocacy groups and facilitators helped the workers to frame their special status as the backbone of the American economy: by caring for the children of the professional middle classes, they made all other work possible. Both groups were portrayed as hard-working immigrants who desired to attain the American Dream. This chapter and the next focus on what happened to these movements in the post-2006 period when they increasingly became drawn into the instrumental goals of foundations, political strategists, and nonprofits—and sometimes challenged them.

NARRATIVES AND STRATEGIES IN THE DOMESTIC
WORKERS BILL OF RIGHTS CAMPAIGN

The exploitation and mistreatment of domestic workers has become common in global cities like New York, where a burgeoning service sector of low-paid and manual work held by mostly migrant women has arisen to meet the needs and lifestyles of a growing professional class generated by the global economy in fields such as international finance.[15] Saskia Sassen argues that there is an increased demand for female professionals whose households must function like clockwork in order to ensure the functioning of globalized sectors like finance, and the low-wage domestic worker is brought in to maintain the household infrastructure.[16] Childcare needs more generally have not been met by a downsized neoliberal state which fails to offer publicly funded childcare for working parents.[17] The demand is met by migrant women from third-world countries who are themselves forced to migrate in search of work as a result of economic crisis and rising unemployment caused by the expansion of free trade policies and structural adjustment measures.[18] The domestic work industry has provided low-cost, migrant female labor through informalization, downgrading the tasks of reproductive labor.[19] Because of the undocumented status of many workers, employers can also use the threat of deportation to keep them captive in exploitative situations.[20] Silvia Federici argues that the new international division of labor in reproductive tasks is a "colonial" solution to the housework question that occurred because the feminist movement failed to make the state recognize reproductive labor as work and to subsidize it.[21]

Among domestic workers, new forms of political action have also arisen to address and improve their conditions. The organization Domestic Workers United (DWU) was founded in 2000 as a collaboration between three organizers: Ai-jen Poo, Carolyn de Leon, and Nahar Alam. Poo, who would become the Executive Director of DWU, was a second-generation Asian American college graduate with a degree from Columbia University. Her parents, a prominent scientist and oncologist, had migrated from Taiwan in the early 1970s. Poo had been organizing domestic workers with the Committee against Anti-Asian Violence (CAAAV) Organizing Asian Communities since 1996. De Leon, from CAAAV's Women Workers Project, and Alam, from Andolan: Organizing South Asian Workers were both domestic workers. De Leon was a Filipina domestic worker who left the Philippines at the age of twenty-three to work in Hong Kong and was then brought to the United States by an American family. She was isolated in the suburbs of New York and denied basic items such as a winter coat, until she finally left her employer.[22] Alam had a similar story. She was living in an abusive marriage with a police officer in Bangladesh, and after trying to escape unsuccessfully six times, she was granted a visa to the United States. She moved to Astoria, Queens, and found work as a domestic worker, earning as little as $50 for twelve-hour days.[23] Both de Leon and Alam had left their situations of abuse and were now domestic worker organizers. In the first meetings of DWU, the women talked about the devaluation of domestic work as women's work performed in the home and the vulnerability of workers due to their immigration status. They also discussed the unique organizing challenges faced by domestic workers, given the private and individual nature of the workplace. Because of the structure of the industry, they thought that a legislative strategy might be a way to mobilize workers and win lasting changes.

Over six years, DWU enlisted a multiethnic coalition of organizations in the New York City to work on a Bill of Rights campaign, including CAAAV, Andolan, Haitian Women for Haitian Refugees (HWHR), Unity Housecleaners Cooperative, Damayan Migrant Workers Association, and later Adhikar for Human Rights and Social Justice. As one of the main groups driving the coalition, DWU had an expansive vision of worker rights. In member workshops and trainings,[24] they discussed how the domestic work industry was shaped by class exploitation, racial oppression, and patriarchy. They talked about the main goal of DWU to dismantle systems of oppression such as globalization and imperialism.[25] At a retreat in February 2004, workshop leaders noted the need to go beyond legislative actions to address the root causes of oppression: "No matter what law we pass, oppression/injustice/inequality will continue unless we address the root causes and build movements that can disrupt, dismantle those systems of oppression."[26] At its four-week leadership training programs, launched in 2004, DWU used Marxian frames of analysis to understand the primary struggles in which workers were engaged, such as "immigrant labor vs. US capitalists." DWU sought to locate worker struggles in a larger neoliberal economic system where manufacturing is moved overseas and the conditions are created for migrant workers to be highly exploited. They discussed the need to fight both the state and also multinational corporations, who demand profits at any cost.[27]

Given the multiple languages spoken by domestic workers, organizers had to come up with strategies for communication. Ninaj Raoul from HWHR was a Haitian American who had worked as an interpreter and health counselor for Haitian refugees detained at Guantanamo in the 1990s. On her return to New York, Raoul cofounded HWHR to respond to the needs of refugees fleeing persecution. She described how language barriers had always existed for groups representing non-English-speaking populations, but by using "relay interpreting" during the Bill of Rights campaign, they were able to translate from Haitian Creole to English and from English to Spanish. Raoul recalled when De Leon visited HWHR and talked about the US occupation of the Philippines: "It was like she was talking about Haiti, everything she talked about. And everybody got it, and we're sitting here translating, but everybody got it."[28] DWU provided their globalization trainings for groups like HWHR, which also helped to draw Haitian domestic workers into the Bill of Rights campaign.

At the start of the Bill of Rights campaign, the coalition of organizations saw the legislative arena as only one of many sites of struggle. They argued that existing labor laws and government protections were vastly out of sync with workers' realities. The Fair Labor Standards Act (FLSA) and the National Labor Relations Act (NLRA) were based on long-term employment at large, single firms, a reality that has long ceased to describe the conditions for vast numbers of workers.[29] The NLRA, which guaranteed workers the right to organize, specifically excluded domestic workers. The proposed Bill of Rights would include such rights as mandated health insurance, notice of termination, personal days, severance pay, and a minimum wage of up to $16 per hour. These demands were first articulated in the "Having Your Say Convention" on November 1, 2003, where over two hundred domestic workers came together to outline their vision for an ideal Bill of Rights. These "dream" provisions eventually became the Domestic Workers Bill of Rights. DWU drafted the bill into formal legislation with the help of the New York University Immigrant Rights Clinic. In January 2004, the groups took their first trip to the state capital of Albany to meet with legislators.

On August 31, 2010, Governor David Paterson signed a much watered-down Bill of Rights into legislation. During the campaign, many of the provisions of the original bill were removed or weakened. Most of the resources and energy of the movement went into the legislative campaign, and alliances with institutional actors such as legislators, formal sector unions, and employers were promoted over grassroots base building. How did the campaign move from such an expansive notion of rights and possibility to one that became so narrowly circumscribed?

DWU was never strongly oriented toward mass mobilization and base building, but during the campaign the organization began to transition more toward a movement of worker-leaders sharing their stories through lobbying.[30] The stories aimed to promote the dignity and recognition of domestic workers, but the constructions of workers in the stories—bound by legislative protocols and geared toward a mainstream audience—reinforced rather than challenged the structural conditions of their work. Storytelling helped domestic workers to win recognition in broader society, highlighting a need for labor laws that would include them in basic provisions and emphasizing the value of their work. But as the campaign progressed, and the organization received more foundation grants for their legislative work, a wedge was driven between these symbolic struggles for recognition and battles for redistribution of economic resources, with the utopian visions and systemic critiques of the early days being gradually replaced by a more pragmatic approach. Coming out of the private spaces of the home, domestic workers gained public visibility, but by re-entering into the New York State Legislature, they were subject to new forms of constraint that narrowed their political vision.

Organizers in the Bill of Rights coalition had different visions for change and different analyses of the causes of domestic worker exploitation, which led them to promote distinct strategies. Ai-jen Poo was a proponent of legal advocacy in pursuit of cultural and legal recognition for domestic workers. She made the argument that domestic workers were a unique case, that they could not engage in direct labor market intervention such as strikes because due to the structure of the industry, workers were isolated in the homes of individual employers in situations where they lacked bargaining power.[31] She argued that the exploitation and vulnerability of domestic workers were due to this isolation and their exclusion from labor protections, and fighting for legislation would be a first step in challenging their exploitation. Poo explained her strategic vision in a later piece reflecting back on the New York Bill of Rights campaign together with the California organizer, Andrea Cristina Mercado, the granddaughter of a domestic worker whose parents immigrated from South America, and who held a college degree from Brown University.[32] In their piece, Poo and Mercado refer to the hostile contemporary political terrain where organized labor struggles to make gains, collective bargaining has been undermined, and strike activity has dramatically declined. They argue that despite the limitations of legislative change, it is a means to "bring domestic workers into the public conversation, and to win dignity and respect." These leaders were aware of the trade-offs required by a legislative strategy, but they saw it as the best chance to win changes for domestic workers in a hostile political climate.

By contrast, leaders from some of the other organizations in the coalition, several of whom were domestic workers with histories of radical organizing outside the United States, did not always share these pragmatist visions. For instance, Raoul did see the strike tactic as a possibility for domestic workers, although she argued that there would need to be a greater depth and breadth of organizing work to pursue a strike. She referred to the successful mass transportation strikes in Haiti as one model.[33] Linda Oalican from Damayan also believed that domestic workers could engage in strike activity given the right moment and level of unity. Oalican had been born to a family of poor farmers in the north of the Philippines and received a scholarship to study at university. During the extreme political repression by Ferdinand Marcos in the early 1970s, she joined thousands of students who left the campuses to become community organizers living among the urban poor. She later helped organize pickets and strikes with stevedores and factory workers under conditions of martial law. In her forties, she went to the United States and worked as a live-in domestic worker in New Jersey and New York City to pay for her children's education back home.[34] Both Raoul's and Oalican's experiences in Haiti and the Philippines led them to a more critical vision of what was possible for domestic worker organizing, and they situated their analysis of the industry in broader understandings of global politics.

Domestic workers in DWU also shared some of these organizing backgrounds in radical politics. For example, Christine Lewis was raised in rural southern Trinidad, and her father was a shop steward and political organizer among oil workers. Lewis was a calypso singer and dancer who became politicized by the Black Power uprising in Trinidad in the 1970s, when students forged alliances with striking transport workers. In her late twenties, Christine migrated to the United States with her four-year-old daughter and began working long hours as a domestic worker while also caring for her child. She later joined DWU. Other workers in DWU came from countries where they had organized strikes in maquiladoras and export processing zones. Silvia Medina, a Mexican domestic worker and member of DWU, saw direct strike action as feasible for domestic workers today. She argued that:

> We count on [a labor force of] more than 200,000 domestic workers and if they should have this awareness. If we all united, I think that all of us domestic workers would have a much greater force. . . . if for example they didn't pay us fully or if they were abusing us and all the workers said that today we're not going to work because we want a fair salary. If nobody turned up to work then we could do like a strike. That is how our voices would be heard. Because they need us. They need us because they would also lose a lot of money. We would lose a small amount that would be our daily or weekly salary, but they would lose a lot more because they wouldn't earn. They don't make what we make. . . . Even the government would lose money.[35]

Although DWU had followed the advocacy path, voices within the coalition and even within the organization were raising the question of alternative strategies and paths to what the leadership was proposing. But as Raoul said, some people "want quicker successes," and mobilizing people into mass strikes as in other countries can take a lot longer. If DWU had put its resources toward mobilizing and organizing direct labor market inter-ventions like strikes, how might that pressure have created a new terrain of struggle where domestic workers' voices could really be heard?

Several earlier generations of domestic worker organizers had also proposed or engaged in direct labor market interventions. Tera Hunter describes how African American washerwomen in Atlanta in 1881 formed an organization known as the Washing Society, and they went door to door soliciting support and organizing a citywide strike of three thousand domes-tic workers in demand of higher wages.[36] Hunter argues that, in the face of entrenched hostility and reprisal, and not long out of slavery, the women exercised remarkable leverage.[37] They drew on community networks that had grown out of shared work routines and living space to build a base for political action. The strike was also made possible by the broader political climate of heightened black political struggle. Premilla Nadasen gives the case of black household worker organizers in New York of the 1970s. She cites one of these organizers, Carolyn Reed, who believed that the potential for domestic workers to strike came from the indispensable labor power that they provided. Reed felt that it was only through the collective power of strike action that wages and working conditions could be improved.[38] Although the outsourcing of domestic labor to women from the Global South weakened the position of domestic workers vis-à-vis their employers in the decades to follow, some workers continued to believe that building worker power in the form of labor market intervention would give them a better chance at raising worker consciousness and demanding changes in the industry.

Foundations played a crucial role in directing DWU leaders away from labor market interventions based in a critique of underlying structures toward a legal advocacy approach. As Erica Kohl-Arenas has argued, given that foundation endowments consist of profits made in private industry, it is not surprising that they don't fund interventions like strikes and boycotts.[39] During the Bill of Rights campaign, the legislative component attracted increasing amounts of funding. While grants to the smaller organizations in the coalition remained negligible, in the year that the Bill of Rights was passed, DWU was awarded $482,000 in grant funding from the NoVo Foundation, Surdna Foundation, and the Foundation to Promote Open Society, some of the funds earmarked specifically for the implementation of the Bill of Rights campaign. At the same time, foundations were giving large grants to the National Domestic Workers Alliance (NDWA), which was formed by a loose coalition of domestic worker groups at the US Social Forum in Atlanta in 2007. After the Bill of Rights was passed in New York in 2010, Poo was appointed as the director of NDWA. She pursued a strategy of cultivating relationships with funders and seeking large grants to support local coalitions to win Bill of Rights campaigns in other states. Between 2008 and 2013, the Ford Foundation gave several grants to NDWA under the approach of Advocacy, Litigation, and Reform.[40] In 2013, NDWA received at least $4,754,250 in grants from a variety of foundations[41] and in the same year, they regranted about $896,810 to twenty-nine organizations.[42] Thus, the pursuit of foundation funding reshaped NDWA from a loose coalition of domestic worker organizations into an organization with a more strongly top-down, directive leadership and a stronger focus on pursuing legislative bills.

DWU and then NDWA also began to shift their priorities in line with foundations to focus on securing a well-trained workforce to meet the needs of domestic employers. Between 2008 and 2011, the Ford Foundation began giving grants to NDWA specifically for the development of a National Training Institute for domestic workers.[43] Foundations such as Surdna were also giving funds to NDWA to "advance quality jobs and career ladder models for domestic workers." It seems that one objective of foundations in their funding of DWU and NDWA was to improve the access of employers to a steady supply of well-trained domestic workers.[44] Just like the nineteenth-century domestic work reformers who, as Peggie Smith describes, sought to regulate domestic service in order to guarantee the supply of black women's labor for white, middle-class employers,[45] so, too, foundations have been concerned with regulating and professionalizing the domestic service pool.[46] Similar to the efficiency trainings sponsored by the nineteenth-century reformers, the training institutes and household management courses promoted by foundations and some domestic worker organizations were also about improving the household skills of workers to meet the needs of high-end professionals and middle-class families.[47]

Leaders made storytelling central to their legislative advocacy approach. Initially, the campaign had sought to make a technical argument about why basic rights were necessary for domestic workers. But after becoming mired in frustrating debates with a small number of legislators, Poo felt the need to shift the debate away from legal fine points and technicalities toward human rights and to change the perception of domestic work outside of Albany. She said, "The problem was that domestic workers were so dehumanized and invisible in popular consciousness; the problem was that it was hard to see the connections between the issues facing domestic workers and the issues facing all New Yorkers."[48] To build broader support for domestic workers, Poo argued that the campaign would have to humanize the workers and show their interconnection with others, and storytelling would help them achieve that. Poo frequently told her own story of realizing the interconnectedness of humanity when her grandfather was paralyzed by a stroke and cared for by a home attendant.

Stories were utilized for movement-building activities. Meetings and rallies were a site for internal sharing of stories and witnessing. These internal movement stories were rich and complex accounts that helped to inspire other domestic workers and bring them into the campaign. As the domestic worker Jennifer Bernard related, when she attended her first DWU meeting, she heard a story that moved her:

> I found myself there, very excited and enthused and hurt at the same time, because I was sitting there listening to the story of a domestic worker who, when she came to this country spoke very little English, and now had enough English to tell her story, and every domestic worker in that room, in that meeting, had tears in their eyes. It was a story of not just physical abuse, it was sexual abuse, it was abuse in every form, and it was very painful. And after listening to her that day I just knew that I wanted to be a part of this movement that makes changes.[49]

Speaking aloud the stories for the first time was not just therapeutic for the women who had often suffered alone, but it was the basis for their organizing efforts. Raoul described the experience of sitting with Haitian domestic workers and trying to prepare stories for the 2005 Human Rights tribunal:[50] "All of us were breaking down because the stories were so emotional."[51] Haitian workers originally felt ashamed and afraid to tell their stories, but over the course of the campaign they became more outspoken. Nahar Alam and Chitra Aiyar speak about how the organization Andolan started with groups of domestic workers sitting around Nahar's kitchen table and telling their stories to each other.[52] There was a power and value to this internal storytelling in helping to build and unify the movement.

Storytelling was also used in legal hearings, press conferences, and media interviews to promote the Bill of Rights campaign. In these venues, domestic workers recounted detailed narratives of their lives and the abuses that they had suffered. They sent written copies of their stories to legislators in Albany. The workers shared their stories in rallies, demonstrations, and conferences. Over the course of the six-year campaign, domestic workers shared hundreds of stories. What emerged through the testimonies was the portrait of a class of people treated as less than human beings. The Filipina domestic worker Mona related that her employers flung dirty clothes in her face, threw stale pizza on a table for her dinner, and accused her of stealing a box of $2 Niagra cornstarch. Another Filipina domestic worker, Zelem Guerrero, told how her employer referred to her as a dog, and shortly before she was fired, Guerrero overheard the employer telling a friend that she needed a new dog because she was not happy with her dog.

There were numerous stories of abuse—Angélica Hernández and Patricia Francois were both physically beaten. One employer frequently exposed himself to all of his domestic female employees. There were also stories about racially motivated abuse. Carolyn, a West Indian domestic worker, recounts her treatment at the hands of her employer, a self-defined "upstanding citizen of Massapequa Park": "While she was beating and kicking me, she was saying to me I was 'nothing but a nigger' and she wanted me off her property . . . she was cursing and saying that she had wanted to call me a nigger for three years." Stories like these helped to expose the crimes and abuses that took place in private homes, bringing them into public awareness.

In the Domestic Workers Bill of Rights campaign, stories were used for building alliances with employers and formal sector unions, in creating sympathy for the cause among prominent media outlets, and in convincing legislators to pass the Bill of Rights. Stories helped to bring domestic workers a sense of visibility and recognition in broader society. As Oalican stated, "Before, women workers were very scared. So this movement addressed fear and shame in the industry. I think it really lifted domestic work. Reclaimed the dignity of the work and dignified the workers."[53] The campaign highlighted the value of the work done by domestic workers. But the cost of this recognition was a need to conform to the dominant myths and tropes that would resonate for a mainstream, white liberal audience. In media interviews, workers were often required to present themselves as isolated, helpless, and powerless, and they had to excise emotions such as anger for fear of appearing violent. In the legal hearings, they were asked to focus on the conditions of their work, leaving out an analysis of the broader conditions of inequality that structured their work, thereby making it seem as though the problem was bad individual employers rather than a system of exploitation. The need to appeal to both Democratic and Republican lawmakers during the legislative debates over the bill imposed restrictions on the kinds of representations that domestic workers could fashion. Lawmakers and workers themselves drew on myths of social mobility and assimilation. In the end, these limited representations actually worked against the building of a class-based movement that could draw on existing bases of solidarity among workers and challenge the underlying system of exploitation.

Tropes of Domestic Work in Campaign Messaging and the Media

During the Bill of Rights campaign, leaders like Poo drew on narratives and tropes that would appeal to a white, middle- to upper-class audience. This messaging helped them to secure coverage in a series of prominent

New York Times op-eds. Early on in the campaign, a *Times* op-ed by Steven Greenhouse on June 1, 2007, quotes Poo, "These workers play a very important role in the state economy. They work for the state's professional class—lawyers, doctors, financial people, media people—and their work makes it possible for all these people to go to work every day."[54] DWU leaders and legislators appealed to the niche status of domestic workers, emphasizing that the work done by domestic workers allowed highly paid professionals to do their jobs and thereby kept the state's economy functioning. The campaign used the slogan: "the workers who make all other work possible." This was similar to the nineteenth-century reformers who Smith describes as fostering an "ideological understanding of domestic service as labor that enriched the economy."[55] Although the idea of domestic worker labor as foundational for the economy was an important move to challenge the devaluation of household work, it also celebrated the role of migrant women in carrying out reproductive tasks, rather than challenging the global division of labor and making demands on the state to pay for reproductive work.[56] In the same Greenhouse op-ed, Assemblyman Keith Wright is quoted as saying, "These folks are the invisible cogs that make the economic engines of New York work." There is no analysis of why and how those economic engines function to exploit certain people, but only a consideration of how they could be made to function better by treating domestic workers well.

The campaign messaging and the op-eds assumed that the employer was upper middle class, professional, and white, thereby erasing working-class parents of color and their childcare needs.[57] DWU focused many of its outreach and community events in wealthy, gentrified enclaves like Park Slope in Brooklyn, and their main employer allies, organized through a group called Jews for Racial and Economic Justice (JFREJ), were white. In a *New York Times* op-ed published on September 23, 2007, in support of the Bill of Rights, Lucy Kaylin, an executive editor of *Marie Claire* magazine, refers to her own middle- to upper-class milieu as "the vast majority of us who employ nannies."[58] Kaylin speaks about the "ambivalence we feel about turning over the care of our offspring to a stranger while we go off to earn and schmooze and fly to Dallas for a company party." The "we" invoked in the op-ed is a class-specific group of employers who have the financial means to fly to Dallas for a party and "schmooze" while leaving their child in the care of third world immigrant nannies, "chased here by wars and economic collapse." By focusing on the needs of professional, wealthy employers, the DWU leadership and its supporters in the media ignored vast arenas of childcare in New York City, such as the daycare workers and childcare providers who serve low-income families in places like the Bronx, who provide their labor to subsidize underfunded public childcare programs, and who would be unable to demand higher wages from the poor families that could not pay more. The erasure of working-class parents of color points to the much bigger care crisis, one which could not be resolved by legislative reforms.

These *New York Times* op-eds focus on the importance of recognition and dignity for domestic workers, but do not question the work itself or the gendered and racialized underpinnings of the work. In an editorial on June 8, 2008, titled "Women's Work," the *Times* editorial team encourages passage of the bill as "a long-overdue affirmation of the fundamental value of a belittled profession."[59] But despite the provocative title of the piece, the editorial actually ends by reaffirming the need to appreciate domestic workers for their "skills at keeping a home" and their role in "caring for children and the elderly," rather than challenging these tasks as women's work. This ideology of domesticity within the occupation dates back to the time of slavery when, as Thavolia Glymph argues, it camouflaged contentious labor relations within the plantation household.[60] Similarly, in these op-ed pieces exploitative caregiving relationships are depoliticized through references to the home as a site of care and nurturance. These op-eds fail to interrogate the assumption of migrant and black women as appropriate caretakers for the children of white professionals. Domestic work is women's work—that is not questioned.

In June 2010, at a turning point in the campaign when the revised bill was to go before an unpredictable State Senate, there was a flurry of media attention. The *New York Times* published a strongly argued op-ed piece by Ross Buettner on June 2, entitled "For Nannies, Hope for Workplace Protection."[61] This was followed by an interview with DWU leaders on WNYC's Brian Lehrer show and an online discussion forum about the proposed bill on the New York parenting website Urban Baby. In the *Times* op-ed, Buettner opens by saying, "In a city of secret economies, few are as vital to the life of New York as the business of nannies, the legions of women who emancipate high powered professionals and less glamorous working parents from the duties of daily child care." This statement makes quite clear the class sensibilities of media elites in pushing for reforms—it is about the "emancipation" of the middle and upper classes from the shackles of domestic duties and not about the emancipation of migrant domestic workers or working-class parents.

Some of the organizations in the coalition like HWHR rejected the strategy of appealing to papers like the *New York Times* precisely because they were aware of the ways in which the media could distort and manipulate their message. Raoul said, "In the Haitian community, we didn't trust the *New York Times*. We've had such a bad experience with the *New York Times*. We've had protests in front of the *New York Times* because of the way that they wrote stories about Haiti."[62] She related an experience when a *Times* reporter interviewed a Haitian man and put his photos in the paper without his permission and then the police turned up in Haiti looking for his family with a copy of the *Times* in their hands. Although the man's life was in danger, the journalist would not retract her statements. During the Bill of Rights campaign, Raoul saw the strategy of appealing to the *Times* as one that was impressive to foundations, "It's almost like a requirement sometimes." But she refused to answer the phone to *Times* reporters. Instead, HWHR spent a lot of time on local Haitian community radio, subcarrier radio stations that broadcast in Haitian creole and are widely listened to in the Haitian community. In this way they reached a large number of Haitian domestic workers and employers, educating them about the Bill of Rights campaign, but without the narrow messaging that DWU leaders created in order to get their issue into the *New York Times*. Working out of their office in the working-class Brooklyn neighborhood of Flatbush, HWHR's constituency was also quite different from the wealthy white parents who formed the base of the DWU constituency.

Patricia Francois's Story

One of the stories to receive significant attention during the media coverage of June 2010 was that of the Trinidadian domestic worker and DWU member Patricia Francois. In December 2008, Francois was assaulted by her employer of six and a half years after she had an argument with him while standing up for his daughter, an eight-year-old girl under her care. I first met Francois just weeks after the attack when contacts in DWU recommended her to look after my infant daughter one morning a week while I attended a seminar. At first, she didn't mention anything about the attack, and there was not much physical evidence because her face had mostly healed, but slowly she began to tell me the details and I came to know about her case.

In 2009, Francois filed a lawsuit against her employers, Michael Mazer, a filmmaker, and Sheryl Shade, a sports agent representing prominent athletes. The lawsuit, which included such heartbreaking details as Francois's young charge testifying against her in court, played out alongside the Bill of Rights campaign. Francois was profiled in an extensive feature story on domestic workers by the reporter Jennifer Gonnerman in the *New York Magazine* that came out on June 6, 2010, at the climax of the media attention for the bill.[63] The article made mention of the fact that Francois was a strong supporter of the Domestic Workers Bill of Rights and had made twenty-five visits to Albany to lobby for it. Gonnerman narrates Francois's story in a strongly sympathetic and moving rendering of the events:

In Francois's version of the story, the father came home in a bad mood and began berating his daughter for not practicing her lines for a holiday skit. Even after he took her to another room, Francois could hear the girl crying.

"Mr Matthew, stop it!" she shouted.

"It's my child!" he said.

"I don't care!" she said. "I'm taking care of her too!"

She was about to leave when she overheard him tell his daughter she was going to have to do without her nanny from now on. Hearing the girl's sobs, Francois went to comfort her, and that's when, she claims, things escalated. According to Francois, her boss called her a "stupid black bitch" and told her he hoped she died "a horrible death." She shouted back and he slapped her, she claims. When Francois tried to call 911, he grabbed her hand and twisted it. She fell, he lost his balance, too, and then he punched her in the torso and the face. She struggled to get free and rushed out the door.

The reporter uses narrative devices such as direct speech, suspense, and a subjective third-person point of view to draw the reader in. Although the reporter uses the qualifier "she claims" several times, the way the events are narrated builds a picture of an incident that actually transpired rather than simply being alleged. Among the thirty-some postings on the website of the article, most people did sympathize with Francois and not with her employer. As Polletta argues, when audiences read news stories profiling an individual story, they tend to take that person's point of view as persuasive.[64]

The photographs of Francois's face, bruised and swollen after the attack, were also used widely in the campaign to convey the nature of the violent attack on her and the vulnerability of domestic workers. Like the photographs of mass graves in the Guatemalan Truth Commission, visual imagery in the Bill of Rights campaign was used alongside written or verbal narrative as a means of storytelling.[65]

But although the Gonnerman article and other media stories profiling Francois's case presented Francois as assertive and not a helpless victim in the events—she told her employer to stop berating his daughter and she defended herself—winning the sympathy of a liberal readership did require sanitizing the events. There was one detail that had been left out of the media stories. In a personal interview with Francois, she told me that in her interaction with Mazer, she called him a bitch as well:

That night in particular, I was called a stupid black bitch. Well, it went backward and forward because I let him know he was the bigger one, and he asked back for his keys and his phone which I presented to him. But after I—he called me a stupid black "b," and I told him he was a bigger "b," he punched me in my face. And when I said I'm not taking this and grabbed the phone, he grabbed onto me and—up until now I still have a little scar on my hand—grabbed onto me and told me don't use his phone. But it so happened I was screaming and yelling for help, "somebody help me," because he—after punching me—he turned around and asked me if I could afford a lawyer. So my answer, my response was, if you paid me right, paid me my overtime, I'd be able to pay my rent on time and afford a lawyer as well. So that's how my six and a half years job as a nanny ended.[66]

The information about Francois cursing back at her employer was left out of Gonnerman's article discreetly—either omitted by Francois herself or by the reporter—most likely in an effort to maintain the reader's sympathy for her and her story. However, as a result of this omission, we have less of a sense of Francois as a real person, with her own frustrations, anger, and pain. She is supposed to have the upper hand by maintaining her composure, and the evidence of her own anger cannot be contained within this particular narrative.

Compare this coverage of Francois's story with the reporting about Yoselyn Ortega, the nanny accused of murdering the two small children under her care in October 2012. Although the nanny's family members and neighbors spoke to the media of Ortega's untreated mental illness, stress, and work overload, the media itself used phrases like "killer nanny," and Internet discussion forums exploded with stereotypes about the "violent and bloody culture of Mexicans," even though the nanny was Dominican. Parents on the blogs and parenting forums were understandably distressed, but there was no place to understand the anger that may have been behind the tragic events, as this was not seen as befitting the character of a nanny.

While the media presented certain images of Francois that would garner sympathy, these are not necessarily the images that Francois herself wanted to convey with her story. A short 2010 film *In Our Care* by Selena Rhine narrates Francois's story alongside other stories of domestic workers. In one scene Francois is looking tired and emotional, with tears running down her face. Photos of her battered face appear on the screen as she relates the sadness of her fiftieth birthday, which took place just days after the attack. But at the end of the film, Francois is wearing a bright-blue, tie-dye dress and applying mascara in front of a mirror. As she attaches dangly gold hoop earrings, she says, "Your face tells a story, and with my face I always wanted to tell a good story." Then she attaches a badge to the front of her dress that reads, "Domestic Workers United for Dignity," and she goes for the final event of a training workshop. The story of abuse and victimhood is not the only story that Francois wants her face to tell.

Like the other workers who suffered abuse at the hands of their employers, Francois was brought out in hearings, press conferences, and lobbying visits to tell her story over and over. On June 13, 2012, two years after the passage of the Bill of Rights, Francois received the verdict in her case. The verdict included only a very small payout for Francois, representing a loss after all she had endured. But NDWA published a piece on their website with the heading "Domestic Worker Wins Justice, Finally."[67] Francois's supposed victory is connected to the victory of the Bill of Rights campaign. The article notes that "Pat shared her story countless times so that lawmakers would feel the urgency of providing domestic workers with rights and protections." But not only did Francois fail to get justice, she also faced the indignity of having her loss paraded as a success by the organization.

The Generic Power of the Legal Hearing

Alongside the media profiling of domestic workers' stories, one of the other main arenas for storytelling during the campaign was the New York State legislature in Albany. The testimonies given by workers were situated narratives produced within the context of the legal hearing. While the testimonies reference the actual experiences of domestic workers, these stories are also dialogic,[68] contextual, and strategic.[69] The workers told thickly descriptive accounts using literary techniques that invited listeners to enter into the worlds that they depicted. They circulated, retold, and refashioned their narratives in other arenas, such as marches, rallies, conferences, and meetings. Analyzing workers' testimonies as literary texts can help us to understand how they made their stories resonate with lawmakers and allies in what was initially an unfriendly space. But these stories are not unmediated windows into the real lives of domestic workers; they are narratives that are shaped by the generic power of the legal hearing itself. For purposes of legal testimony the workers were given specific protocols to guide their storytelling. They had to condense their stories, to leave out the broader conditions and focus only on technical employment issues, and to present themselves as isolated victims of unscrupulous employers. Although the stories were useful in appealing to the sensibilities of lawmakers, they narrowed the ability of the workers to collectively analyze and challenge deeper structures of oppression.

When the domestic worker activists made trips to Albany to meet with individual Republican and Democratic lawmakers, they initially encountered a hostile environment. This is not surprising, given that state legislatures have been actively enacting laws that criminalize and expand policing powers over the undocumented. The New York state legislature in particular has been described by political scientists as one that frustrates change: "a limited suffrage, an inattentive electorate, and an ossified party and pressure system combine to make sure that this year's policies will look pretty much like last year's."[70] A bill introduced in New York State has a chance of about one in thirty of becoming law.[71] Many legislators, Republican and Democratic, themselves hired domestic workers to care for their children or elderly parents, or to clean their homes. In the beginning this was not an asset to the campaign because legislators were concerned that a bill might impact their own access to domestic labor.

Domestic workers were made aware of the state legislature as a strongly racialized and gendered space. Medina related how she was singled out and treated differently from the other workers because she was Mexican. She described a particular meeting in Albany, where the group of workers was being addressed in English by a Puerto Rican female legislator. According to Medina, when she indicated that she wanted to speak, the legislator told her in Spanish, "You, shut up. Just as I can defend you, I can also throw you out, so you shut up."[72] Medina was the only one who was treated so rudely by the legislator, and since she was the only Latina in the group, she concluded that it was because of her ethnicity. Lewis found that it was hard to adapt to the cultural norms of Albany: "I might go in with my feisty self, sometimes you have to tone it down. You don't pound the table, I want this right now."[73] The workers had to be subservient and obedient, qualities that the movement had encouraged them to overcome.

During the campaign, Bill of Rights activists travelled to Albany to meet with legislators more than forty times. By 2008, the leaders of the organization were able to meet directly with the Speaker of the Assembly. At an Assembly Labor Committee hearing on the conditions surrounding domestic employment in New York, held on November 21, 2008, testimonies by domestic workers, academics, and labor allies were presented. The hearing was a crucial one for the campaign. It was presided over by Susan John, the chair of the Assembly Labor Committee, who opened by expressing her desire to know more about working conditions in the industry to bring about the necessary legislative action. The general atmosphere of the hearing was sympathetic and open, as the three members of the Assembly present were all supporters of the bill.

Domestic workers were given a protocol to follow for submitting their testimonies. The notice stated that "Oral testimony will be by invitation only and limited to ten minutes duration."[74] Assemblyman Keith Wright emphasized to the presenters that they were on a "very tight schedule" and that people would have to stick to the schedule. Four domestic workers presented their testimonies at the hearing and another submitted written testimony.[75]

The domestic workers used the legislative hearing as a site to stage their stories of abuse and mistreatment. The narratives garner sympathy not by overwrought and sentimental evocations of the traumatic events, but rather by matter-of-fact prose that invites the listener to watch the scene unfolding.

The domestic worker Angélica Hernández related how she began working for a family in Manhattan in 2007, cleaning their house. She then started looking after their child, cooking, and going food shopping for the entire family, working twenty-hour days for a low salary. When Hernández started attending DWU meetings, she was fired from her job. She describes the physically abusive actions of her employer in language that is controlled and spare:

> The employer scolded me for not taking the child to the park. She was furious and yelled at me. I asked her to stop. She continued insulting me and pushed me. She insisted that I return the keys to the apartment. I understood then that she was firing me, that I had to leave and that I should gather my things. So she grabbed me by the hair, slapped me, and punched my arm. She grabbed my things and threw them on the floor, yelling and stomping on them. She said that I was born to be a servant, not a nanny. And that Domestic Workers United didn't know what they were talking about because I did not have rights.

Hérnandez does not describe her own feelings and responses, but simply relates the actions of her employer. The absence of affect in her account evokes the normalization of violence against domestic workers.

Hernández's story of physical abuse and harassment had echoes in the stories of other workers such as Elizabeth, who detailed the sexual abuse that she suffered from her employer. Elizabeth was working for a family in Manhattan with eight other workers, all of whom were sexually harassed by their male employer. She related a few examples:

> The second day on the job, the employer started in on me. I was in the living room when he went to shower. From there, he called out to me, "Elizabeth, please get me the phone." I entered the room and responded, "Where are you?" "In the shower," he answered. When I entered, he had the curtain opened completely. I was shocked. I grabbed the phone and threw it. I was furious.

The use of pointed dialogue to convey this experience of sexual abuse helps to set the scene and place the listener there. Elizabeth uses short sentences to build to the climax: "He had the curtain opened completely." Rather than passively accepting or ignoring the violation, Elizabeth shows her anger toward her employer by throwing the phone.

But even more powerful than the traumatic instances of shocking abuse are the routine, mundane kinds of mistreatment suffered by the workers. It is the specific details and images in these parts of the narratives that are so effective in conveying their situation. Freda says that "The husband hardly said 'Hi' or 'Good morning' to me. He would just walk straight past me."

When Mona relates that she was accused of stealing a box of "$2 Niagra Cornstarch," the vivid details of the brand and the cost of the product have more impact than if she had simply said that she was accused of stealing a cleaning product. Elizabeth describes pay day at her job: "Every Friday, when he paid us, he would have his penis out." The potent image of the male employer exposing himself to his female employees comes as a shock because it is expressed in a simple sentence about the regular experience of pay day.

This cataloguing of details is also present in Joycelyn Gill-Campbell's testimony, describing her work in 1998 for a family in Manhattan:

> I was made to wear a white uniform like Florence Nightingale, white shoes, white pants and shirt. The only thing that was missing was the little white hat. I was taking care of one little girl. They also had two dogs; however, one of the dogs developed cancer in one of his legs and could not walk, so my employer went out and bought a double stroller which meant that I had to push the little girl and the dog through the streets of Manhattan in this stroller.

There is an element of humor in Gill-Campbell's testimony, which invites her listeners to laugh with her at the excesses of her employers. The narrative conveys her humiliation at being forced to wear a white uniform while pushing a dog and a child in a stroller.

Personal stories were highly effective in communicating the conditions of domestic work, even more so than just facts and statistics on violations. But the stories were also strongly circumscribed by the legal hearing itself. The strict time limits of the testimonies and of the hearings themselves often meant that there was little room for the complexity of the women's stories. The protocol at the 2008 Labor Committee Hearing required workers to address certain "selected issues" that fell within narrowly defined boundaries, including typical hours and schedule, benefits, relationship with employer, grievance procedures, and how New York State can improve working conditions. Workers were instructed to focus on the technical conditions of employment rather than the broader structural context of their industry. As a result, the abuses seemed to be the consequence of individual bad employers who could be reined in by tighter regulations, rather than part of an entrenched system of exploitation.

While some workers recounted standing up to their employers, most of the stories end with the worker being fired or subject to ongoing harassment. Although several of these cases involved lawsuits against employers or demonstrations and protests outside their homes, the stories did not make mention of these facts. For the purposes of the public hearing or press conference, the employers reign supreme in their position of control while the worker has been taken advantage of. Many of the narratives end with reference to the bill, and how this bill will improve their situation, but the stories do not give the satisfaction of seeing the employers made accountable for their acts. Like the adult survivors of child abuse who were required to give performances of fear, grief, and shame in court in order to prove victimhood and win compensation, domestic workers were also required to present themselves as victims of unscrupulous employers who get away with exploiting workers.[76] The liberal script of the bad mistress and individual victim is one that has its roots in slavery and the plantation household, where acts of abuse were presented as an aberration among otherwise benevolent mistresses.[77]

Social movement organizations seem to accept that the nature of legal advocacy requires this frame of victimhood. But like the child abuse survivors, domestic workers could find other outlets like marches and protests to speak of their empowerment. At rallies for the Domestic Workers Bill of Rights, chants included: "Are we right or wrong? We're right! Are we weak or strong? We're strong!" And although the testimonies often appealed to legislators to protect vulnerable domestic workers, in campaign slogans it is the domestic workers who are schooling legislators. In the "Domestic slide" dance performed in Albany by West Indian domestic workers, they sang: "You gotta move—We'll educate you from our side. And we will teach you, teach you, teach you—So you can pass our Bill of Rights." In their cultural actions, the workers reversed the paternalism inherent in the legal process.

Another limitation of storytelling in the legislative arena is that the stories presented in support of the bill may not fit all of the experiences of those the campaign claims to represent.[78] For instance, at the Labor Committee Hearing, many of the stories of domestic workers referred to their isolation. One of the experts called in to provide testimony, the historian Premilla Nadasen, also emphasized the isolation of domestic workers: "They have no opportunity to organize and little opportunity to speak out on their own behalf. They are isolated from friends and family. And in many cases have no one to turn to for support."[79] While this may be the case for some domestic workers, especially the ones that testified at the hearing, this may not be the case in general. In her ethnography of West Indian domestic workers in Brooklyn—a key constituent of a group like DWU—Tamara Mose Brown found that the workers never mentioned isolation.[80] They had built strong communities of trust through their gathering in public places like parks, through food sharing, informal systems of saving money, and cell phone technology. Although the legislative focus on isolation may have been a strategy to prove the inability of these workers to engage in collective bargaining, by constructing domestic workers as isolated and unorganized, the testimonies may have reinforced the workers' powerlessness rather than the existing bases of collective strength that could be the grounds for organizing work.

An exception among the testimonies was one submitted by Damayan, a Filipino migrant workers organization. Damayan wanted to include a discussion of the global conditions of exploitation, and its leaders faced some resistance but ultimately submitted testimony as a written document. The testimony is from an anonymous domestic worker testifying on behalf of a fellow Filipina domestic worker, Marichu Baoanan. She recounts that Baoanan was a nursing school graduate who was subjected to forced labor and racketeering by the former Philippines UN Ambassador. She then goes on to address the global conditions of domestic work:

> Marichu and I are part of the global crisis that enslaves Third World women into dehumanizing conditions—working in a foreign land as second-class immigrants. We are two of the 10 million Filipinos abroad who are treated as products in the global market. We prop up the Philippines economy with more than $20 millions in remittances. We also contribute to the annual $952.6 billion that is generated by the New York City's economy. We not only shoulder the crisis of our homeland, but we also carry the weight of the deepening crisis in the US. Billions of dollars turn into profits as a result of our labor and at the expense of our dignity and humanity.

Unlike the other testimonies, this one links the personal story of abuse of Baoanan to the double neoliberal crisis that both impoverishes third-world nations like the Philippines and creates domestic economic hardships. The labor of Filipina women is used both to bolster a failing economy back home and to meet a care crisis in the United States. Underlying this narrative is the analysis of labor exploitation as generating vast profits for the wealthy. In this testimony, cases like that of Baoanan are not individual instances but, as the testimony puts it, part of "a system that perpetuates abuse and violence against women workers like me." In the conclusion to the story, the narrator informs us that Baoanan "managed to escape and is now fighting for her rights." Unlike the other stories where the workers are portrayed as victims, in this account Baoanan is a survivor and a political organizer.

Legislative Debates and the Myth of an Immigrant America

Ellis Island was a symbol mostly for European refugees. Blacks, "we blacks," had known rougher ports of entry.

Teju Cole, *Open City*

In the legislative debates that followed the Labor Committee hearing, legislators reframed the stories of domestic workers using dominant tropes of the American Dream and hard-working, deserving immigrants. During the Senate debate on June 1, 2010 in the New York State legislature, senators in support of the bill presented domestic workers as just another group who wanted to access the American Dream. The legislative debates and stories were framed by the construct of what Bonnie Honig refers to as the "myth of an immigrant America," or the belief that "America is a distinctively consent-based regime, founded on choice rather than inheritance, on civic rather than ethnic ties."[81] Senator Eric Adams drew a genealogy dating back from earlier immigrant groups like Italian and Irish Americans to contemporary immigrants, saying that they've all made this pilgrimage, and like them, "we too love America."[82] In the news conference held beforehand, he affirmed that "from the board room to the boiler room, everyone will have the opportunity to participate in the American Dream."[83] The universalizing discourse of the American Dream obscured the class-based rights that domestic workers were seeking.

By drawing on the myth of an immigrant America, the legislators framed the debate using discourses of social mobility. Several senators, including Bill Perkins, Eric Adams, and Thomas Duane, testified about the experiences of their own immigrant mothers and grandmothers who had worked as domestic workers.[84] Senator Duane described how his great aunt worked as a domestic and then had become a public school teacher. Adams told the story of his own mother, a domestic worker who saw her son "go from being a cop to a state Senator," and that, for him, is the American Dream: "That's what your dreams and hopes are, that's what America is about." Adams argued that current immigrant groups are identical to earlier ones: "There's nothing different from this group that's here." At a time of downward mobility for most Americans, Honig argues that the myth of an immigrant America helps to keep alive the idea of the American Dream and a meritocratic economy.[85] The myth of a nation of immigrants also obscures the ways that the American nation was not founded only on immigration, but also by conquest, slavery and annexation.[86]

Domestic workers themselves drew on nationalist myths of the American Dream and an immigrant America to win over conservative and Republican legislators to the bill. Jennifer Bernard related her experiences during a lobbying visit with one Republican senator who would not tell her where his parents emigrated from. "I kept at him until I found out that his fore parents were Polish," she said. "And so then I said, 'You're a product of immigrants.' And they cleaned houses and different things for a living, and so I said, "Oh, so you're a product of a domestic worker.'" Bernard recalled how she told the senator that it was immigrants and domestic workers who brought him to where he was now, and he should be commended for achieving so much in life. She said to the senator that she too is raising her son, hoping not that he'll be a legislator per se, but that he will also be an important person like the senator. Other domestic workers such as Monica Díaz made reference to the American Dream during the news conference. She talked about the abuses committed against Indonesian domestic workers, referring to "the suffering they went through when they came for their American Dream."[87] The domestic workers' use of these myths was strategic, but the nationalist frame also worked to paper over racial and class cleavages by presenting social mobility as the ultimate goal of the campaign.

Moreover, the language of the striving immigrant that underpinned both the legislators and domestic workers' narratives worked to create a division between "good" immigrants, who are hard-working, employed, and desiring assimilation, and "bad" immigrants who are unemployed, do not embrace American values, and do not desire assimilation. Jennifer Gordon describes this same dynamic in the successful campaign for New York's Unpaid Wages Prohibition Act more than a decade earlier.[88] Republican senators were prepared to approve labor rights for undocumented workers as long as they were hard working and productive. "Bad" immigrants, conversely, were seen as "takers," who wanted a handout. This division between "good" and "bad" immigrants can also function to set immigrants against African Americans, often stereotyped as "freeloaders" who are lazy and dependent on public welfare.

The need to win bipartisan support from both liberals and conservatives led supporters of the bill to link their stories to nationalist rhetoric about the American Dream, an immigrant America, and the hard-working, deserving immigrant. In other contexts such as a direct action strike, rather than trying to win over the conservative Republicans, they might instead be exposed for their narrow class interests. Yet in the legal arena where bipartisan support is necessary for the passage of legislation, there is an emphasis on building consensus and finding common ground with one's opponents. Poo spoke about the role of stories in producing a sense of connection and interdependence, and how the campaign was energized by employers, legislators, unionists, and others seeing how their own life stories were connected to the stories of domestic workers.[89] But although the discourse of "our collective humanity" was important in garnering widespread support for the campaign, the compromises and bargains that had to be struck to please all parties meant that the original demands of the domestic workers were watered down to be little more than a symbolic victory.

The Senate bill, approved after a two-hour debate with a vote of 33 to 28, itself reflected the competing interests at the negotiating table. Although the Senate version of the bill was more expansive than the version passed in the Assembly, it was much more watered down than the original proposal. Once the Assembly and Senate bills were reconciled, the final bill that was signed into law removed even the paid sick days, vacation days, and notice of termination that the Senate version had provided, on the grounds that domestic workers should not be entitled to special provisions not available to other workers. And without the rights to collective bargaining that other workers had, it would be hard to raise basic standards without further state legislation.

When the cuts to the bill were presented to the groups in the coalition in June 2009, there was disagreement about whether it was worth continuing with such a compromised bill, but after a vote they went ahead. Legislators themselves were eager to push the weak bill forward in order to have a success that they could parade to their constituencies. Two of the coalition groups that raised concerns were Damayan and HWHR. HWHR was occupied with working in Haiti after the January 2010 earthquake, so their attention was somewhat diverted from the campaign during a crucial period when the bill was up for debate. But Raoul was aware that with mobilization and mass action, it would have been possible to push for something better. In the late 1990s, Raoul had been involved in a campaign for a Haitian Refugee Immigration Fairness Act, passed in 1998, and they got a bill on the table only because of initial efforts in the Miami Haitian community that drew crowds of seven to eight thousand Haitian immigrants, many undocumented, demonstrating outside of legislators' offices. Based on her experience with mass action in the Haitian immigration campaign, Raoul felt that the Bill of Rights campaign could have pushed for more.

In assessing the final bill that was signed into law, the legal scholar Terri Nilliasca said that what were touted as legal gains were mostly symbolic and duplicative of legal rights that were already codified in laws such as the FSLA and New York law but not enforced.[90] Nilliasca also argues that the Bill codified an exclusionary definition of domestic workers by excluding those who provide "companionship services." The bill expands coverage to those domestic workers who care for the infirm and the elderly under state minimum wage law (most other domestic workers were already covered under minimum wage laws), expands overtime pay to live-in domestic workers, and legislates benefits such as an unpaid day of rest each week and three days of paid vacation after working for the same employer for a year, as well as protection for workers from sexual or racial harassment. But overall, Nilliasca says that "the Domestic Workers Bill of Rights establishes a very low floor of protections and yields limited concrete benefits for the black and immigrant women who labor as paid caregivers."[91] In fact, some groups in the coalition were concerned that codifying such a low floor might actually worsen the conditions of their members in the workplace.

The final bill appeared to concede to the demands of workers and the bill sounded progressive, but ultimately it reinforced the neoliberal logics and outsourcing practices of the state, as Monisha Das Gupta has argued in relation to an earlier 2002 New York City council bill to regulate the agencies that employ domestic workers.[92] Just like the City Council bill, the Domestic Workers Bill of Rights does not change the privatized mechanisms through which the state depresses women's paid reproductive labor.[93] Neither bill requires the state to change its practices, to become accountable, or to make any investment in services or enforcement that would be needed to free domestic workers from exploitation. The Bill of Rights campaign actually used these arguments to appeal to legislators. A "Talking Points" flyer that was widely circulated by the campaign claimed that "The Bill of Rights is smart economic policy:" "In a time of tight state budgets, the Bill of Rights will not cost anything for the State of New York."[94] While the campaign brought about an awareness of the conditions of domestic workers, the final bill had little impact on the economic conditions of workers and it failed to challenge the deeper structure of the work or make demands on the state.

Domestic workers who had told their stories during the campaign were skeptical of what benefits the whittled-down bill had brought them. Reflecting back on the campaign several years later, Francois said that the Bill of Rights "did nothing to change my working conditions or working conditions of the hundreds of thousands of domestic workers in NY."[95] DWU cofounder De Leon argued that symbolic victories were not enough: "As workers, we don't need symbolic victories, we need tangible changes."[96] She said that while middle-class women were making the decisions to follow the legislative path; it was third world women workers who were suffering the brunt of the outcome. Gill-Campbell was doubtful that the claim of recognition was even a reality. She believed that without any lasting organizational structure or support, "the recognition of the domestic worker has yet to be addressed."[97] As domestic workers were well aware, the pursuit of recognition without accompanying structural changes is by nature limited, as cultural categories and discourses are buttressed by institutions, and you cannot change one without changing the other.

A few years after the passage of the Bill of Rights, DWU went through a series of tensions and conflicts, with some domestic workers feeling that the non-domestic worker leadership needed to allow more space for leadership by workers. After Poo left to direct NDWA, DWU suffered a major decline in funding and membership. Some local members of DWU felt that their labor, stories, and effort of years of organizing mostly went to build the political capital and prestige of NDWA and its leaders, leaving them with few tangible changes in their lives.

After the legislative win in New York State, NDWA pursued Bills of Rights campaigns in several other states, including California. The New York Bill of Rights campaign was widely touted by NDWA as a model for the other campaigns and for low-wage and immigrant organizing in general. In 2013, NDWA produced a handbook for how other states could design their Bill of Rights.[98] For the most part, this guide begins with the low floor of protections that was established in New York. It does not include a minimum hourly wage or health insurance that the Bill of Rights campaign had originally put forth. It also includes such redundant clauses as "Written Notice and Wage Statements" and "Recordkeeping by Employers," which are already required by most state laws. Raoul says that when she saw some of the bills that were being proposed, she questioned why they were even starting with such minimal policies.[99] "Why not try to get a better bill than New York got?" she asked.

THE "BE THE HELP" CAMPAIGN: FICTIONAL PORTRAYALS OF DOMESTIC WORKERS

Besides using stories at the legislature and in the media, domestic worker organizations used fictional portrayals of domestic workers in order to boost their visibility and build awareness about the conditions of workers. During the California campaign, the organization launched a media and storytelling campaign around *The Help*, a Hollywood movie released in 2011 about domestic workers in the Jim Crow South that was based on a bestselling novel by Kathryn Stockett. Like the legislative and media stories, the fictional portrayals, which drew on highly contested Hollywood representations, presented the lives of domestic workers through limiting and narrow tropes. By reinforcing dominant misconceptions about black domestic workers through their campaign, the NDWA distanced themselves even further from minorities and lost a key opportunity to educate their own membership base about black and civil rights history.

When *The Help* was released, there was an outpouring of criticism from African Americans. The Association of Black Women Historians (ABWH) issued a statement calling out the film for its resurrection of the mythical "mammy" stereotype: "Portrayed as asexual, loyal, and contented caretakers of whites, the caricature of Mammy allowed mainstream America to ignore the systemic racism that bound black women to back-breaking, low paying jobs where employers routinely exploited them."[100] The statement also criticized the film for its caricatures of black vernacular, distorted and misleading images of black male characters, its comic treatment of the very real violence and abuses faced by domestic workers, and for centering the plot on the triumphs of a young white benefactor, Ms. Skeeter, who writes the women's stories. The ABWH pointed out the silence on the history of black women's civil rights activism, even though in Mississippi of the 1960s when the film is set, black women were agitating for change and registering to vote. African American public figures from former MSNBC host and professor Melissa Harris-Perry to actor Wendell Pierce were outraged at what they saw as Hollywood's caricature of the lives of black domestic workers. Pierce, who saw the movie with his mother, called the movie "Jim Crow lite," and said that it didn't express the pain and anger that his mother had experienced as a domestic worker.[101]

Despite these public criticisms of the film, NDWA chose *The Help* as a major campaigning tool as they made a push for a California Domestic Workers Bill of Rights. Even before the film came out, NDWA produced a short YouTube video called "Meet Today's Help."[102] The video refers to the movie as a "courageous story about domestic workers in the Civil Rights era." But forwarding fifty years on, the video emphasizes that domestic workers are still not covered by labor laws. The video shows a broad range of domestic workers of different races and ethnicities, and argues that they are in need of legislation to protect their rights. The NDWA created a Facebook page and used the Twitter hashtag #BeTheHelp in advance of the Oscars. When Octavia Spencer won the Academy Award in 2012 for Best Supporting Actress in the film, NDWA had organized parties of domestic workers all over the country who cheered her on. At an NDWA fundraising gala in November 2012, the organization honored two other actresses from the film, Viola Davis and Cicely Tyson. Poo noted that the film was "a huge opening to create space in the public imagination for domestic workers today."[103] And just as the movie and novel reached millions of viewers and readers, so too the NDWA YouTube video received over 10,000 hits while short videos of today's domestic workers created by Participant Media—one of the producers of the film—received over 100,000 hits.[104] When Spencer won a Golden Globe award, she referred to "domestics in this country—now and then" in her acceptance speech.

NDWA's Be The Help campaign tried to challenge the idea encouraged by the film that domestic worker abuse is simply a thing of the past. Rather, through videos and testimonies, they show the ways in which this abuse continues today. But some critics such as Tamara Nopper have pointed out the political opportunism of NDWA in using the film for its own ends, thereby silencing the outpouring of critique by African Americans. Nopper argued that NDWA was actively engaged in what she calls "black disappearance" in multiracial progressive politics.[105] Nopper describes how NDWA, together with movie studios, political consultants, strategists, and Hollywood directors, crafted a new storyline about *The Help* that constructed African Americans as heroines of the "unfinished" struggle of the civil rights movement, which today will be carried on by immigrant domestic workers. This narrative erases black domestic workers in many ways, including those African Americans who continue to work as domestic workers today, and those who still experience racism and organize against it. In such narratives, argues Nopper, African Americans exist only in the past, where they can be allies or sentimental inspiration.

NDWA pushed back against charges of political opportunism by deploying black Caribbean workers such as Barbara Young to silence the critics. In a panel on the Melissa Harris-Perry show, where Harris-Perry and her two other panelists air their critiques of Ms. Skeeter as the agent for the women to tell their stories, Young reaffirms the role of Ms. Skeeter in the film, discrediting the views of the others by claiming to represent the viewpoint of "real" domestic workers: "I am the real-life domestic worker, and I see what she did in the movie, because she tells her story at the end and the love she had for the woman that takes care of her and today, her story was giving those women a voice. And today domestic workers are finding their voice."[106] Yet if domestic workers today are finding their voice, is this at the expense of earlier black domestic workers, whose stories remain untold and misrepresented?[107]

In the marketing of NWDA's Be The Help campaign, partners such as Participant Media spoke of storytelling as empowering for the black women in the film and for today's domestic workers: "In *The Help*, a group of women risk everything to tell their stories. Through the process of storytelling they become empowered and, in turn, inspire and empower others."[108] Yet not only is it likely that domestic workers in the Jim Crow South would have faced brutal retaliation for telling their stories, but for present-day domestic workers, there was a sense that in marketing campaigns such as these, their stories had become commodities. As Christine Lewis noted, the hype of the film created a frenzy of reporters and writers wanting to speak with contemporary domestic workers and get their story: "We're so in vogue now. Everyone wants our story, everyone wants a DWU story, so they come and put a microphone in your face. And these were the same stories that the women couldn't speak about back in the sixties, who were still in the backwaters of Mississippi or Alabama."[109] Lewis identifies the experiences of contemporary domestic workers who have somebody come in to "take our story and twist it and turn it and tell the story" with the domestic workers in *The Help* who had a white woman come in and take their stories: "You have people who capitalize on the story, on our stories, so I see it as *The Help* all over again, in a different era."[110] Both past and contemporary domestic workers had someone else profiting from their stories.

The engagement of NDWA with *The Help* raises questions about how immigrant worker organizations deploy civil rights analogies. NDWA presented the film as a jumping-off point for a deeper engagement with the lives and histories of African American domestic workers and the legacies of slavery within the industry. Yet in reality, the campaign failed to engage with the silences and exclusions contained in the portrayals, thereby reinforcing the silencing of black women and furthering the gap between immigrant domestic workers and African Americans. In pursuit of a high-profile campaign, NDWA missed a crucial opportunity to educate its membership about such harmful stereotypes as the mammy, the history of civil rights, the trajectory of black domestic workers, and the ongoing racism and institutionalized exclusions faced by African Americans today.

Through the Bills of Rights campaigns, NDWA leaders presented storytelling as an empowering act that would help to communicate the plight of current-day domestic workers to broader publics. And although the various high-profile media and outreach campaigns did bring modes of coveted mainstream recognition to domestic workers, they did so at the expense of forging more radical and oppositional ties with groups such as African Americans and other undocumented people who didn't fit the models devised by the campaign. The choice to identify with a highly problematic film about black domestic workers was not simply a bid for major publicity, but it was revealing of the limitations of the strategy itself, which was about the recognition of one group of niche workers, and not the challenging of broader dynamics of class and racial power.

Like other domestic workers, Lewis was critical of what she saw as middle-class women setting the agenda for the domestic workers movement, while workers were brought out to tell their stories and do cultural performances. In reference to an academic conference held on domestic work, where the panels consisted of mostly academics and middle-class leaders while local domestic workers were relegated to a postconference performance, Lewis remarked that "We are whittled down to culture, brought out to do the jigaboo dance. We are not allowed to organize and strategize."[111] Out of the spotlight, Lewis and other domestic worker leaders like Patricia Francois have been working to restructure DWU, as an organization independent of NDWA. Along with other long-time domestic worker members of DWU, these leaders have a vision for DWU as a truly worker-led organization, focused on member outreach, direct action tactics, and relying on volunteer labor and community resources rather than large foundation grants. DWU has been supported by a range of smaller grassroots organizations such as HWHR, which continues to carry on its work in the outer boroughs and in the working-class, migrant enclaves of the city.

Domestic workers from DWU have turned to alternative forms of storytelling that engage deeply and critically with the broader global structures that perpetuate the care industry. At a Worker Writers event organized by poet Mark Nowak at the PEN World Voices Festival on May 9, 2015, Lewis spoke movingly about the university students in her country of Trinidad who gave their lives for the revolution against British rule in the 1960s. "Their bones and blood and bodies littered the landscape of this lush twin island republic," read Lewis.[112] And even in the postindependence period, she says, the oil and sugar continued to be pillaged by foreign companies. Another domestic worker and DWU member, Lizeth Palencia from Guatemala, talked about how ex-President Ronald Reagan promoted genocide in her country by providing military aid to the brutal right-wing regime in the 1980s. Through tears, Palencia spoke about the indigenous children being slaughtered in the northern mountain highlands, whose "blood ran like water." Rather than celebrating the work that domestic workers do to keep our economy running, these workers are revealing the violence of global inequality that fuels the care industry. For these workers, a radical restructuring of domestic work would mean envisaging and working toward an alternative kind of global order.

Domestic workers from other groups in the Bill of Rights coalition, like Andolan, also reflected back critically on the storytelling advocacy approach. In a piece entitled "The Power of Complicated Stories," DWU cofounder and Andolan leader Nahar Alam and Chitra Aiyar, an Andolan volunteer, describe how domestic workers were sought out by the media who were looking for simple narratives of egregious exploitation and victimhood followed by empowerment and upliftment. They argue that publicly speaking about abuse can backfire for workers who may have a harder time finding work, and that even after supposedly successful legal campaigns, some workers are still consigned to underpaid domestic labor.[113] This came home to them after Andolan suffered cuts in funding and lost their full-time organizers and office space. Yet with this loss of funding came liberation: "Andolan has in some ways been forcibly returned to our roots with meetings happening again at Nahar's house; women workers gathering to share food and stories." They worked toward a theatre production called "Claiming Our Voice," in which they realized that not all domestic workers want to talk about domestic work. Some prefer to go "off message," to talk about their families, or the Liberation War in Bangladesh. Like the DWU women, these workers want to tell stories about the complicated nature of transnational lives.

CONCLUSION

Although I have argued in this chapter that storytelling at the legislature narrowed the goals of the domestic worker movement, could this history be told another way? Could it be, rather, that it was the growing orientation of the domestic worker movement toward a nonprofit model heavily reliant on foundations that led them to neglect grassroots base building and pursue high-profile legislative wins? Is this the more familiar experience of the professionalization and cooptation of a movement organization by the state and foundation funding? Do stories really matter in this account? I believe that stories do matter, both for the successes achieved by the campaign as well as explaining the limited goals that it ended up embracing.

The campaign for a Domestic Workers Bill of Rights helped to draw attention to the plight of domestic workers. It was in the public rallies and media campaigns that workers gained a sense of themselves as political actors and the abuses in the industry became more widely known and acknowledged. Stories played a central role in humanizing workers, revealing their mistreatment by employers, attracting media and legislative attention, and ultimately convincing the broader public and their representatives that change was necessary. The symbolic injustices faced by domestic workers were rooted in patterns of invisibility, misrepresentation, and disrespect that the movement sought to challenge by broad dissemination of personal narratives.

At the same time, campaign leaders channeled the energy of the movement into more limited avenues of legislative reform, trading deeper critique and direct action for higher profile in the media and policy settings. Domestic worker stories were publicly disseminated through limiting media tropes, they were reframed using hegemonic myths in legislative debates, and they were couched in the language of Hollywood narratives. Stories in the media and legal hearings relied on a liberal framing, as individual workers exploited by deviant bad employers, that dates back to slavery and colonialism. These stories were severed from the root causes of injustice, and from strategies to address these causes. By driving a wedge between goals of recognition and redistribution, the campaign did little to change the deeper crisis of care under neoliberalism or the structures of global inequality that underlay the lives of domestic workers. In fact, as the political scientist Joan Tronto has argued, globalization is often seen as a means to resolve existing care crises by providing new sources of caring labor.[114] There was no attempt to challenge the racialized and globalized division of labor that produced migrant and black women as carers for a predominantly white, professional middle to upper class.

Through the act of storytelling, a new subject was created in the upwardly mobile, hard-working domestic worker, a subject whose limited legal rights would not threaten the apparatus of privatized and globalized care. As domestic workers in the campaign embraced these subjectivities created through storytelling, some shifted their goals away from the earlier expansive visions of possibility, to more pragmatic and constrained outcomes. However, within the campaign there were always dissident voices, and in the aftermath of the campaign many domestic workers openly critiqued the role of middle-class leaders and their benefactors who were making decisions about the direction of the movement. These workers have sought to break away from structures of philanthropy and create worker-led movements based in more complex kinds of storytelling.

The example of the Dreamers explored in the next chapter shows how stories of undocumented students scripted by advocacy organizations similarly worked to orient the movement toward limited and class-based projects that would benefit only a small minority. But as the Dreamers came to reject these kinds of narratives, and sought to define their own movement, I also ask, can these actors narrate their lives in ways that do not feed into dominant tropes? How might stories enable a project of transformative redistribution that goes beyond recognition? Or might we need to look beyond storytelling itself?

CHAPTER 5

Sticking to the Script

The Battle over Representations

Estrella was a seventeen-year-old undocumented student whose mother carried her as a baby over the US-Mexico border into Southern California from her home town of Arroyo Seco in Michoacán. She relates that her two younger sisters were involved in a Mexican American street gang called *Norteños* and her sister Adriana was suspended from school once. One time her sister got in an argument with someone from a rival gang, *Sureños*, and Estrella was drawn into the fight as well; consequently, she was called before the gang prevention officer at her school. In her story, which she relates through an oral history project called Voice of Witness, Estrella says that she plans to go to community college, although she doesn't know how she will pay the fees.[1] Estrella tells how she joined the mega-marches in 2006, walking off campus on May Day with all of the other Latinx students, including elementary and junior high school students. Although the teachers and principal were taking pictures to see who was walking out, and threatened the marching students with detention, Estrella and her friends and family took the risk and marched for equal rights for migrants.

The stories of Estrella and her siblings stand in contrast to the stories of the undocumented students known as Dreamers, who were presented as the acceptable face of the immigrant rights movement. The Dreamer stories, told in Congressional hearings, media reports, and on websites, presented undocumented students who were model citizens, striving for upward mobility and personal advancement. Dan-El Padilla was an undocumented classics major at Princeton who turned himself in after winning a two-year scholarship to Oxford University. The undocumented Harvard biology student Eric Balderas was detained when trying to board an airplane in Texas.

Jose Godinez-Samperio, a law student, valedictorian, and National Honor Society scholar, had to go before the court when it came time for him to apply for admission to the Florida Bar. The stories of Dan-El, Eric, and Jose are some of the ones that received prominent media attention during the campaign to pass a DREAM Act to provide a path to citizenship for undocumented students. Other stories like that of Estrella and her siblings with their less acceptable experiences of gang involvement and street protests were to be silenced from the narrative of the deserving immigrant.

This chapter will look at how the attempt by advocacy organizations to produce narrow scripts of undocumented students as deserving and innocent immigrants met with opposition from some students. The Dreamers category came into being as a social category through the messaging strategies of mainstream immigration organizations in the new millennium. The students were given scripts to follow that emphasized their achievements, assimilation into American society, and rejection of their home culture. In the lead-up to the 2008 national election and the subsequent push for Comprehensive Immigration Reform (CIR), this group of young people was mobilized in mass storytelling trainings across the country to support the electoral and legislative agenda of mainstream organizations. Scripted stories and storytelling trainings aimed to channel the energy of the youth into narrow advocacy campaigns that would build the Latinx voter base for the Democrats. Eventually, many young people rebelled against this orchestration and sought to take control over their own representations. Some even began to move away from storytelling as a mode of political engagement altogether.

Storytelling was a key component of the "Movement Building Trainings" devised by political strategist Marshall Ganz. Ganz, along with a range of nonprofits and foundations, presented these trainings as helping to build capacity, promote participation, and develop social capital in the immigrant rights movement. I see these storytelling trainings as a disciplinary technology that helped to channel stories toward utilitarian ends and enabled neoliberal subject-making. The trainings explored in this chapter bolstered a particular class project, one that favored incorporation for a small minority of upwardly mobile immigrants over legalization and justice for the vast majority of working-class migrants.

Individuals, presented as the authors of their own stories, are seen as active agents in their own advancement. In line with the notion of neoliberal subjectivity offered by Wendy Brown and others, I argue that undocumented youth involved in the crafting of their stories become self-actualizing and active in the regulation of their own conduct.[2] By constructing themselves within the binary formulations of immigrant rights discourse as hard-working, innocent, deserving immigrants, they signal their own status as ideal citizen subjects and distance themselves from African Americans, who are stigmatized by tropes of criminality and welfare dependence.[3] The emphasis on migrants as free-willed individuals guided by their choices ignores the hierarchical US racial order and the broader global capitalist system that positions migrants within a set of unequal relations.

THE DESERVING AND THE INNOCENT: EARLY DREAMER STORIES

The category of the Dreamer was created in 2001 by immigrant rights organizations such as the National Immigration Law Center (NILC), the Center for Community Change (CCC), and others. Drafted by NILC, the Development, Relief, and Education for Alien Minors (DREAM) Act sought a path to citizenship for undocumented university students and youth engaged in community service.[4] The DREAM Act was first introduced into Congress by the Republican Senator Orrin Hatch on August 1, 2001. Undocumented youth were hand-picked by advocacy organizations to tell their stories to Congresspeople and the media. There were certain themes that were emphasized by legislators and echoed in the stories of the youth. The students were always high achieving, usually valedictorians of their classes, and shown as being "of good moral character" and "hard working." They were presented as fully assimilated into American culture and society with few ties to their birth countries; as innocent of the crime of illegally entering the United States, which was blamed on their parents; as seeking meritocratic success, in line with American values and ideals; and as patriots, who were willing to defend America. Although the aim of these narratives was to mark out some immigrants as deserving and worthy of citizenship, the effect was to draw a class distinction between those upwardly mobile, assimilated, and self-reliant immigrants whose stories could humanize them, and the anonymous, foreign, and lower-class undocumented laborers who filled the ranks of an informal and exploited labor force.

Narratives of deserving and undeserving immigrants, and the prototypes they are based on, have a long history in the United States. Susan Coutin describes how Central American asylum applicants in the 1990s were classified by suspension hearings as either deserving or undeserving subjects.[5] Prototypes of undeserving subjects were "the public charge, the nonachiever, the unassimilated, and the unrooted." Judges and attorneys posed specific questions to witnesses that were designed to determine the prototype of an applicant. Those who were deserving had to demonstrate that they were being singled out for political persecution or were uniquely needy, such as AIDs patients who couldn't receive treatment in their home country or battered women undergoing counseling. They could not simply claim economic hardship.[6] These prototypes are revived in the case of the Dreamers, who seek to show their deserving-ness and exceptionalism by focusing on their assimilation, high achievements, and roots in American culture.

Despite the support of key Senate and House Democrats throughout the decade of the 2000s, the original DREAM Act failed to pass, as did subsequent DREAM bills—both stand-alone and in combination with broader legislation. At the same time, in the post-9/11 climate where immigration and terrorism were coupled, several repressive immigration bills were passed, leading to an acceleration in deportation rates.[7] When the CIR bill failed to pass in 2007, the DREAM Act was reintroduced into Congress as a stand-alone bill by Senator Dick Durbin, who had championed the bill since its inception. The legislators who promoted the bill presented it as a measure to enhance border security. At a congressional session on October 24, 2007, the Republican senator Charles Hagel emphasized that "Obviously border security is the core, the beginning of immigration reform."[8] He noted that in July, the Senate had approved another $3 billion for border security, bringing the total funding for homeland security to $40.6 billion. Just like the CIR bill, the DREAM legislation was also presented to a conservative Congress as a means of improving border security, but due to staunch nativist opposition, the bill did not gain the traction it needed to pass.

In this section, I will explore the stories that were told by Dreamers in the early period of 2007 to 2008 in congressional hearings and the media. Congressional hearings are ostensibly sessions where decision makers seek information and promote discussion about proposed legislation, although the anthropologist Phyllis Chock argues that we can better see them as quasi-rituals, where divisive issues and cross-purposes are brought under control through the use of myths.[9] Like in the case of domestic workers in the last chapter, the stories that were told by undocumented youth were shaped and ordered by such dominant myths as the opportunity myth, the myth of an immigrant America, and the "search for freedom" and legalization narratives that various scholars have identified.

The young people who told their stories to Congress were acting as self-regulating subjects who sought to define themselves as law abiding and deserving of citizenship. Several undocumented youth told their stories at a Congressional Hearing before the Immigration Subcommittee on May 18, 2007.[10] The hearing was introduced by California representative Zoe

Lofgren. She framed the students as "innocent children" who should not be penalized for the unlawful actions of their parents and who should be given a chance to become productive members of the society. After this introduction, the undocumented youth presented their stories and then answered questions from legislators. The first person to present her testimony was the college student Marie Gonzalez. In her introduction, Sheila Jackson Lee, a representative from Texas, presented Gonzalez by listing her civic involvement: "She was a member of the National Honor Society, the Foreign Language Club, the tennis team, and the track team." When she gives her testimony, Gonzalez draws on the tropes given by the senators. She emphasizes that her parents had entered the country legally from Costa Rica, but later entered into undocumented status. Upholding the notion of undocumented immigrants as lawbreakers, she states, "When they came to the US, they had no intention of breaking the law, or of making an exception for themselves." She says:

> Their plan was to become US citizens so we could one day all benefit from living in the land of the free. We sought to live the American Dream —the promise of a better education, a better life, and altogether, a better future, what any parent would want for their child.

Drawing on nationalist mythologies of "the land of the free" and "the American Dream," Gonzalez aligns herself as a patriot who came to America seeking freedoms not available in her home country. Gonzalez relates the battle of her and her family to stay in the country, facing deportations and appearing on national television. She ultimately became a national symbol for the DREAM Act after giving the valedictorian speech at the mock graduation at a DREAM rally in front of the Capitol. Gonzalez emphasizes that despite her Costa Rican birth certificate, she considers her only home to be the United States: "I love this country. Only in America would a person like me have the opportunity to be standing in front of you." Her story follows the conventional script of what Chock calls the "myth of opportunity:" they are about individuals who arrive in America for betterment, strive in adversity, and put down roots in the country.[11] Opportunity stories are about individual heroes, rather than social structures or histories.

Part of the importance of congressional testimony as myth-making derives from the performance of feelings such as patriotism. Gonzalez speaks of her aspirations to one day be an American citizen. In a cross-questioning by Jackson Lee later in the proceedings, Gonzalez is interrogated over the veracity of those feelings:

Ms. Jackson Lee: My next question, do you feel a sense of loyalty and patriotism and pride about America?

Ms. Gonzalez: Oh, my goodness, yes, every Fourth of July I stand up there and cannot wait until the day that I am a citizen and can proudly say that I am.

Ms. Jackson Lee: I have been to those ceremonies. They are emotional. The tears come to your eyes. Are you a teary person about patriotism and loyalty?

Ms. Gonzalez: I am very much.

Ms. Jackson Lee : You feel it in your heart?

Ms. Gonzalez: Oh, I do. Hard core.

It is not enough for Gonzalez to proclaim her loyalty to the United States; she must perform it, by speaking about tears and her emotions. These spectacles aim to demonstrate the patriotism and pride of undocumented youth as aspiring American citizens.

The mythologies of opportunity and the "land of the free" are frequently invoked as Cold War tropes in reference to immigrants arriving from Communist countries. Tam Tran, an undocumented student whose parents had arrived in the United States from Vietnam via Germany, also spoke at the hearing. Tran's parents had applied for asylum in the United States because "they no longer considered Communist Vietnam as their home." The story of refugees fleeing from non-free Communist countries fits the Cold War trope of America as the land of the free. This trope is emphasized again and again in the hearing, with Steve King, a representative from Iowa, claiming that "you are all here to escape the lack of rule of law in the countries that you left." Like Gonzalez, Tran emphasizes her American-ness— she considers herself culturally American and not Vietnamese, she has been "American-raised and educated for the past 18 years," and she graduated with honors in American literature. In her story, Tran makes reference to American cultural icons, as a way of proving her American-ness: "I grew up watching Speed Racer and Mighty Mouse every Saturday morning." The narratives render the youth familiar, "just like us," as compared to those who are not and do not desire assimilation. Tran also went on to become a symbol of the movement, and even to enroll in a PhD program at Brown University, before her untimely death in a car accident in May 2010.

These kinds of curated narratives, presented at Congressional hearings, were also told to the media and at rallies, collected in numerous books, and featured on the websites of legislative leaders. The stories did not intend to convey the complexity, texture, or ambiguity of the lives of undocumented youth; rather, they were intended for the purely instrumental goal of

winning legislation. On Senator Durbin's website, numerous stories are col-
lated.[12] The stories are framed in the same way as the congressional stories,
emphasizing the exceptionality of the youth who will contribute to America
and as innocent young people who "should not be punished for their parents' mistakes." The stories refer to the youth as "model Americans," honors
students, and valedictorians; they list GPAs, SAT scores, and civic involvement. The stories make a virtue out of the American-ness of the students,
and their lack of any connection with their home culture. As Mexican-born
student Benita Veliz relates in her story:

> I was recently asked to sing the national anthems for both the US and Mexico at a Cinco
> de Mayo community assembly. Without missing a beat, I quickly belted out the Star
> Spangled Banner. To my embarrassment, I then realized I had no idea how to sing the
> Mexican national anthem. I am American. My dream is American.[13]

In Veliz's story, her lack of knowledge about the Mexican anthem is to be
celebrated. As part of the opportunity myth, family narratives and history are presented as irrelevant; what matters is whether they are putting
down roots in the country.[14] The American-ness of Veliz is again touted
in a *New York Times* op-ed on March 28, 2009, entitled "Don't Deport
Benita Veliz." The piece claims that "By all detectable measures, she is an
American, a Texan." It ends by saying that this country should "accept
Benita Veliz as the American she is." The logic of this argument is that
those who are not assimilated, not American like Veliz, do deserve to be
deported.

The framing of the stories upholds the dogmas of neoconservative
scholars such as the late Samuel Huntington by reproducing the idea
of an American national culture as static and reified, and asserting that
these immigrants will not be a challenge to this culture because they are
fully assimilated into it. The retired high school teacher Allan Cameron
presented his testimony at the Immigration Subcommittee hearing about
his mentoring of a group of undocumented students known as the Falcon
Robotics Team, who beat out schools such as MIT when they won an
acclaimed science competition with an underwater robot. Cameron
describes the all-American nature of these students who "repeat the Pledge
of Allegiance, liberty and justice for all. They root for their favorite baseball
and football teams." Cameron's testimony, just like the film produced about
this team, repeats the meritocratic mantra about American uplift: "Hard-
working kids who can overcome all obstacles and compete with the best
is an American tale. The gritty students of the Falcon Robotics Team have
become role models to young people nationwide, positive examples of the
American can-do spirit." In a House debate in December 2010, Colorado

representative Jared Polis similarly referred to Dreamers injecting an "infusion of ingenuity" at a time when the country suffers a "national malaise of laziness."[15] In these narratives, immigrant youth are not only examples of uplift, but they are used to discipline minorities and the poor who are seen as lacking in the American entrepreneurial spirit.

Early Dreamer stories tended to downplay the complex causes of migration, emphasizing the United States as a promised land for migrants escaping violent and impoverished homelands. Eithne Lubheid refers to this narrative of movement from repression to freedom as one that appropriates migrants for foreign policy objectives and reinforces dominant US nationalism and imperialism.[16] There is no reflection on the role of US intervention abroad or global neoliberal policies contributing to the harsh conditions that people may face in their home countries. Rather, America is seen as a benefactor nation that serves as a refuge of freedom for those coming from culturally backward and illiberal nations.

An edited collection of early Dreamer stories from undocumented UCLA students reflects this narrative emphasis.[17] Mariana Zamboni tells the story of Grace Lee, who migrated with her family from Korea in 1997. Zamboni relates that Lee and her family lived a fairly comfortable existence until her father's company, like many others, started going bankrupt, and the country had to borrow money from the United States and the International Monetary Fund (IMF). In Zamboni's account, the IMF is presented as a benevolent institution helping Korea, and there is no analysis of the global causes of financial collapse. Erika Perez tells the story of Mario Escobar, who fled to the United States from El Salvador in 1993. The conflict in El Salvador is described neutrally as a civil war between the government and Communists. Although Perez does mention that Mario decided to join the revolution and fight for social justice, she does not mention that the El Salvadoran military suppressing the revolution with violent and brutal tactics were being funded by the United States as part of a Cold War policy to contain Communism. Likewise, narrating the story of Argentine student Nicolas Cervantes, Fabiola Inzunza points to "Argentina's old labor laws" and "economic recession" to blame for his father's unemployment, without any analysis of the IMF–imposed neoliberal policies that had caused external shocks and capital flight, leading to unprecedented economic collapse.

Only one story in the volume speaks directly about US imperial power and involvement, and interestingly, it is one that is narrated in the first person by Gregory Allan Cendana, a Filipino American. He speaks about his conflicts with his parents who were pressured to assimilate into US culture and politics, and who did not understand his reluctance to enlist in the military as his father had done. He discusses the effects of US imperial power both in the Philippines and on communities in the United States. He says that he sees the connection with stories his fellow undocumented students from Central America and Mexico tell him about fleeing from "American-supported wars that devastated their countries" and trade agreements that force people to migrate. Although the curated stories in the legislatures, media, and books do not often tell these kinds of histories, they were being discussed by undocumented students who did not all necessarily believe in the Dreamer script.

These stories are presented as the voices of undocumented youth, but to what degree are the youth themselves agents in the crafting? Walter Nicholls argues that during this stage of the Dreamer movement, the stories were largely scripted by legislators and mainstream immigration organizations, with undocumented youth brought out as mouthpieces for the stories.[18] But while the idea of Dreamers as "mouthpieces" assumes an authority who is orchestrating the events, I suggest we rather see the students as self-regulating subjects who themselves take on the task of producing discourses about their lives. The handpicked students involved in the early campaigns were high-achieving individuals whose parents had stressed the importance of academic success and adapting to American culture. In his study of Dreamers in Massachusetts, Thomas Piñeros Shields found that they often came from families where parents had emphasized English language acquisition and math skills, and had created incentives for reading.[19] Youth presented themselves as being worthy because of their academic success, even though they may not have been fully aware of how these narratives result in the labeling of others, mostly anonymous migrant laborers and African Americans as criminal and undeserving.[20] In trying to cleanse themselves of stigmas of criminality, they legitimate the targeting of those other black and brown bodies that should be targeted instead.

STORYTELLING TRAININGS AND THE ELECTORAL TURN

But look how they treat us, make us believers
We fight their battles, then they deceive us.
Try to control us, they couldn't hold us
'Cause we just move forward like Buffalo soldiers

K'Naan, "Wavin' Flag"

In 2009, the National Organizing Institute (NOI) founded by Marshall Ganz produced a short promotional video to showcase the storytelling trainings that they had carried out with thousands of undocumented youth across the country that year. They chose the song "Wavin' Flag" by Somali rapper K'Naan as the background to the video, which was ironic because just a year later the mainstream DC-based organizations that had sponsored the trainings would be accused by undocumented youth of using them as pawns for their own electoral and legislative agenda. Though this meaning was unintended, the song could not have been more appropriate.

Whereas in the early period, Dreamers presented their stories to Congress in an attempt to win legislation giving them legal status, after the 2008 elections when Democratic president Barack Obama was elected to office, there was a shift to training large numbers of undocumented youth to tell their stories in support of CIR, following the model devised by Ganz in the Obama election campaign. Dreamers were showcased as the respectable face of the immigrant rights movement and were channeled into a narrow, foundation-driven politics that focused on winning CIR and building the Latinx voter base for the Democrats.

The harnessing of the immigrant rights movement for electoral gains took place in two stages. First, following the mass-based migrant rights marches in 2006 that arose in opposition to the punitive Sensenbrenner bill, mainstream organizations like CCC and the Service Employees International Union (SEIU) promoted a coalition known as Somos America (We Are America) and the Kennedy-McCain bill that would provide a path to citizenship in exchange for greater punitive measures. The more radical sectors of the mass movement were isolated from policy discussions, and the mainstream organizations began to funnel activism on the streets toward their agenda of electing Democrats, with this slogan: "Today We March, Tomorrow We Vote." The Democratic Party apparatus and liberal foundations began providing the logistical support for this coalition.[21] At a time when Republicans were vigorously pursuing anti-immigrant policies, the creation of a large base of Latinx voters was crucial to the outcome of the 2008 election.[22]

Second, after Obama was elected in 2008, with a Democratic supermajority in Congress, mainstream organizations perceived a window of opportunity to pass CIR. CIR proposals would offer a long and uncertain path for some immigrants toward a greencard while preserving the homeland security state and the global economic system that penalize and exploit migrant labor.[23] In 2009, a coalition of organizations encouraged by major foundations came together as Reform Immigration for America (RIFA) in order to push through CIR. Foundations contributed $3.5 million in funding for the coalition. The main members of RIFA were groups like CCC, National Council of La Raza (NCLR), and the National Immigration Forum. Smaller groups like the National Day Laborers Organizing Network (NDLON) also tried to influence the process by being members of the coalition, but over time they were marginalized from policy discussions.[24] The key strategy of RIFA was to mobilize the members of organizations across the country to put pressure on Congress in order to adopt immigration legislation and to build a voter base for the 2012 elections.

While early Dreamer narratives drew a class distinction between upwardly mobile, assimilated youth and an exploited, anonymous laboring class, the post-2008 push for CIR transformed that distinction into two class projects. William Robinson and Xuan Santos describe these projects as "the former, those middle class strata who aspire to remove racist and legal impediments to their own class condition; the latter, a mass immigrant working class that faces not just racism and legal discrimination but as well the acute labor exploitation."[25] The CIR strategy that was being pushed by the Democratic Party and mainstream immigration organizations was key to the former class project, one that enabled greater militarization of the border and repression of migrant communities in exchange for legalization of a small number of upwardly mobile migrants. The latter class project had been represented by the direction of the mega-marches of 2006, which sought legalization of all undocumented migrants, and by a number of smaller organizations who preferred to fight local and state-level repressive policies that criminalized undocumented migrants.

Those groups pushing for CIR sought to incorporate the DREAM Act into their campaign, with Dreamers as the palatable face of the immigrant rights movement. In 2007, CCC and NILC had created a network called the United We Dream Coalition, later known as United We Dream (UWD). Another large coalition of DREAM groups in California was the California Dream Network. These coalitions provided an ever-expanding network of undocumented youth through their own members and affiliated organizations who could be drawn into RIFA's campaign for CIR. Based on instructional manuals devised by Marshall Ganz and used in the Camp Obama trainings described in Chapter 2, the NOI came up with three-day Movement Building Trainings that taught skills in storytelling as a way to mobilize young people for CIR. The trainings were collaborations between CCC, NOI, RIFA, Ganz's Leading Change project, and UWD. Ganz and others based the CIR campaign directly on the model that they had devised for the election of Obama, with a self-regulating network of volunteers telling their stories to recruit supporters. The trainings were first used with the Massachusetts-based Student Immigrant Movement (SIM), of which several key leaders had attended Ganz's Public Narrative course at Harvard. In May 2009, eighteen leaders from SIM chapters across Massachusetts were brought together for a full-day leadership retreat.[26] One of the leaders from SIM who had studied with Ganz later went on to be the national organizer for UWD, where he adapted the trainings for the DREAM Act.[27]

The first storytelling training was held in August 2009 in Florida with thirty youth leaders. These leaders went on to recruit and train other leaders, and training sessions were scheduled across the country. Between 2009 and 2012, there were more than 1,200 immigrant leaders trained in eight states.[28] Even outside of these official training sessions conducted by NOI, many Dreamer groups took the manuals used in the sessions and adapted them for their own use. Mohammad Abdollahi, a former founding member of UWD, described how they would take the training manual and turn it into a day-long training for use with other groups.[29] The trainings were conducted in a highly top-down manner, with all materials provided by NOI, exercises such as role playing scripted in advance, and talking points and messages already determined by the RIFA leadership.

The training manuals used the same formula of Story of Self, Story of Us, and Story of Now that Ganz had developed in his Public Narrative course at Harvard and then applied to the Camp Obama trainings in 2008. After the election of Obama, these trainings were reworked for use by a broad range of organizations pushing for policy change, and they were drawn into the same mode of lobbying and advocacy as the immigrant rights movement. Just like the Camp Obama trainings, the Dreamer trainings also emphasized values over ideas or political analysis. These values were amorphously defined as faith, hope, and family.

In addition to the blueprint of storytelling and leadership training provided by NOI, immigrant rights organizations came up with the talking points and framings contained in the manuals. The discourse of these talking points resembles closely the early Dreamer discourse that emphasized assimilation, criminalization of some migrants, and the broken immigration system. In an April 2010, Dream Team LA (DTLA) Training Manual, under a section titled "The DREAM Act Supports America," it says that the DREAM Act "helps pave the way for CIR by highlighting a group of immigrants that promote a positive image of successful immigrant integration."[30] Those immigrants who deserve citizenship are assimilated and also upwardly mobile, those who "epitomize the American Dream." The introduction to the manual uncritically reproduces an opinion piece by Senator Durbin, where he speaks about the need for secure borders to prevent people from crossing illegally.[31] An August 28, 2010, manual used in Arizona and titled "Live the Promise: Paz Movement Building Training," reinforces the language of the "broken immigration system" that needs to be fixed, rather than, as more critical advocates have pointed out, a system that is not broken but actually works well to provide a steady stream of highly exploited labor for corporations.

Through the storytelling trainings, the manuals also emphasize the immigrant uplift story. Just like the Camp Obama trainings, the immigrant trainings draw on Obama's speech to the Democratic National Convention in 2004, presenting Obama as a model for immigrant uplift. At a movement building training session in Ithaca, New York, in January 2010 that included both immigrant youth and older immigrants, the trainer Joy Cushman compares winning CIR to electing Obama and then shows a video of his speech.[32] When she asks people to discuss the video, an older black immigrant woman makes the connection that Cushman is looking for:

> I'm just saying, him standing there after telling what his father did, and his mother and all
> of that. I can't believe I'm seeing someone whose grandfather was a goat herder should
> be standing on the national stage. It shows you that everything is possible.

Obama's uplift story fits neatly into the Dreamer discourse of upwardly mobile immigrants who achieve distinction based on their own merits. Cushman replies to the woman, saying: "Does that give you some hope? Does that take some courage?" Another older white woman replies to Cushman, saying, "I don't think that he played the race card in that story. What he did was he married the immigrant story to American traditional values." Cushman agrees with her. To make racial and immigrant issues nonthreatening for a mainstream white audience, they must be couched in this language of uplift, American values, and assimilation.

The manuals and the trainings created a narrative that connected the mega-marches of 2006 to CIR and the election of Obama, countering the narrative put forth by more oppositional groups that the CIR campaign was an attempt to co-opt the potential of the marches. Under the heading "Yet change can come—if we fight for it!" the DTLA manual says:

> In 2006, we made our problem the nation's problem by mobilizing millions to fill the
> streets across America. In 2007 we built on that success by fighting for legislative reform.
> And in 2008, when that was not enough, we turned to the polls and helped elect Barack
> Obama. Youth in California had a special role in electing President Obama; many trav-
> eled to other states and were successful in turning traditionally red states into blue states.

The statement suggests that the "we" referred to is the youth, but more broadly, the "we" is the coalition of RIFA organizations that is responsible for all of these actions and the entity that links these disparate events together. In this narrative, the goals of mobilization are restricted to the narrow ends of pushing for legislation. At the Ithaca training, CCC trainer Sean repeated the same narrative: "We have to remember back to 2006 when millions of people turned out in the streets to make clear demands on their legislatures."[33] Again, he claims for CCC the credit of bringing people out onto the streets: "The fact that we mobilized so many people . . . " Sean concludes his talk by repeating the Somos America mantra that mass mobilizations are not enough and they must be followed up by voting; that is the true "people power." By contrast, Alfonso Gonzales argues that if the migrant rights movement of 2006 had not been co-opted by the reformers and had kept up their mass actions, they could have pressured the president to act sooner and under different terms.[34]

The training in how to tell your Story of Self followed this same trajectory toward an end of legislative or electoral action. Much like the Camp Obama trainings, the immigrant rights/Dreamer trainings presented storytelling as a means to link the personal details of one's life with immediate goals of voter recruitment and influencing legislators. The Coaching Tips for telling your Story of Self in the manuals provide a fairly conventional structure of a storyteller who faces a challenge, must make a choice, and then an outcome results from that choice. An NOI Powershift Handbook used in the Northeast trainings gives the following description of story structure: "A Plot: something happens to the character, and then the character needs to make a choice, then that choice yields an outcome—and that outcome teaches a moral."[35] Rather than being open ended, the guide says that stories must result in a specific outcome that teaches us something. That is, the training presents storytelling as something that must in the end have a clear and defined moral outcome if it is to be useful. Piñero Shields, who attended the early Massachusetts training, described how leaders shaped the stories of the participants to fit these components.[36] A student named Dee told her story of coming to the United States from Chile to join her father, and then her father passed away and she and her mother suffered financial hardships, with barely money for food. Dee was encouraged to rewrite her story and to focus more on the choice she made and the outcome. Another participant Pedro, who was not undocumented, told a story of two friends who were not able to enroll in tech college because of their status. The trainer kept pushing him, asking him to name the challenge, and asking him over and over "Why do you care?" In the Ganz model, the neoliberal discourse of individual choice produces the subject as one who is responsible for her own actions and shapes her destiny.

One of the stories presented frequently in the trainings as a model is that of Tony Fierro, who told his story at a RIFA vigil in Phoenix to oppose anti-immigrant bill SB1070 in 2010. Participants in the workshops are asked to watch the video of Fierro's story and identify his choice points, values, and moral outcome.[37] Fierro relates the story of his best friend, who was pulled over on the road by police and deported to the Mexican town of Nogales. While trying to get money to return, the friend was murdered. Fierro relates that "At his funeral, I stood up on his casket and held his cold hand. At that moment, I was very angry. At that moment, I had so much frustration because I did not know what to do. The only thing I could think of was retaliation and hurting somebody else." But instead, he looked at his friend's mother and realized he couldn't do it. "I decided to turn that pain and that anger into power," he says. Fierro ends his story with a clear step for action—registering voters: "Come November, we will go out and vote, because that's what we've been building up to do. We will go and we will have our voices heard." Just like in Sean's talk, in Fierro's story, voting is equated with power and having your voice heard. The story is one that is personal and resonant, and perhaps familiar to people at the vigil. Yet just like the anger of the movement is channeled into more respectable channels of electoral politics, so too, Fierro's story and his frustration are contained by the neat and prescriptive ending. But as Francesca Polletta argues in her study of social movement narratives, stories are made compelling by their "engaging ambiguity" rather than these kinds of clear moral objectives.[38] Although Fierro's story presents the perfect model for the RIFA trainings, it's not clear that the contrived ending resonates in the same way as his experiences.

One of the objectives that is mentioned in all of the training manuals is that of "creating measurable actions." As a result of the "audit culture" discussed in Chapter 2, where foundations and nongovernmental organizations require constant assessment and evidence of impact, these highly funded trainings must also give quantitative proof of their effectiveness. The intense focus on metrics also comes from the model of the Obama electoral campaign, which generated detailed daily reports on field metrics to evaluate the performance of organizers and make the case for more resources.[39] The manuals all contain numerous references to specific numbers both of what they have accomplished and what they expect to achieve. For example, the DTLA manual states that as part of the RIFA campaign, UWD has "generated 503,000 faxes, letters, and emails, 1,000 house meetings and over 229,000 calls into Congress and the President."[40] The yearly reports of the various organizations such as CCC are filled with boxes that report statistics with headings such as "Real Change," which indicate how many media hits they received, how many voters they registered, how many pledge cards they had signed, and even down to the number of hours volunteers spent knocking on doors. For the purposes of audit culture, everything must be quantified and registered. The DTLA manual states that organizing campaigns must be based upon electoral campaigns, which "enjoy the advantage of very clear outcome measures."[41] Such quantifiable organizing campaigns which focus on moderate electoral and legislative goals are much more fundable than open-ended movements on the streets that mobilize people for multiple ends that are not always determined in advance.

The trainings provided a highly scripted and carefully controlled method of imparting skills in storytelling and movement building with the aim of legislative action. The handbooks suggest that the participants should engage in role playing to practice how to tell their stories to Congresspeople. The 2011 Northeast Powershift Training manual contains an example skit with a script about "Organizer Mara" who goes to visit "Congressperson Renata." The script is written exactly as it was enacted in the Ithaca training session in 2010.[42] The narrator begins by addressing the audience: "Organizer Mara has heard too many stories about families in her community being torn apart by ICE raids,[43] deportations, and the almost impossible work of becoming a US citizen." Because she knows that those in Washington have the power to change the laws, she decides to visit her Congressperson. Organizer Mara falls into various traps, like trying to do everything herself, and having too many individual leaders, and having no strategy, but when she finally learns to delegate and coordinate and devise a strategy, they approach Congressperson Renata. The narrator engages with the audience, asking questions such as "When Congressperson Renata arrives, what do you think she finds?" These questions are carefully framed so as to elicit stock answers. When the organizers meet the Congressperson, they ask if she will vote for CIR. The narrator says, "Congressperson Renata is impressed with the organization and number of people at the event. Since she's running for re-election next fall and knows she needs the Latino vote, she says . . . yes." Even if the exact same skit is not reproduced by participants in the trainings, the basic structure is one of organizers who must approach their congressional representatives in order to achieve change. The role playing is intended to train the participants to learn about congressional lobbying as a solution to the ICE raids, deportation, and other problems in their communities.

In addition to the role-playing exercises, the manuals and trainings contain numerous activities to train people in how to use their stories to recruit people to the CIR campaign, and how to do voter registration. The manuals contain a phone recruitment script, where they must create a call script and use their stories to role-play a phone call with a potential recruit. The stories are used in order to motivate people. The manuals and the trainings use the language of participation, mobilization, and decision making, but in fact, there is no room for debate over the proposed goals of the trainings. Participants cannot question the framing of the talking points that are given; they cannot criticize CIR or propose alternatives to Congressional lobbying. Those fundamental decisions have already been made. Even the ways that stories are to be framed are decided in advance, by Ganz, by funders, by mainstream organizations and those who are funding the trainings. People are encouraged to fit their stories into the narrow frameworks that are provided to them.

Stories were used as a key part of CCC's Keeping Families Together Day of Action on March 22, 2013. On the YouTube video of the visit to John McCain's Washington, DC, office, the caption says that "Immigrant families visited the offices of several members of the Senate's Gang of 8 to tell their stories and push the urgency of dropping a good immigrant reform bill this month."[44] The video consists of activists speaking with staffers and each telling short two-minute stories about their experiences and why they need a CIR bill. One of the activists, Petra Falcon, introduces herself to a staffer as a member of the organization Promise Arizona, part of the RIFA coalition. She describes spending the entire day telling stories to Congresspeople: "We've been visiting members of Congress and senators all day long. We actually had a hearing here in the building at 1 pm with members of Congress and senators, and . . . we've just been telling our stories all day long." There is a tone of weariness that accompanies the rote recitation of stories for an entire day. Similarly, at a National Coming Out of the Shadows Day rally in Chicago in March 2010, Thomas Swerts observed that one of the students, Claudia, was interrupted by organizers while telling her story. She was told to do "less acting," and they prodded her and asked, "You felt frustrated, but why?" Claudia was crying and saying, "It's just so difficult to have to tell my story over and over again."[45]

The question arises of how successful these trainings were. The organizations running the trainings show how they were able to recruit voters, organize events, join new members, and so on. But I am more interested in how successful they were in creating a Dreamer subject who would not only tell stories about being an exceptional immigrant but also would channel those stories into lobbying and electoral paths of change. The training videos seem to show participants who largely toed the line and followed the instructions that they were given. But there are moments where we can see ambivalence or conflict, even among the trainers themselves. For instance, at a training session in Tempe, Arizona, in July 2010, NOI staff member Michelle Rudy opened with a story about her ancestors who came as Jewish immigrants from Russia, fleeing Nazi persecution.[46] She then went on to describe her feelings about the Obama campaign:

> Hearing people tell their stories made me feel hopeful and made me think of another time I felt hopeful [smiles]. Any of you a part of the Obama campaign? I worked my ass off on the Obama campaign because I believed that Obama would pass immigration reform. . . . But you know what? Obama didn't do it.

As she was speaking, Rudy became emotional and had to pause. It was a line that did not fit with the ideological tenor of the trainings, and so she quickly composed herself and moved in a different track, asking: "What other pain is happening in your community that is not resolved?" These ambivalent feelings are never allowed to be expressed more fully within the space of the training. Rather, Rudy repressed the thought and asked the participants to close their eyes and imagine the 177,000 people who they are going to register to vote. The question of why they should vote if politicians don't follow through on their promises is not addressed.

Dreamers themselves also expressed some hesitations about the trainings. Andrea Leon Schettini, who organized trainings with the New Jersey DREAM Act Coalition, said that she found the trainings helpful but also a bit monotonous, especially after going through a lot of them: "So after doing like five trainings of Story of Self, you get it." She also found it a challenge to fit her personal story into the two-minute format: "It's hard to put it in two minutes because there's so many events in your life. You're just like, wait, but this changed me, but this changed me too, but this motivated me, so it's like, which one do I choose to make it the most powerful?"[47] Abdollahi was at the first Florida training, and he referred to the trainings as a "circus show." Although he thought that people did find the trainings beneficial, he also thought that the organizers did not get out of it what they wanted.[48] Although the organizations were able to provide "measurable data" about the numbers of people who were recruited, trained, and registered to vote as a result of the trainings, their success in winning people to their particular reform agenda was not so measurable or obvious. This was to become clear as Dreamers rejected the leadership of the mainstream organizations and politicians.

UNDOCUMENTED AND UNAFRAID: DISSIDENT DREAMER NARRATIVES

By 2010, a shift in the immigrant rights movement was underway with Dreamers becoming increasingly vocal and independent from mainstream associations. As Dreamers publicly accused large immigration organizations of demobilizing them by pushing for CIR, and as they began to engage in contentious, direct actions, they also put forth new kinds of narratives that brought out the silenced dimensions of earlier narratives. Under the banner of "Undocumented and Unafraid," the narratives that Dreamers told at rallies, meetings, and in creative arts projects were similar to the coming-out narratives of queer activists. They told more nuanced and in-depth narratives than the Ganz trainings stories, they gave broader context, and they identified with their parents' struggle, but they still often remained within the confines of the good-and-bad-immigrant frame that had been set up by earlier advocates.

One of the turning points came in March 2010 when RIFA orchestrated a large-scale and lavishly funded demonstration in Washington, DC, in an attempt to convince Obama and Senate leaders to make a move for CIR. Alfonso Gonzales argues that there were two separate movements taking place: the hundreds of thousands of migrants who were protesting and the carefully choreographed rally taking place on the stage.[49] Labor organizations passed out American flags and asked those with Latin American flags to put them away. But the failure of the march to garner any significant media attention or reaction from Congress led to a questioning of RIFA's goals, and a number of smaller immigrant rights associations switched their attention from achieving CIR to mobilizing against state- and federal-level anti-immigrant measures.[50] Groups such as NDLON and the Mexican American Legal Defense Fund (MALDEF) argued that while RIFA was putting all of its resources toward a losing battle for CIR, anti-immigrant groups were slowly passing measures to roll back the rights of immigrants.[51] In the "Live the Promise" movement building training manual, RIFA advocates themselves relate that on April 10, 2010, they mobilized 9,000 activists from Arizona and elsewhere to go to Las Vegas in order to pressure Senate Majority Leader Harry Reid to pass CIR, and while they were occupied extracting "empty promises" from the senator, legislators back in Arizona were taking advantage of the vacuum there to pass anti-immigrant bill SB 1070.[52] NDLON, MALDEF, and others devised a strategy to fight local enforcement measures and push for smaller wins, and as Dreamers started campaigning for a stand-alone DREAM Act, these smaller organizations provided support for them.

Dreamers started to carve out their own independent path with a series of actions in the Spring of 2010 that began with a march by four undocumented students from Miami to Washington, DC, known as the "Trail of Dreams." In May, Dreamers carried out acts of civil disobedience, with five undocumented youth holding a sit-in at the office of Senator John McCain. In a bid to bring the DREAM Act back into public visibility, undocumented students across the country organized under the name "The Dream Is Coming." The escalation of the movement by undocumented youth continued into the summer, with hunger strikes in New York to convince Senator Charles Schumer to support the DREAM Act. The direct actions won the attention of the media with major newspapers publishing editorials in favor of the DREAM Act. Nicholls describes how the approach of groups like NDLON, MALDEF, and the UCLA Labor Center differed from the large immigration organizations in that they provided logistical support to Dreamers while also respecting their autonomy.[53] The balance of forces started to shift away from RIFA and their CIR strategy toward an empowered Dreamer movement pushing for stand-alone DREAM legislation.

The real rupture with mainstream groups and with the Dreamer discourse established in the earlier period came in September 2010, when five Dreamers published a manifesto-like statement in *Dissent* magazine.[54] Opening with a quote from Martin Luther King speaking on direct action, they identified their own rebellious stance with King and the Birmingham youth activists. The statement outlined the problems with the leadership of the immigrant rights movement, who the youth activists referred to as the "social justice elite" and the "nonprofit industrial complex." The activists outlined several aspects of a new politics that was going to shape and redirect the Dreamer narrative in coming years.

In the opening paragraphs, the dissident youth describe their mobilizations and the confronting of their own fears in order to declare themselves "Undocumented and Unafraid!" In contrast to earlier stages where Dreamers were told to follow the lead of the mainstream organizations and many were afraid to give their real names, they were now openly declaring themselves undocumented, in a coming-out process both linked to the queer movement and inclusive of those queer and undocumented within the movement. The statement outlined a new confrontational stance where young people were willing to put their bodies on the line, risking incarceration and deportation. They identified with the civil rights movement but also with the Chicano movements of the 1960s, associating themselves with a history of struggle that earlier narratives had silenced. They proposed a broader global and historical perspective that saw attacks on undocumented migrants and refugees as linked to histories of imperialism, nativism, and the criminalization of communities of color. Rejecting the frame of the assimilated American youth, they openly declared themselves to be the "displaced youth from across the Americas, Asia, and Africa." They pointed to US Empire, "American-funded violence," and capitalist expansion through globalization as reasons for their displacement.

One of the key interventions in the statement concerned the issue of representation.[55] The authors charged that the leadership of the immigrant rights movement was mostly documented and, as such, should "not have the right to say what undocumented youth need or want." The opposition to the DREAM Act by allies is, they say, a paternalistic act that assumes that documented people know better than undocumented youth themselves what is right for them. The heart of their argument comes in a paragraph written in all-caps:

WE DO NOT WANT IMMIGRATION RIGHTS "ADVOCATES" SPEAKING FOR US ANY LONGER. WE DEMAND THE RIGHT TO REPRESENT OURSELVES!

After being paraded by politicians, legislators, and advocacy organizations, and being told what to say and what not to say, the dissident Dreamers were taking back the means of representation and defining themselves on their own terms.

One of the responses to this statement by CCC staff member Sally Kohn demonstrated the paternalism that the Dreamers were criticizing. Kohn's response was entitled "DREAM Act Students Causing a Nightmare."[56] Kohn questions the Dreamers' connections to the civil rights movement, which she describes as "beautiful, powerful," in comparison to undocumented immigrants marching in the streets who she says don't "have the same visceral power" and actually inspire a backlash rather than compassion. In derisive and patronizing language, Kohn refers to the activists as "kids" and then as "petulant children." When the Dreamers are obedient, they are referred to as model citizens, but when they choose to speak out against the mainstream groups who try to control them, they are infantilized. As one person notes in the comments section to Kohn's piece, "Comparing a group of mostly brown adults working for change to 'petulant children' smacks of racism." Kohn, a white American citizen, admits that the paid leadership of the advocacy organizations are documented and sometimes white, while the grassroots volunteer leaders are undocumented migrants. But her strategy is to pit these grassroots leaders, the "low wage workers struggling to make a living," against the Dreamers, as "kids on a more elite path," saying that the DREAM Act was never going to help those workers.

Following the failure of the DREAM Act to pass again in December 2010, youth activists embarked on a campaign to pressure Obama to grant Administrative Relief to young undocumented people. Neidi Dominguez, one of the authors of the *Dissent* statement, led an investigation into how they could present a viable case. With the legal and infrastructural support of groups like MALDEF, and a campaign that continued the direct actions, sit-ins, and solidarity actions in swing states, the Dreamers won the passage of Administrative Relief.[57] On June 15, 2012, Obama announced the Deferred Action for Childhood Arrivals (DACA) policy that gave a limited subset of Dreamers a temporary work permit and reprieve from deportation.

An analysis of the narratives being told in the rallies and congresses of the various Dreamer organizations during this period of 2010–2011 can give a sense of the shift that took place after the rupture. In contrast to the heavily scripted congressional stories and the two-minute recruitment stories told in the movement building trainings, the dissident Dreamer narratives were more in-depth stories that gave voice to alternative perspectives and histories that had been silenced in earlier Dreamer narratives.

One of the major currents to emerge within the Dreamer movement was queer identity, and queer undocumented youth became prominent leaders of the movement. As Nicholls argues, while earlier messaging tried to play down issues such as sexuality as a distraction from the main goals of the campaign, Dreamers began to publicly reclaim these other identities.[58] The term "Undocuqueer" came to represent those who identified as both undocumented and queer, and the slogan "Queer, Undocumented, and Unafraid" was popularized by smaller organizations such as the Immigrant Youth Coalition (IYC). Even more mainstream Dreamer groups such as UWD embraced queer identity as part of the Dreamer narrative and started up projects such as the Queer Undocumented Immigrant Project.

Narratives from queer undocumented youth emphasized the struggles they faced being undocumented in broader society and for being queer within their communities. On a video entitled "Our Stories—Our Power: Queer, Undocumented, and Unafraid," three activists tell their stories.[59] Nicolas Gonzales relates how he was kicked out of home when he came out to his parents. He describes how you must come out twice, once as a queer person and also as undocumented. But even within the Dreamer movement, there are stigmas and prejudice attached to being queer. "You always hear negative things about being queer," he says, "or like joking, people joking about it, and to us it's been really important to talk about that." The queer Dreamer youth, often students influenced by critical race theory on university campuses, used terms such as "intersectionality" to describe the ways that they experienced their multiple identities.[60]

It was no surprise that queer youth became leaders of the movement during this period. "Coming out" as undocumented strongly resonated with "coming out" as queer. However, there were also tensions between these identities, and undocumented queer youth faced discrimination not only within the immigrant rights movement but also in the queer movement. A Dreamer activist relates on a video how youth from UWD's Queer Undocumented Immigrant Project were invited to speak at a rally to repeal the Defense of Marriage Act (DOMA).[61] He says that prior to getting on the stage, his speech was revised and he was told not to share the realities of being an undocuqueer immigrant. "Our real-life struggles and daily challenges as LGBTQ people are not acknowledged but rather continue to be pushed into the closet and excluded from the dominant narrative," he says on the video. At certain times, Dreamers found some components of their identity more acceptable than others.

The resonance of "coming out" for undocumented activists was demonstrated at the UWD National Congress in Kansas City, Missouri, in December 2012, when the Managing Director Cristina Jiménez made the analogy in her keynote speech.[62] Jiménez relates her own trajectory as a young undocumented student to the trajectory of the movement. She begins with an anecdote that is common to many Dreamer narratives, being told that her advisor couldn't sign off on her college applications because she didn't have a Social Security number. Her advisor told her, "I'm sorry, Cristina, I cannot sign off on this application and you can't go to school." She recalls, "It was a painful moment." Jiménez describes how at that time she was always afraid:

> When I was nineteen, I was very afraid. Afraid of sharing my story. I was afraid because
> I did not want to put myself and my family at the risk of being deported. . . . I was a
> closeted Dreamer.

This changed when her husband, Walter, was detained on his way to a national immigrant rights meeting and put into deportation proceedings. At that point, she says that she lost her fear and told her story publicly in the *El Diario* newspaper in New York. Her use of the phrase "closeted Dreamer" and her descriptions of coming out of the closet and declaring herself undocumented signal her affinities with the strategies of the queer movement.

Jiménez reflects on the use of storytelling in the movement, how it is one of their most powerful tools, but also how Dreamers were expected to recite scripts. "When I started to do this work," she relates, "I got talking points. And the talking points were, 'I'm Cristina Jiménez. I'm from Ecuador. My parents brought me to this country. I want to be a lawyer. I'm an honor student. I want to contribute to this country. Please pass the DREAM Act.'" Jiménez recites the litany of discourses that Dreamers were required to repeat. She talks about the contradictions that this presented to her:

> But you know, let me share something with you. Every time I shared my story, I felt
> weird because I never talked about my mom and my dad and my family and all of the
> sacrifices and the fact that my dad drives scared shitless every day to work because he
> doesn't have a license and I didn't talk about the struggles of my mom either.

Jiménez invites the youth at the Congress to write their own stories, to be the authors of their own stories: "Are you willing to write a new story? And what does that story look like?" In these later narratives, Dreamers sought to humanize their parents as good and hard-working people who acted in the best interests of their children, as compared to the earlier narratives that criminalized parents and disassociated children from the acts of their parents.

Dreamers also began to engage in more creative projects of storytelling, using video, spoken word poetry, and song to give voice to an array of repressed identities. These stories were marked by a refusal of the class project as it had been articulated through the CIR campaign; they attempted to come up with new forms of political subjectivity that are not bound by nationalist identifications or assimilation paradigms. As compared to the good immigrant subject of the early Dreamer narrative, following Alicia Schmidt-Camacho, I refer to these alternative subjectivities as "migrant" subjectivities.[63] Undocumented activists related how reporters would often push them to conform to a narrative of upward mobility, and would pick and select the parts of their identity that fit this narrative. The undocumented activist Prerna Lal, who had migrated to the United States from Fiji, recalled when *US News and World Report* came to her house in 2007 to interview her for a story on the DREAM Act.[64] They took photos of an "'ego wall' with plaques, degrees, and medals," but they discarded photos that depicted her cultural background in order to construct a "Dreamer" identity: "an identity that leaves out the parts of me that make me a complete human being." Reporters would push her to narrate a "linear 'rags to riches' story" and take out any mention of her love for Fiji. She concluded that "Not everyone has the same linear trajectory of immigrant success packaged as the 'American Dream.' Some of us don't even want any part or parcel in the nationalist project. Most of our lives don't follow those trajectories." In retelling their stories on their own terms, activists sought to fill in those parts of themselves that were left out of the dominant narratives.

Alternative migrant subjectivities can be seen in a creative project known as Dreamers Adrift, where artists upload videos on its website telling stories through music, spoken word, visual arts, and poetry. One of the videos on the site is a collaboration between two undocumented artists: the poet Yosimar Reyes and the visual artist Julio Salgado, entitled "The Legalities of Being."[65] The video opens with Salgado sketching images on a mounted sheet of paper while Reyes narrates his story in a voiceover. Salgado draws a picture of an older woman holding a sign that reads: "Reality." "My grandmother has never used the word undocumented to describe her existence," begins Reyes. Salgado sketches a group of students wearing caps and gowns—a symbol used by the Dreamer movement—and he draws a large question mark in the center of the image. Reyes says that he does not define himself by laws that could never summarize his existence. He finds labels such as "Dreamer" and "illegal" to be "stagnant, that in no way, shape or form speaks truth about the complexities of being and the connections that we have as humans beyond borders and political systems." Unlike the striving, model Dreamers who are made to feel inferior or excluded because of their status, especially in relation to more privileged peers, Reyes and his friends were all undocumented, so their status was seen as "a simple reality and not our identity."

They all knew where to get fake work documents and they never felt alone. "We were more than the lack of a social security number," he says. While the Dreamers hold up visibility as one of the key goals of their movement, Reyes, his grandmother and his friends on the block have no wish to make themselves legible within the dominant order.

Reyes questions the myths he has been made to believe about his homeland and the illusion of America as a place of freedom and justice that will grant him a proper education. He asks: "Why is it that every time I think about my home, my heart stops at the idea of living in poverty, when in reality I have been living below the poverty line my whole life." Salgado sketches a picture of a girl with her hands behind her back in handcuffs, and Reyes says: "We're still at the same place as when we arrived, under attack, caged, profiled, subjugated to unjust loss." In the next screen, Salgado draws a picture of a girl surrounded by words in block letters and exclamation points: "DACA, APPLY NOW!!! DREAM ACT NOW!!! APPLY APPLY NOW NOW." Reyes says he feels bamboozled by the constant requests to tell his story, to speak about his experience. There is "a trend of folks writing about us, documenting us, wanting to hear us, wanting us to come out of the shadows, wanting us to feel empowered." Just like the domestic workers who felt bombarded by a demand for their stories, so too artists like Reyes feel bewildered by the demand for stories about "being undocumented." Reyes asserts himself not as "undocumented," but rather as part of a collectivity of "migrants, displaced people, folks whose hearts have been broken by America's lies."

In the final part of the video, Salgado draws an image of Reyes's grandmother standing behind a politician with a sign reading, "Vote for me." Reyes shifts into Spanish, emphasizing the nontranslatability and illegibility of his grandmother's experiences into the dominant Dreamer discourse: "*Ella no tiene la lengua para explicarle al presidente de sus milpas de café*" (She doesn't have the language to explain to the president about her fields of coffee). He continues: "She is not a Dreamer. There is no Deferred Action for her, no immigration reform for her. She will never be American." Reyes's grandmother's story becomes a reflection on the alternative migrant experience, as one who is not striving for social mobility and assimilation into middle-class American life but rather yearns for her homeland:

> One day she will pack her bags, purchase a plane ticket, and return home. She will look at the streets, try to remember how things used to be, but time has not passed since she left. Her comadres have passed. Su casita fell. She will look at the dirt, try to remember where she gave birth to her firstborn, look at the face of a son she has not seen in decades. She will be weak, spending her days remembering. Abuelita will slowly dig her grave, crawl back into the land that brought her to this journey, return to the center, and

migrate to the spirit world. There she will no longer need papers, no longer be poor, no longer ache, no longer be broken-hearted. There, she will whisper to me, and remind me that all this is a dream, that one day we will wake up to a place more beautiful than this.

The grandmother's *milpas de café*, her broken heart, these are things that she cannot explain. The tortured reconnection with the homeland is present in these stories, but even it does not provide the release that the grandmother will find only in death. Through his grandmother, Reyes is asserting his own connection to his country, and his grandmother's story as a part of his own.

The Dreamer discourse began to embrace rather than criminalize parents, connecting the struggle of Dreamers with the low-wage undocumented population. But despite these shifts, the Dreamers had still not found a way to make connections with minorities, particularly African Americans. At a UWD congress in Memphis in March 2011, Dreamers reported more ties with queer groups than with African American groups.[66] The early Dreamer discourse that sought to differentiate good and bad immigrants still influenced the Dreamer movement and more broadly the immigrant rights movement. The Dreamer identity was still distanced from those perceived as criminals, gang members, and the incarcerated, emphasizing the educational aspirations of many Dreamers. But as deportations rose in record numbers under the second term of the Obama administration, and more money was funneled into the private detention industry, some groups found a way to build solidarity with black struggles by focusing on deportations and the criminal justice system that criminalized and imprisoned migrants and minorities.

MIGRANT AND BLACK SOLIDARITY: MASS INCARCERATION AND DEPORTATION

Storytelling has not been a strong focus of the antideportation movement in the same way as it was instrumental for the legal advocacy campaigns, and the kinds of narratives that are told are quite different to those of the early Dreamers. A notable feature of these stories is that they challenge the notion of some migrants as criminals, and hence deportable. Zé Garcia tells his story on a blog.[67] He relates how he was convicted of two separate cannabis possession charges in his youth. When returning from Mexico one summer, he was apprehended by immigration officials at Chicago's O'Hare airport and after being held in custody and paroled into the country, he was given a Notice to Appear before the Department of Homeland Security. At the time of writing his story in February 2014, he was awaiting his final court date in 2017. Garcia accompanies his narrative with a critique of immigrant advocacy organizations and politicians such as Senator Durbin proposing CIR, which he says will afford millions of dollars through contracts to private companies like the GEO Group and Corrections Corporation of America, who would benefit from the building of detention centers. He points to the eagerness of such immigrant advocates to promote the militarization of the US-Mexico border, the expansion of the state security apparatus, and the adoption of new qualifications of criminality, all in exchange for the legalization of some categories of immigrants, as well as an increase in funding to those nonprofits who can show a willingness to help funnel immigrants into prisons. Another key distinction between Garcia's narrative and the earlier narratives is his challenge to antiblack racism: "I will not be joining the chorus of liberal prison apologists for whom the caging and disposability of mostly brown and black bodies with less digestible narratives remain permissible." Garcia sees this criminalization and disposability of immigrants and minorities as providing the grounds of solidarity.

Another story is narrated by the Families for Freedom organizer Aarti Shahani, who relates her own politicization after the detainment of her Indian immigrant father. She recounts the story in a book, although it is a story she has told many times at rallies and speak-outs.[68] Shahani's father ran a wholesale electronics store with his brother, and both men were arrested for not properly reporting foreign sales to the Internal Revenue Service. After serving two years of jail time, some of that in the notorious Riker's prison, instead of the eight months he was given, due to a clerical error, Shahani relates that the federal government planned to send her father back to India, where he had not lived since the 1950s. As she worked to halt the deportation, she found that immigrant organizations did not challenge the good immigrant/bad immigrant binary, but rather just changed who fell where. By joining antideportation networks, she said she found a "home of sorts, because it was the only space to embrace people like my dad and uncle, with rap sheets, the so-called Bad immigrants."[69] Like Garcia, the purpose of Shahani's story is to challenge the binaries that make certain immigrants deportable and criminal.

As deportations were on the rise under the Obama administration, several organizations sought to bring attention to this trend under the Twitter hashtag #Not1More. The Moratorium on Deportations campaign, centered in Chicago, held education workshops to explain the ways in which the proposed CIR bill would increase the possibility of immigrant detainment and deportation. The group was successful in its campaign to halt construction of an immigrant detention center in Crete, Illinois.[70] Undocumented youth organizations like the Chicago-based Immigrant Youth Justice League (IYJL) and the National Immigrant Youth Alliance (NIYA) began collaborating with the National Day Laborers Organizing Network (NDLON) in anti-deportation campaigns. Like Garcia, some of these organizers sought to find common ground between African Americans and migrants based in their experiences of criminalization and incarceration. Others such as Black Alliance for Just Immigration (BAJI) worked to build solidarity between black immigrants and African Americans through a shared understanding of racism and economic globalization that deprives people of the ability to earn a living in their home countries.[71] BAJI's search for alliances is predicated on an analysis of structural racism and the causes of migration under neoliberal capitalism.

The question of solidarity between immigrants and African Americans was raised in August 2014, when the fatal shooting of a black teenager Michael Brown by police in Ferguson, Missouri, sparked outrage and ongoing protests on the streets. Some groups, like the DC Center for Immigrant Justice, called on mainstream immigrant organizations to stand in solidarity with the protests. They charged these organizations with co-opting the black civil rights struggle to legitimize the immigrant rights movement with little reciprocity, ignoring the plight of black immigrants, failing to offer support to black communities under siege, and embracing antiblack rhetoric to present themselves as worthy of American citizenship.[72] For the DC Center, challenging deportations is not enough. Rather, they state:

> We must challenge racist notions of criminality that are being used to justify the militarization of local police in an effort to antagonize and destroy Black life. The same legal apparatus that unjustly detains and deports millions of immigrants and militarizes the US-Mexico border is the same apparatus that profiles, harasses, arrests, incarcerates and murders with impunity Black people in America.

Some mainstream organizations like NDWA and the Dreamer coalition United We Dream (UWD) released statements and sent organizers to participate in the protests. NDWA used the frame of motherhood to connect domestic workers with Brown's mother, Leslie McSpadden. UWD used the Twitter hashtag #OneFight to identify the struggles of migrants with that of African Americans. This move was criticized by Prerna Lal and others, who resisted such easy identifications and called for more nuanced analyses of the connections between migrants and African Americans.

Some of those involved in the antideportation movement felt that it was necessary to tell the stories of deportees. Abdollahi said that within the immigrant rights movement those are usually the stories that are silenced or hidden from the public.[73] But other antideportation activists moved away from telling stories altogether and claimed that the participation of grassroots immigrant activists was often limited to storytelling. In an opinion piece on the state of the immigrant rights movement, UCLA Labor Center

Project Director Victor Narro urged the mainstream leadership to step back and "allow undocumented community leaders to assert themselves as more than just storytellers, as people who can stand and act on their own behalf."[74] This sentiment was repeated by Lal, who tweeted:

> We're not just good for telling our stories, and being tokenized. Perfectly capable of mak-
> ing strategic decisions about our lives. #Not1More
>
> @prernaplal, July 28, 2014

Organizations such as NDLON started calling more directly on prominent organizations to stop negotiating with the White House on behalf of migrant communities. In summer 2014, they proposed a boycott of the White House until undocumented leaders, directly impacted by immigration policies, were given a seat at the negotiating table.

Although the Dreamers had managed to carve out a somewhat independent space and partially win some victories, and many of the more radical undocumented youth groups were closely allied with workers' centers like NDLON, they still encountered tensions with the class project of the mainstream immigrant organizations, who continued to promote messaging about deserving immigrants and model citizens. When Obama announced a new measure of reprieve in November 2014 for undocumented parents of US citizens, he drew on the very binary terms that immigrant organizations had constructed, describing the target of enforcement actions as "felons, not families" and "criminals, not children." The noncitizen, the outsider is characterized as the "felon," "criminal," or "gang member," labels comprising the more than two and a half million deported under the Obama administration. But in the battle over representations, undocumented youth had made it clear that they were not prepared to buy into these binaries or to have their stories used as pawns in larger power struggles, particularly when they were not treated as equals at the bargaining table.

In November 2015, Sonia Guinansaca, who identifies as a migrant queer poet activist and organizer, was invited to speak at a TEDxCUNY event on borders and belonging. In a blog post, she relates how her aim was to show the resistance, resilience, and creative work of her migrant community through reading a poem and giving a talk.[75] Over several rehearsals her script was approved, but shortly before the event, Guinansaca was asked to remove the talk and to share two or three poems. She chose not to remove her talk, and at the final dress rehearsal, she was berated by a white male staff member who told her that her talk was not innovative, that no one wanted to hear a list of migrant artists, that they wanted a "heroic" story. In her blog post, she recounts: "What they continued to ask of me was a boot-strapped, singular narrative that just isn't the reality nor lived experiences of migrant communities." Although Guinansaca wanted to show that the work of undocumented poets is a collective work grounded in a community, the organizers were looking for an individual heroic tale. Guinansaca says that she was reminded, yet again, of "the ongoing commodification of migrant stories in a particular, comfortable and sellable package that does not disrupt privilege, white supremacy, and misogyny." She concludes her post with a poignant question: "Who exactly does this benefit and at what cost?"

CONCLUSION

Although telling stories was presented by mainstream immigration organizations as the way to win legislation that would empower undocumented youth, in fact, storytelling tended to build the political capital and electoral goals of these organizations while not resulting in substantive changes for youth most affected. The various approaches employed by organizations like CCC, from Congressional stories to two-minute Ganz recruitment stories, reinforced myths about the hard-working, upwardly mobile Dreamer. These stories were crucial to a class project that sought power for a small minority of immigrants and their allies while intensifying the exploitation and criminalization of the majority of low-wage undocumented migrant workers.

The attempts by immigrant rights organizations to use storytelling trainings to mold an upwardly mobile Dreamer subject who was oriented toward moderate Congressional reform and voter recruitment had a mixed degree of success. The trainings were able to reach a large number of groups, and through the recycling and sharing of training manuals an even larger number of organizations disseminated the Ganz doctrine of Story of Self, Us, and Now. The effects of those trainings are still apparent even in the more dissident storytelling work. But the attempts by mainstream organizations to control the direction of the Dreamer movement also produced a backlash and led undocumented youth to explore different kinds of storytelling that rejected the script of the model, aspiring American and presented connections to parents and homelands, as well as identities such as queer identity, as a key part of the narratives. After the passage of DACA, and given the rise in deportations, many undocumented youth rejected the "good immigrant" trope that had guided much of their public image. Some even began to reject storytelling altogether, wanting to be seen as participants and strategists on their own behalf, and not simply puppets of the immigration organizations.

The example of the Dreamers shows the ways that storytelling can be drawn into dominant class projects, while still retaining neoliberal discourses of participation and empowerment. The youth at the base of the movement showed that stories could be resuscitated for a more dissident project as well, and their creative projects sought to find a different model of storytelling that allowed them to represent themselves on their own terms. But the youth also express a certain weariness from telling their stories over and over, as they were required to do throughout the years of the campaigns. In this context, it's possible that refusing to tell your story may be the more radical act. In the next chapter, I look at storytelling workshops under the government of Hugo Chávez in Venezuela. In a different context of highly mobilized and collectivist social movements under post-neoliberal conditions, what alternative kinds of narrative models and forms of consciousness and agency might be available?

CHAPTER 6

Rumbas in the Barrio

Personal Lives in a Collectivist Project

This book has focused on the ways that storytelling has been reconfig- ured in a neoliberal era and employed in the service of statecraft, soft power, and advocacy. The Afghan women, domestic workers, and undoc- umented youth who told their stories on websites, at legislatures, and in voter recruitment drives were learning to be upwardly mobile, entrepre- neurial, and self-reliant neoliberal subjects who exercise choice over their destiny. But the contemporary era has also seen significant challenges to neoliberalism in many parts of the globe, starting with the massive waves of antiausterity strikes and mass mobilizations that swept Latin America over the last few decades and brought to power leaders who enabled a transi- tion away from the neoliberal model. Under these conditions of heightened social struggle and post-neoliberal governments, what kinds of storytelling projects do we find and what forms of agency and subjectivity are possible? Could we find some examples of alternative and subversive storytelling projects that allow for complexity and context, in pursuit of a politics of transformation?

In this chapter, I look at the state-sponsored storytelling workshops con- ducted through the Misión Cultura program in Venezuela in the mid-2000s under the radical leftist leader Hugo Chávez. Before his death in 2013 due to cancer, Chávez had pursued a program of regional integration and national redistribution based on the vision of the nineteenth-century independence leader Simón Bolívar. The autobiography workshops of the Misión Cultura were instituted in 2005 as part of a broader Bolivarian project. Barrio resi- dents, workers, indigenous people, and peasants across the country were engaged in writing their personal narratives and local histories under the guidance of trained facilitators. Alongside the other government-sponsored social missions that provided healthcare, literacy training, soup kitchens, and subsidized groceries, the Misión Cultura aimed to "give words, voice, to us, those always silenced."[1] The mission sought to build up a popular alternative archive of people's stories and histories, alongside the official archives that have traditionally defined the national history.

The anti-neoliberal orientation of the Chávez government[2] and its alliances with social justice movements in the country and across the region enabled distinct options for grassroots social action, and that range is also apparent within the Misión Cultura storytelling project. One option that the Bolivarian project made available was a revolutionary subjectivity with Chávez's life story as a model. But I argue that this revolutionary subjectivity tended to reproduce racialized and masculine forms of agency and consciousness that construct actors as self-reliant and independent. While placing emphasis on the awakening of class consciousness and the importance of political struggle, revolutionary subject-making in the Bolivarian frame is still grounded in the idea of the sovereign liberal individual subject. Another option that the Misión Cultura made available was an alternative register for narration that allowed for a decentering of the unitary subject and its location in broader community networks. These two options were taken up in various ways by the participants of the Misión. While some participants modeled their life stories on Chávez's epic tale of revolutionary conversion, others, often those with a strong base in mobilized barrio movements, linked their personal experiences to the collective register— identified by Alessandro Portelli as the life of the neighborhood and collective participation.[3] It is this relinking of the personal, political, and collective registers that has made possible alternative modes of storytelling in post-neoliberal settings.

Do these latter collective modes of subject-making signal a return to the earlier community-based genre of *testimonio* produced during the 1970s and 1980s era of radical social movements in Latin America? These storytelling practices do revive the testimonial form for a contemporary resurgence of left-wing politics in the region, but they have taken somewhat of a different form, especially as these governments did not as yet face the heightened situation of counterinsurgency that earlier radical and socialist governments encountered. In cases such as the Misión Cultura project, the purpose of eliciting stories is less for international circulation and more for building a collective consciousness tied to a left-wing nationalist project. While earlier *testimonios* relied on Western solidarity activists as intermediaries to record, edit, translate, and publish texts, in the contemporary context of Venezuela and other countries in Latin America life stories are recorded and disseminated locally through digital media, the Internet, and community-based radio and television stations.[4] In this chapter, I pay particular attention to the ways that the stories are structured, the narrative modes of telling, and the kinds of subjects-in-formation to understand the liberatory potential of the stories. Just like with the earlier genre of *testimonio*, it is those stories grounded in collective movements and struggles of everyday life that contain the seeds for more oppositional modes of agency.

THE MISIÓN CULTURA AND STATE-SPONSORED STORYTELLING

The underlying utilitarian goals of the Misión Cultura storytelling project are expressed in its mission statement and storytelling manuals. The Misión Cultura project is based on a static notion of culture as a set of traditions that need to be rescued in order to fulfill certain goals such as promoting literacy, bolstering electoral participation, and fostering identification with the Bolivarian project. The storytelling component of the mission was oriented toward producing engaged Bolivarian subjects who would mobilize to defend Chávez and a state-led project of social transformation.

This mobilization of storytelling by left-wing projects in contemporary Latin America differs from the instrumental use of stories by the earlier radical social movements in the region who were facing dictatorial and genocidal regimes. As regimes in countries like Guatemala and El Salvador launched violent counterinsurgency operations against local indigenous and peasant populations in the 1970s and 1980s, US solidarity movements faced the urgency of getting their own government to stop providing military aid to these regimes and to secure international condemnation of their actions. Narratives like the autobiography of Guatemalan indigenous activist Rigoberta Menchú gave personal accounts of this offensive against people's movements, and they required the collaboration of international supporters to edit and circulate the narratives for a broader audience.

The contemporary context of Venezuela and other radical leftist governments in the region such as Bolivia and Ecuador is quite different to this earlier period. Having consolidated electoral office through the power of mass movements, and having drawn on these same movements to defend themselves against right-wing coup attempts, in the mid-2000s left-wing forces were less urgently concerned with international public opinion and more focused on consolidating hegemony domestically against insurgent oppositions through cultivation of support from popular sectors and grassroots organizations. In Venezuela, the poor and marginalized majority aligned themselves with Chávez to wrest control of the state, and its considerable oil resources, out of the hands of the country's transnational wealthy classes. After the elections of 1998 when Chávez was voted into office, ongoing struggles included an opposition-led coup attempt in 2002, a recall referendum in 2004 when the opposition attempted to legally remove Chávez from office, and a general election in 2006. On each of these occasions, the Chávez government mobilized the urban and rural poor to defeat the opposition. This chapter deals with the era of the mid to late 2000s under Chávez. After his death a similar dynamic of struggles over the state apparatus continued under his successor Nicolás Maduro, although the less charismatic Maduro faced greater economic crisis and less popular support.

While Chávez's first period of office was marked by a continuation of his predecessor's policies, by 2001 he was ready to make a break with macroeconomic adjustment policies. In the wake of the failed 2002 coup, the Chávez administration exercised increasing control over the state-owned oil company PDVSA. Boosted by a spectacular rise in oil prices, the Chávez government announced a new social plan based on the universalization of social rights, reduction of wealth inequality, and the public realm as a collective good.[5] At the center of this new social policy were the missions, a series of publicly funded and administered poverty alleviation programs. Following from the adult literacy and elementary education programs, Misión Robinson I and II, as well as the work study program Misión Ribas and the university program Misión Sucre, the Misión Cultura program was introduced later in 2005. The mission consists of a program of study to train teams of cultural promoters who would work to educate people about local and regional cultural traditions. The program was piloted in the Caracas parish of Macarao with fifty-one participants. Shortly thereafter it spread to other parishes and sectors across the country, with local facilitators guided by DVDs, workbooks, and other materials. In 2005, the government allocated $US 5.58 million (Bs 12 billion) to the mission, and in 2006 that amount went up to $US 8.37 million (Bs 18 billion).[6] As of 2008, there were some 32,335 promoters receiving training in the mission, beyond the figure of 28,000 that was initially projected.[7]

The overall goals of the mission were fairly broad but fit closely with the aims of cultural policy that had been set out by the Chávez administration in the Project of the Organic Law of Culture (Proyecto de Ley Orgánica de la Cultura, PLOC) in 2000. Elsewhere, I have described shifts in cultural policy under Chávez toward increased state patronage of culture, with the aim of promoting culture as a tool for national cohesion and political integration. But at the same time, under PLOC, I show how the field of culture continued to be oriented toward private investment, which led to a utilitarian approach to culture as a service or product with the aim of enhancing economic growth.[8] I have argued that under the cultural legislation of the Bolivarian state, these distinct instrumental approaches toward culture overlap and combine, creating a set of conflicting rationalities in the field of cultural policy.

In its mission statement, the Misión Cultura applies these cultural policies toward specific programs that promote the "cultural development of the Venezuelan people."[9] The notion of culture employed by the mission is static and reified, as compared with the more fluid understandings of culture that are employed by cultural producers in Venezuela. The verb *rescatar*, or rescue, is used frequently in the mission statement. "The citizen must be involved in the rescue of the values, beliefs, dances, their patrimony," says the statement in the introduction. It goes on to say that the Bolivarian revolution comes to "rescue the national identity, values, and creations of the Venezuelan public." It is also local identity that must be rescued, as the mission statement says: "provide professionals to the community to rescue the identity of the residents of the parishes" and "rescue the traditions of the parish." The project of writing personal and local histories is directly related to the "rescue of memory." Rescue implies loss, and the statement attributes the loss of these items to the adoption of foreign customs by Venezuelans. Ironically, one of the suggested activities of the mission is to distribute to every sector a copy of *Don Quixote*—a Spanish novel seen as one of the founding works of the Western literary canon. The statement sets up an opposition between the national and the global, with a fortified national identity acting as a bulwark against neocolonialism and globalization. The complex ways in which globalization has bolstered and constituted forms of local and national identity are missing from this conception.

Who are the agents doing the rescuing? At times it is the citizens, or professionals, or the Bolivarian revolutionaries, as described earlier, who are rescuing cultural traditions. At other times it is an "alternative cultural educational project that rescues our national identity." Although state agents are not directly seen as responsible for rescuing cultural traditions, the association of "rescuing culture" with "educating the people" implies that this is a top-down process whereby people must be instructed in what their culture is. This notion of an a priori existing culture that has been lost, and of a professional or expert who needs to step in to re-educate the community in their cultural traditions, runs counter to the history of cultural movements in Venezuela, which have syncretically created and re-created their practices by drawing on elements from their past and present.

The procedures for rescuing culture are quantitative and classificatory in nature, much as James Scott describes the rationalizing functions of modern statecraft.[10] The mission statement lists the following as its objectives: "Detect, know, and adequately register all of those cultural manifestations that are characteristic of each place and have meaning for its population" and "Elaborate an exhaustive registry of cultural patrimony, with emphasis in the values of each region and community."[11] The mission purports to undertake the first-ever census of Venezuelan Cultural Patrimony. These procedures set up hierarchies of knowledge production, where quantified and codified forms of knowledge are held above those that are already latent in the historical memory and shared practices of different urban and rural communities.

The Misión Cultura views the rescue, classification, and reconstitution of cultural traditions as justified by certain instrumental ends. One of these ends is economic, oriented toward "incentives of tourism, the generation of employment, and the improvement of the quality of life of human beings." According to the mission statement, the planning of the mission in each sector must be accompanied by a socioeconomic census that indicates the needs of the community and develops projects that resolve the issues being faced by the community. Another one of the ends is political. Through strengthening regional cultural traditions, the mission aims to promote national cohesion and identity. It encourages the participation of the people in electoral processes, as part of a "new electoral strategy." Given the focus of new leftist governments in the region on attaining and wielding the tools of liberal democracy, including elections, and constitutions to enact change, they have also sought to channel the energies of organized popular movements into an electoral agenda.[12] Social movements for their part have sought to maintain their autonomy while collaborating with the state. The tensions produced as a result of these countervailing tendencies are reflected in the Misión Cultura storytelling project. Whereas the Misión seeks to harness the stories of the urban and rural poor toward a nationalist project of state-led transformation channeled through electoral politics, social movement actors produced narratives that were part of a broader activity of building spaces of popular power based in the networks and experiences of everyday life.

The Misión Cultura trainings aim to produce a team of cultural promoters who will graduate after four years with the title of Bachelor of Education, specializing in Cultural Development, from the Simón Rodríguez National Experimental University. As part of their training, the promoters pass through four stages. These include the writing of their personal stories or autobiographies in the first three months of the program; the construction of a personal educational profile that identifies educational achievements and areas where training is required; the accreditation of learning that has been gained through experience; and finally, the carrying out of neighborhood projects that propose solutions to local issues. During the course of study, the promoters must also carry out a census of cultural patrimony in their neighborhood, interview residents, and write a local history of their community. The initial idea was that the personal and local histories would form part of a new national and popular archive in the Biblioteca Nacional in Caracas. However, these stories were never collected and so there is no repository of them available in any one place.

TRABAJO CON AUTOBIOGRAFÍA: NARRATIVE MODELS IN THE TRAINING MANUALS

The Misión Cultura produced a workbook called "*Trabajo con Autobiografía*" or Work with Autobiography, to be used by the facilitators in the story-telling trainings. The authors of the workbook identify themselves as belonging to the Experimental Center for Lifelong Learning (Centro de Experimentación para el Aprendizaje Permanente, CEPAP). Under a section entitled "Elaboration," the manual describes one method for writing one's personal story as the "life line" method.[13] Participants are asked to draw a line on a sheet of paper to indicate the trajectory of their life and then they mark the most significant events that have happened to them, with successes noted above the line and their challenges below the line. Examples of these significant events may be graduating from school, getting married, death of a grandparent, and so on. This linear method for mapping one's life fits with another notion emphasized in the workbook, that of self-discovery. The workbook describes an interpersonal notion of self-discovery as part of the reason for writing one's story: "It is a real and sincere meeting with ourselves and others. It is a pretext for true communication, the exchange in real human encounters, the meeting (of me) with myself, the meeting (of you) with yourself."[14] Various events in one's life are presented as catalysts for self-discovery, and the recording of these moments in autobiography provides further opportunity for self-reflection.

The idea that one's life can be mapped out as a progressive linear path with successes, failures, and moments of self-discovery along the way corresponds to the epic narrative form. The workbook introduces the quasi-religious idea of "rebirth" as another element of the life story.[15] Shifts in consciousness as a result of momentous life events are often presented in epic terms as a rebirth and Chávez's own life story is given as an example of this epic narrative in the workbook. According to Daniel James, the epic form "implies the individual's identification with the community and its values, and leaves little room for the expression of individual identity."[16] Chávez's epic narrative emphasizes uplift through education, evangelical discourses of rebirth, transcendental choices, and moments of self-discovery as key to developing revolutionary agency. The manual draws on Chávez's life story from the text *Chávez Nuestro*, edited by Rosa Miriam

Elizade and Luis Báez.[17] The book consists of a series of interviews with Chávez's friends and family, followed by a personal recounting of his life history by the former president himself to the editors. In a brief introduction, Elizade and Báez recount that the interview with Chávez lasted six hours, which they edited down to a sixty-five page narrative. The narrative presents a masculine model of revolutionary subjectivity that Josie Saldaña has identified in the case of earlier Latin American revolutionaries Che Guevara and Mario Payeras as being "a risk taker, an advantage seeker, flexible and highly mobile."[18] But whereas Guevara and Payeras receive their "baptism by fire" in the guerrilla struggle of the 1950s and 1960s, Chávez has his transcendental awakening two decades later through becoming a soldier in the military and staging a coup. Also, while for Guevara and Payeras becoming a guerrilla is based on the transcending of difference,[19] Chávez asserts early on the importance of his ethnic and racial heritage to his political identity.[20]

Chávez's self-recounted narrative begins with his childhood memories of rural poverty in the state of Barinas. He grew up in a palm-thatched hut with mud floors where, as he recalls, water used to enter during the rains. Chávez's rise from humble origins is part of the Chávez myth and differentiates him from establishment politicians who are mostly from elite backgrounds. His connection to the Llanera region as symbolic of national identity helps to strengthen the populist myth. One of the recurrent themes in Chávez's autobiography is his love of baseball, which helps to establish his credentials as a man of the people. He also signals early on his identification with his great-grandfather Maisanta, a general who revolted against the military leader Juan Vicente Gomez. Chávez narrates his journey of self-discovery alongside his quest to discover his links to Maisanta, connecting his political awareness to the epic myths that undergird his own genealogy.

The narrative arc of Chávez's story emphasizes both his innate political acumen and also his awakening through the military and education. He describes as a child helping his father who was a vendor in the streets. He enjoyed the work because "it was an opportunity to speak with the people and above all wander around town." Chávez's natural garrulousness and curiosity are seen as part of his political style, apparent from early on. He gives his first speech while in the sixth grade, when he was invited to say some words in honor of the first bishop to be named in Barinas. Afterward he was told by one of his mother's friends that "Huguito is going to love giving speeches, look at how well he does it."[21] From a young age, Chávez also describes an affinity for military life: "From childhood I liked the military life: we invented military forts with zinc cans and boards, and we launched them for conquest." [22] He says, "I felt like a soldier from the beginning."[23] But while Chávez yearns to join the military life, he makes it clear from the start that he was also a rebel. His grandmother Rosa Inés, who was like a mother to him, disapproves of him joining the military, saying, "It is dangerous, and moreover, you, Huguito, are a rebel; some day you are going to get into trouble."[24] The seeds of Chávez's spectacular rise to power from rural poverty to the highest office in the country are seen as innate and apparent from his early childhood experiences.

The backbone of Chávez's life story is the trajectory of his political awakening. He describes several factors that lead to his politicization, including the influence of his brother who was a militant in the Revolutionary Left Movement (Movimiento de Izquierda Revolucionaria, MIR), his participation in the education unit Plan Andrés Bello within the armed forces, and his discovery of Simón Bolívar. Chávez first encountered Bolívar in his study groups in the army, which is not unusual given the presence of Bolívar in a range of official sites as part of a cult of progress and order.[25] Fernando Coronil and Julie Skurski argue that the epic story of Bolívar's struggle against the Spanish colonizers is a "master narrative for nationalist discourse."[26] Bolívar, as patrician hero, wins independence by shaping the anarchic energies of the masses into a liberal national order. At the same time, Bolívar had been reclaimed within collective popular histories as an anti-establishment figure, and Chávez identified with him as a figure fighting against poverty and misery.[27] Chávez claims that it was in adopting Bolivarian thought that he found a way to reconcile his inclinations toward Marxism with the Prussian formation of the professionalized military.[28] Chávez read Bolívar's biography and his writings, and when he was promoted within the military, his unit was given the name Bolívar and they started referring to themselves as Bolivarians.[29] The revindication of Bolívar, as well as other grand heroes of Republican discourse such as Miranda, Zamora, and Simón Rodriguez, led to the adoption within Chavismo of a heroic concept of politics marked by grand stories of liberation. Magdalena Valdavieso argues that within Chavismo, "politics is constituted and understood as a space of heroic actions, and the privileged protagonist of this mode of doing politics is the man, reinvested with the qualities of the warrior: physical vigor, daring, determination, and being ready to sacrifice one's life."[30] Women, she argues, are limited to actions that are complementary or useful for men.

Chávez locates the first points of his political awakening as occurring within the military. He encountered daily conflicts and situations at odds with the Bolivarian principles that he identified with, and which provoked an uncomfortable question for the military and political elites: "What democracy is this that enriches a minority while impoverishing the majority?"[31] He reaches a moment of transcendental awakening during a training in the mountains one day when he hears Cuban leader Fidel Castro denouncing the Chilean coup on Radio Habana Cuba, and there was one particular phrase that stuck with him: "If every worker had weapons in his hands, the fascist Chilean coup would never have happened." He says, "Those words left such a deep impression that they became a motto . . . If every worker . . ."[32] The defenceless state of the Left in Allende's Chile presented a lesson to revolutionaries in the region about the weaknesses of electoral democracy and the need for self-defense, a lesson that the young Chávez took very much to heart.

His four years of military training are a crucible that transforms the "boy from the mountains," the "rural kid with aspirations of being a professional baseball player," to "a sublieutenant who had embarked on the revolutionary path."[33] It is at the moment of graduation from the military that Chávez enters into an individual and masculine revolutionary subjectivity, referring to himself in the third person: "Hugo Chávez was now the man and his circumstances." He was "someone who had no commitment to anyone, who didn't belong to any movement, who was not enrolled in any party, but I knew very well where I was going."[34] It is the individualism of the lone, self-reliant masculine hero, not tied down to party affiliation or movement, that feeds the myth of Chávez as the outsider who could challenge the corruption of the established two-party system.

Although Chávez identifies his moment of political awakening as occurring upon graduation from the military, he points to his stationing among a local indigenous community at Elorza in Apure state as his moment of self-discovery: "I feel that in Elorza I ended up discovering myself." Chávez recounts that while stationed in Elorza he came to know the local Yaruros and Cuivas.[35] Although he had always known of the oppression suffered by the indigenous population, it wasn't until he was captain of their territory and living among them that he came to "feel their pain in my own soul." Part of his realization came in seeing the ways the indigenous people were treated as animals, and the exclusionary social structure of rural society. The other element came from living among them, "eating and drinking with them, trying to understand their world."[36] One day, after some indigenous people visit his family's house and take some of his children's garments, Chávez explains to his wife that "They have no idea about private property. They have no notion that this is yours and this is mine. They take what they need, like they take the fruits from the trees and fish from the river."[37] Chávez's romantic construction of a primordial indigenous worldview informs his own developing socialist principles, built on the idyllic and harmonious society that he imagines the indigenous communities to embody. Ultimately, however, this vision requires incorporating indigenous people themselves into the military, and Chávez speaks about recruiting some young Indians during his time there.

The autobiography concludes with an homage to the maternal figure of Rosa Inés that is also excerpted in the workbook: "Alongside Rosa Inés I knew humility, poverty, pain, being without food at times; I knew the injustices of this world." Chávez describes how she sent him to bring food to their neighbors who had nothing, even if just a sweet, or oatmeal, or a corn muffin. "I learnt from her Venezuelan principles and values of humility, of those who never had anything and constituted the soul of my country." Above the excerpt from the text is an image of Chávez with his head bowed down and hands clasped in prayer. Ileana Rodríguez speaks of the incorporation of maternal tendencies into a revolutionary subjectivity as the "androgyny necessary for the building of a new society."[38] One of the dramatic focal points in the narrative is the death of Rosa Inés, which enables Chávez to incorporate her maternal attributes into his revolutionary masculine agency.

This epic narrative of Chávez's life story is used as a model in the workbook for constructing stories in the Bolivarian frame. As a so-called life line method, Chávez's story is narrated in a linear fashion, with moments of self-discovery and reckoning, somewhat akin to the moments of choice presented in the Ganz story workshops. Like the other modes of subjectivity explored in this book, Chávez's life story is also one of the sovereign subject who goes through a process of self-knowledge and moves toward enlightenment and participation in civic life. By narrating their own life stories in this epic frame, barrio residents, peasants, and workers come to understand themselves as ideal revolutionary subjects who will fight on behalf of Chávez to promote the Bolivarian political project.

The workbook also presents another nonlinear model for writing personal stories. It is a model that does not follow a chronological or temporal order, and rather represents one's life in terms of spheres, where the individual is at the center and is surrounded by the people, groups, communities, and organizations who have influenced one's life, with the most important influences located closest to the individual.[39] This style is similar to what Marcia Stephenson has described in the case of the Andean Oral History Workshop (Taller de Historia Oral Andina, THOA) in Bolivia, which presented the biography of a leading nineteenth-century Aymara intellectual Eduardo Nina Qhispi.[40] Stephenson describes how the biography which began as a "Western-style biography centered on a unitary subject became instead an extensive collective history of the altiplano region." Writing about Nina Qhispi required writing about his *ayllu*, a traditional Andean unit of governance, and then surrounding *ayllus*. The inclusion in the Misión Cultura workbook of an alternative narrative model that locates the individual among various spheres of people and communities is similar to this decentering of the unitary subject promoted by the THOA. The inclusion of this alternative model is significant, and in the personal narratives that follow we can see how this nonlinear model of storytelling might make available different kinds of registers as alternatives to the epic Bolivarian frame.

One notable feature of the workbook is the emphasis on what the authors call "risky therapy." By this, they refer to the explosion that can happen when people share their feelings, failures, doubts, fears, and sadness. Although such honesty is encouraged by the facilitators, they want to avoid the workshops being converted into large therapy sessions. The authors argue that "We should control this process because it can become excessively long and deviate from the goals for which we are here."[41] Although it is not bad to want to help someone who is bringing up buried or repressed events, the workbook argues that it is risky since they are not trained to do so. This bracketing of the personal and traumatic presents one of the main contradictions of the mission, since the process of encountering oneself and narrating life events is bound to bring up gendered lived experiences of the kind that other movements like the women's movement in the West considered central to political analysis and strategy.

The immediate audience of the narratives is the others in the group, to whom there will be a formal presentation of the autobiography once the writing and revision are completed. And the audience is also more broadly imagined as the community where the participants will go back to work and will share their life story with others. The participants are asked to make three copies of their narratives: one for the facilitator, one for filing with the National Coordinating Academy, and another for the participants themselves. Those sent to the national level were supposed to be stored in the National Archives, but the mission later changed its policies and has not collected or archived any of the narratives. For the most part, the narratives have remained in possession of the individuals or the group facilitators. But the purpose is not to publicize them or make them available to a larger audience, but rather to be shared within the group and community as the basis for promoting interpersonal awareness. As the workbook states, "It is important and obligatory that all participants know the autobiography of every one of their *compañeros*."[42] This sharing of stories and knowledge of one's comrades is seen as integral for the local neighborhood projects that are going to emerge.

In keeping with the message of Chavismo to give voice to the marginalized, the workbook emphasizes the coming out or self-assertion of the invisible poor: "The possibility of giving the word, voice, to us, the always silenced. It is a way of saying, 'HERE I AM. THIS IS HOW I AM.'"[43] Along with the local histories, the mission seeks to build an archive of information about the lives of those in poor and marginalized communities. The personal stories composed through the Misión Cultura workshops can give us insights into the daily lives and histories of those "siempre silencia-dos." But the stories are not simply sources of empirical information, as the facilitators of the mission would propose. Some are shaped by narratives of uplift through education, evangelical discourses of rebirth, and the epic narrative of Chávez's own life story as told and retold in both official and popular venues. Others depart from this epic, linear model to narrate life experiences in unedited prose through the everyday spheres of the barrio, local networks, and activist communities. In these "noncurated stories" we can see how storytelling is engaged in creating new and alternative kinds of political subjectivities.

MICRO STORIES AND REVOLUTIONARY SUBJECTIVITIES

In contrast to the epic model exemplified by Chávez's life story, I explore the stories written in the workshops as examples of what Eric Selbin calls "micro stories," more local and insular stories that are focused on matters of everyday life.[44] While some micro stories are shaped by the conventions of the epic narrative, others may contain the possibility for alternative modes of agency and consciousness. The micro stories also reflect different modes of subjectivity to that made available by Chávez: subjects are dependent and interdependent, some are grounded in community and local move-ments, and some narrate a process of continual change and flux rather than marked moments of transcendental awakening. I argue that what makes these different kinds of storytelling available are the location of subjects within spaces of the barrio, networks of collective culture, and everyday community-based struggles.

Given that the stories from the Misión were never compiled nationally in an archive or database, they were quite difficult to track down. I was able to obtain about a half a dozen stories that were made available to me by friends and on the Internet. This is a small sample of what is a much larger archive of thousands of stories. However, given the length of the stories I obtained, which varied from five to eighty-three pages in length, I still had hundreds of pages of material and the stories presented a fairly broad range. I have selected three stories to analyze and translate into English: one narrative by a woman from the northwest state of Zulia, another by an Afro-descendant barrio activist from the northern state of Carabobo, and a longer narrative by a cultural activist with a physical disability from the barrios of Caracas. These three subjects, and their differential experiences of community orga-nizing, of embodiment, and of life experience, can give us insight into how the Misión Cultura storytelling trainings may enable a range of models of political agency and subjectivity.

Model Bolivarian Subjects and Gendered Experiences

Sara Elena Pérez is from the municipality of Colon, located in Zulia.[45] Pérez begins her autobiography by identifying her place of birth—a southern town in the Andes called Zea, in the state of Merida. The narrative traces her trajectory from rebellious schoolgirl to dignified proud mother to high school graduate and community worker, punctuated by events such as the death of her father and her conversion to evangelical Christianity. We can see several cultural scripts at play in the narrative, including the narrative of uplift through education, evangelical discourses of rebirth, and narratives of gender and motherhood.

Pérez barely remembers her difficult childhood of poverty and tragedy. Her mother tells her that as a child she and her five siblings were moved around a lot, because her parents didn't have a permanent place to live. In 1975, they were victims of flooding and were moved to the Santa Bárbara parish. Finally, in 1978, the family was given their own house in a sector called La Gloria. In comparison to Chávez, who remembers himself and his brother as "two boys very poor, but very happy,"[46] Pérez finds that she doesn't recall much about her childhood and must reconstruct it from what her mother tells her. At the age of eleven, Pérez began to study at the Andrés Bello school. She says that at this stage of her life she was "a very rebellious child and a bit disengaged." She relates that in the fourth grade she made her pregnant teacher chase her through the whole school, in fifth grade she swore at a teacher, and, worst of all, one day she ran away from home with her friend Yaquelin and was found by the police in the Colon walkway. But despite being rebellious, Pérez also worked to help out her family, as her much older father had lost his job due to his age. In the mornings before going to school she would work in the homes of her neighbors for very low pay. She finished six years of primary schooling, but given her need to work and support her family, she was not able to complete even the first year of her *bachillerato*, or secondary education. She dropped out and worked full time in the house of a Señora Brombin. Despite her flouting of authority, Pérez establishes herself in the narrative as a hard worker who deviates somewhat as a teenager but finds a path back to becoming a responsible citizen. But there is also an element of irreverence in her story, which helps her position herself as someone who did not easily accept the status quo.

Pérez describes marriage, motherhood, and evangelical conversion as the three elements that change her life path. After marrying her husband Julio Enrique Pérez Davales at the age of seventeen, and giving birth to a girl, she decides to be baptized in the Emmanuel Church. Soon after obtaining land through an "invasion," or takeover of land by local residents, and constructing a two-bedroom home, Pérez lost her ninety-eight-year-old father. She describes him as a crucial figure in her life: "a man who had concern for each and every one of us, he was a guide, an advisor." By the time shortly thereafter she gave birth to her second child, a boy, Pérez was secure in her "role as a dignified and proud mother." Motherhood is seen as one of the elements that help her to overcome the deviations of her youth, deal with the sadness of losing her father, and to eventually reinvent herself.

The last section of Pérez's life story called "Soñe de Nuevo," or New Dream, is presented in the style of a typical conversion narrative. She recounts that four years after the birth of her son, she felt a restlessness to return to her studies but couldn't figure out how to do it. Then one day she heard Chávez speaking about the Misión Ribas work-study program, and she felt motivated to join. In this section, Pérez describes her educational uplift and political awakening through the educational missions. As part of a community project, she and others restored the library of the technical agriculture school. She graduated from Misión Ribas, with her dream "to have the title that they granted us as high school graduates of the Bolivarian Republic of Venezuela." Pérez's attainment of her degree is strongly associated with her identification with the Bolivarian project. In Pérez's foundational myth of the self, education is the medium through which she becomes politically active. She gives the example of her participation in the "NO" campaign during the recall referendum of 2004 as patrol leader of the Andrés Bello Unit of Electoral Battle (UBE). She was recognized as one of the highlighted "combatants" in the community project and given an award in the amphitheatre of the National Experimental University. Following that, she was the cultural coordinator of the communal council in the sector La Gloria, involving the children of the sector in dance, singing, and theatre.

The life story of Sara Elena Pérez as written in the Misión Cultura workshop reveals the ways in which she constructs her political subjectivity, from a poor child of humble beginnings to a model Bolivarian citizen and student. Through education and self-knowledge she moves toward participation in civic life. The fact that the life story has been written over the course of several workshops, rather than told in one sitting as an oral history, makes it more amenable to being shaped and reordered according to the priorities of the mission. Pérez's story presents an enactment of the prototypical Bolivarian script as modeled on the autobiography of Chávez.

Pérez's story is structured as one of uplift through education and political participation. The evangelical notion of rebirth undergirds her transformation, imagining the Bolivarian subject as reborn and remade anew. But we can also see this model of the epic Chávez narrative as one which can be used by poor women like Pérez as an outline to fill with their own histories, experiences, and emotions. Pérez does not finesse her childhood as one of happiness—in fact, she barely remembers it. Her childhood experiences of domestic labor did not give her the opportunity to practice speaking with the people and being in the city—they deprived her of an education. It is Pérez's ties to the home, to her family and children, that construct her particular revolutionary subjectivity as dependent and interdependent, rather than the universal model based on the life of Chávez as a self-determining, mobile agent.

That Pérez came to support and fight for the Bolivarian project as a result of her involvement in the mission is clear. But her multilayered narrative surpasses the simple tale of political incorporation through a cultural project by also hinting at other darker, undeveloped themes such as her molestation by a neighbor in the Santa Bárbara parish. On this topic, she says very little, only:

> In reality, I don't have many memories of this [her childhood], but I remember we had to live in the Santa Bárbara parish, known actually as the Santa Bárbara School, above all because there, I lived one of the most awful moments of my life when at the age of four I was sexually abused by a man who lived there like us.

This is all she says about the molestation—one of the most awful experiences of her life and the only memory of her childhood that really stands out. The fear of "risky therapy" mentioned by mission coordinators, the need to hold such private and traumatic experiences in check, is at play in this narrative. The structures of gender and sexuality that can be expressed in the stories are limited to available tropes of marriage and motherhood, which provide an acceptable outlet to channel one's emotions. The workings of patriarchy and sexual abuse, as crucial determinants of a poor woman's life story, exist as an undercurrent.

How do we read the multiple themes narrated in the life story of Pérez? James suggests that one of the richest interpretive strategies available for analyzing life histories lies in "probing the relationship between key narrative patterns aimed at creating coherence and continuity and other elements that clarify, obscure, make more complex, or simply leave in the tension-laden coexistence of contradictory themes and ambivalent meanings."[47] In Pérez's story, the molestation is revealed early on as one of the most important events in her life and, like her rebellious behavior and grief for her father's death, remains mostly unexplored. Alongside the upbeat story of overcoming, there is a darker one that can give us a sense of the ways that gendered poverty structures the lives of women like Pérez. The narrative moves between the two registers of her epic tale of education and political awakening, and her personal experiences of gendered poverty. The traumas of abuse and grief are contained by the epic narrative, but that containment is precarious.[48] The elements of "emotion, loss, and mourning"[49] can give us insight into the "siempre silenciados," even more so than the epic narrative.

"Against the Drums of Death:"
Afro-Descendant and Revolutionary

The other two narratives that I will explore in this chapter diverge from the linear, epic model marked by Chávez's life story. Instead of being marked by moments of transcendental change and rebirth, the following two narrators intersperse life events with the people, cultural groupings, political events, and places that they encounter in their lives. In this sense, these narratives resemble more closely the spherical model of autobiography given in the Misión Cultura workbook. Whereas Chávez's life history is expressed as a conversion narrative where his life experiences compel him toward political and electoral involvement, in these alternative narratives it is in the rural, the barrio, and the *rancho* where the struggles of everyday life lead toward forms of cultural and community-based activism. This is similar to the autobiography of Rigoberta Menchú, which Saldaña argues contains no spectacle of transformation, no dramatic moment of revelation of her oppression, or retroactively constructed moment of innocence.[50] Rather, Saldaña draws on Frantz Fanon's idea of "the zone of occult instability where the people dwell" to describe Menchú's location in the "politics of the present," in the "concrete materiality of everyday struggle" through which the possibility for a more radical agency emerges.[51] Rather than a transcendental awakening, or unilinear and messianic revolutionary consciousness, the process of consciousness is repetitive and continual. Political awareness comes as a result of the ongoing interpretation of her life experiences.[52] We can see this as well in these two autobiographies, whose protagonists do not experience transcendental moments of realization or choice but are shaped by immersion in daily life and culture that conditions how they act in the world.

These two narratives have the makings of an alternative form of storytelling that can provide a counter to the neoliberal model of curated stories that I have explored in this book. In these two noncurated stories, there is very little editing; the narratives are written in lengthy sentences with only commas for pause and periods coming mostly at the end of paragraphs. This style gives the texts an oral quality, as if the narrative is being spoken rather than written. In my translations, at times I have added in some periods to make the text easier to read. But where relevant I translate with the original punctuation in place. The lack of editing does not make these stories any more "authentic" than edited stories, because as James, Spivak, and others have noted, the tropes, dominant discourses, and devices found in stories all mediate the subjective experience being related. But at least in these narratives, the chronology, length, and choice of narrative models are priorities established by the writer rather than an outside interlocutor who is interviewing the subject, transcribing their interview, and then preparing it for consumption.[53] Although the immediate audience is not always apparent or consistent across these different narratives, there is more of a sense that the stories are written for local audiences with the aim of contributing to collective histories that can be the basis of place-based, culturally based movements for social change.

The narrative of William Peraza,[54] a sixty-year-old Afro-descendant man from a barrio named Coro in the northern state of Carabobo, begins by him situating himself within his historical lineages. He identifies his maternal grandmother as a descendent of indigenous Caquetia people, who are "today disappeared peoples in Jacura, Falcón state." His maternal grandparents were herbalists "who knew the power of almost all of the plants of the zone." His world moved between the barrio and the countryside, where his family members had small plots of land, and where he is introduced to the medicinal plants and local grains that his family cultivates: legumes known as quinchoncho and tapirama, a medicinal plant known as pira atún, and staples such as quimbombó (okra) and ocumo ñame (tuber).

The early part of Peraza's narrative evokes the life of the barrio, one marked by the traditions of the Afro-Venezuelan fiestas such as San Juan and Cruz de Mayo; the carnivals of December under the almendrón tree; the solidarity and collaboration of neighbors who helped each other out; and stories from elders about the nearby coastal Morón, formerly home to many runaway slaves and a base for organized slave revolts. When Peraza was in sixth grade in 1970, barrio Coro became a base for revolutionary organizing, with residents hiding insurgents who were being hunted by the government. The following year, a young Peraza helped to found the Revolutionary Student Front (Frente Revolucionario Estudiantil, FRE), which won the student elections in his school over the groups from the prevailing political parties Democratic Action (AD) and COPEI. Peraza led the student group in a protest against the contaminated water in the school tanks that was being given to the children.

Peraza's narrative moves fluidly between his cultural activities such as organizing fiestas and founding a local Culture House, his political activism, his entrance into the workplace as a machine operator and union organizer in a paper factory, and his research into Afro-descendant culture and history. The spheres of the neighborhood, the workplace, and the community center are interconnected; they are all sites of daily life and protest that shape his revolutionary consciousness. The personal events in Peraza's life such as the birth of his children are interspersed among the other events, without pause:

> In February 1981 my daughter Anabelis was born I continued with the cultural-political activities, I was newly elected Secretary General of the union, I participated in the second cultural-sporting tour, extending this tour to the states of Falcón, Guárico, Cojedes, Yaracuy, and Aragua, after this I became involved in party activities and in Morón we founded la Causa R and the politics of the new unionism in 1982 my second child was born and we called him Ilich in homage to Wladimir Ilich Ulianov (Lenin).

While the lack of commas and periods gives a breathless quality to the narrative, making it seem as if Peraza is overextended in a number of different activities, in fact, I see this style as testament to the interconnectedness of the spheres of the cultural, political, historical, labor, and personal for Peraza and his comrades. For instance, immediately following this passage, he goes on to describe how his research on the history of runaway slaves in Morón led him to organize a Cruz de Mayo fiesta in his barrio, but how they understood their cultural work as part of broader consciousness raising and as distinct from those who were doing it for commercial gain. Another sentence continues in this same passage: "I began the investigation of the instruments of rites and persecution of those of African origin in Morón, I participated in the Committee for Life and Peace in Morón against the drums of death that they wanted to bring to this people." The past and the present are brought together in the same sentence, allowing Peraza to construct a continuity between both moments—the persecution of ex-slaves and the contemporary struggle to defend Morón from military raids and occupation.

Political work forms a constant thread throughout the narrative but unlike Chávez, Peraza does not identify any moment of political awakening or conversion. Instead, it is a politics of insurgency that is shaped in contention with the police, against the dominant political parties and corrupt, opportunistic politicians. Although he describes his involvement in political activities, this is distinguished from "politicking," as a hierarchical logic of seeking individual gain through electoral politics. Peraza discusses his involvement in the student movement in 1974, and then the civic strike organized against the government in 1976 to protest the lack of water and electricity services, and police repression. In retaliation, he was detained by the intelligence services, and the Culture House that he had founded was bombed by government forces. In February 1992, Peraza participated in the military coup launched by Chávez, for which he was hunted by police and had to go into hiding. A one-and-a-half-page-long paragraph then details his experiences with the elections and his involvement in the Causa R alternative party. In the midst of a stand-off between the military and the activists in Morón, he says that "we took the fiesta of San Juan Bautista out to the streets, the 24th we came out at five in the morning and baptized the saint in the river, with this we said to the government in Morón that we are in the streets defending our rights." Political and party activities are pursued as part of a movement of cultural revindication. The constant narrating of cultural activities alongside political events shows the strong interrelation between them; they cannot be separated.

We also see a reclaiming of Afro-Venezuelan identity in the narrative, and in particular the appropriation of figures such as the rebellious run-away slave Andresote, who was said to have taken refuge in the mountains of Morón. Peraza mentions a talk that he gave at a cultural center in Yaracuy called "Andresote, Rebellion, and Class Struggle." There is an emphasis in his narrative on cultural recognition and rights of Afro-descendants that is tied to a broader movement for economic rights. This portends a revolutionary subjectivity that is not based on transcending one's particularity, as in the case of Guevara or even Chávez, but rather is grounded in cultural identity, knowledge of history, and practices of popular culture.

Peraza constructs his political subjectivity differently to both Pérez and Chávez, in that his awareness of injustice and inequality comes not through a defined moment of political awakening or conversion, but rather as a result of his intertwined experiences of daily life, cultural activities, stories from his elders, and encounters with the police and the military. The lack of editing in the story is crucial, because if it had been edited either according to the linear model of the Misión, or by an outsider with less knowledge of his life, we would miss the convergences between past and present, culture and politics, the barrio and the political sphere that form part of his revolutionary consciousness.

Embodiment and Collective Subjecthood

The autobiography of Ricardo José Guerrero from the parish of La Pastora in Caracas is a longer document than is typical for the Misión—it is eighty-three pages of typed, single-spaced prose.[55] One of the key aspects that differentiate this narrative from the masculinist, epic model presented in the workbook is Guerrero's corporal vulnerability and dependency on others. While Chávez is a self-reliant, independent, and mobile actor, Guerrero suffers a congenital illness known as diastrophic dwarfism, which greatly limits his mobility and makes him more dependent on others. He describes the illness in great detail:

> It involves knotted tendons in all joints of the fingers, elbows and knees, with deformities in the feet and the central trunk of the body. This occurs because of a deficiency of growth hormones, that are generated by a gland called the Pituitary. Here we find the hypophysis which we all have in our brain, that produce the growth glands of the human being.[56]

It is this illness, and the numerous surgeries and hospitalizations resulting from it, that make Guerrero dependent on his mother in a way that at times he sees as unhealthy: "It gave more desire to my mother to overprotect me and spoil me, for most of my life, and often this limited and affected some aspects of my development in my infancy and adolescence."[57] His mother infantilizes and coddles him, partly as a way of protecting him from the hostility and harassment that he comes to suffer as a result of his disability.

Guerrero feels ashamed of his physical difference when compared to his "normal" siblings, and because of the neighbors and friends who continually tell his mother that he is abnormal and needs medical treatment. When he is brought to the local Hospital San Juan Dios in Caracas, a medical priest assures his mother that there is no need to operate, that doctors will only want to experiment with him. God has made him this way, says the doctor, and we should respect it.[58] Nevertheless, with mounting pressure from others, Guerrero's mother takes him to other hospitals where he begins a lifelong experience of medical intervention, surgery, and treatments to correct his disability. As he grows older, he continues to encounter humiliations. The family of his first girlfriend pressures her to end the relationship with him, "simply because I was a midget, deformed, and ugly."[59] These humiliations were combined with the abuse he suffered when his mother worked as a domestic in the home of a wealthy family. He recounts the physical beatings and verbal abuse he received from Erasmo, his mother's employer. At times the abuse was sexual, as when Erasmo was masturbating in the bathroom and called Guerrero to come inside and watch him.[60] Guerrero's mother finally makes the decision to leave after one day Guerrero is in the bath and Erasmo enters and slaps Guerrero on his buttocks with the palm of his hands.

After this experience, Guerrero and his mother moved in with his grandmother in the Caracas barrio of Las Torres in La Vega. It is in the space of the barrio, and the Callejón Ricaute, the alley where he plays with the other children of the neighborhood, that Guerrero comes to learn that he is equal and valued: "In the barrio I learned to feel equal to the rest of my friends. Or rather, they taught me, without knowing or proposing it, to feel myself in conditions of equality, where I often forgot my physical condition, although I was different to them." He was not coddled or treated as lesser in capacity or humiliated for being different. Rather, "If we had to fight, we had to do it with the resources and conditions that we had."[61] Guerrero came to know all of the corners, alleys, sidewalks, and most hidden areas of the barrio, where he played, conversed with the neighbors, and came to feel part of a community. He describes the interconnection of people's lives in the space of the barrio in these terms:

> Every one of the residents was linked together magically, secretly, and in a strange way we all had to deal with one another. There existed ties and affinities that are hard to explain, although every person had their individuality and unique personality, although beyond the door of each house there was a very specific reality, and each of these have very definite shades. Despite everything that can be said of this and that, the barrio is only one. When I go into the streets and begin to explore its places and interact with people, there is another mode of amusement, a motive, a history that connects you with someone or something.[62]

Guerrero is speaking of the space of the barrio as a totality that comprises the unique lives and features of each individual, but that is also a space of interdependence where the social ties and links between these individuals based on history, culture, and coexistence produce a feeling of unity. This notion of interdependence contrasts with the self-sufficient and individualist ethos of Chávez, who emerges from the military as someone who does not need others. At the same time, Guerrero does not idealize this space of the barrio as one of idyllic harmony, which over time he says became the site for gang wars and violence; he recounts that various friends he grew up with were killed by firearms. In his narrative, Guerrero presents what Margaret Mills calls a "networked collective subjecthood," with the extended family and neighborhood as the basic social and economic unit.[63] This collective subjecthood stands in contrast to the individual selfhood presented in the epic Chávez narrative.

Just like for Peraza, Afro-Venezuelan fiestas and culture are profoundly interconnected with Guerrero's community organizing work. From a young age, he recalls his mother taking him to an amusement park called El Parque Mecánico, where he would go on the rides and hear music from the legendary salsa orchestras Sonora Matancera, los Melódicos, Billo Caracas Boy, la Dimensión la Tina, and Beny Moré. Enjoying the fresh breeze high above the city, looking down at the people and cars in the city like little dolls, the music would invoke in him a nostalgia and profound sadness, "perhaps because I was living as a child the complexity of my being."[64] As a child, Guerrero liked to play the drums, and as he couldn't afford to buy one, he made one himself:

> I would take a plastic container, one of those that the Parmalat milk came in, a kilo. I removed the bottom and it became a cylinder. I sanded the edges and I bought a red sheet known as Teype, like those that electricians use. I started wrapping it on one diameter, passing it on all sides, in myriad ways, making the sheet stretch until it covered everything, leaving a uniform skin. This is how I made my first drum.[65]

With few resources, Guerrero created his first drum that had a deep and resonant sound. Along with his friends Gusano and Tico, Guerrero formed a Guaguanco band, where they sang and played. Guerrero also liked to dance and although he danced all different kinds of dance, he was known best as a *rumbero*, a specifically Afro-Venezuelan rhythmic style.

As he grew older, Guerrero came into contact with a wide range of musical influences and cultural activists who encouraged him to pursue a more radical agenda with his performance. One of these was a social activist in his barrio Nelson García, who had formed a Cultural Center Las Torres. The way in which García talked, with a passion and revolutionary fervor, was exciting for Guerrero. He began to formulate a more critical attitude to the world, to express his own ideas, "in other words, I learnt how to become a critical thinker, dialectic, creative, and transcendental, a man who was a fighter, revolutionary, and rebel."[66] He worked with García on a play about social injustice in the lives of street children, and they went all over the city presenting the play in different barrios. Guerrero came of age at a moment of heightened cultural activism and regional political uprisings. He performed at a concert organized by the legendary revolutionary folksinger Alí Primera, and his theatre group dressed as guerrillas in solidarity with the FMLN guerrillas in El Salvador. He performed with the radical cultural grouping Grupo Madera, asking Chu Quintero how to play the bongos. Together with García and another friend Javier Sánchez, Guerrero created a group of clowns, calling himself Payaso Pompon, and this became a way for him to earn an income. By connecting the collective space of the barrio with struggles for social justice, over the course of his story Guerrero transitions from networked collective subjecthood to what Mills refers to as the "activist collective subjecthood of the testimony genre."[67] This represents an alternative form of political agency to that of the self-reliant and individual revolutionary leader.

As the various urban communities confronted government plans for urban remodeling and relocation of barrio residents, Guerrero and García formed a drumming group known as Drummers against Displacement (Los Tambores en Contra de Los Desalojos). Later, with the Experimental Group Example of Friendship (Grupo Experimental Ejemplo de Amistad, GEEA) in the barrio Las Torres, they campaigned to name a park after Alí Primera, who had died in a car accident. Guerrero worked closely with a network of local organizations in Las Torres and La Vega, including the Cultural Center Los Torres and the Grupo Caribes de Itagua of El Gordo Edgar. All of these groups engaged in specific local actions, but they met frequently to discuss and debate ideas, as well as to start up their own newspaper known as *Los Incultos* (The Uncultivated). They also collaborated in the yearly religious festivals of Cruz de Mayo, the Comparasas, percussion workshops, and other activities.

Although Guerrero's cultural activities and political involvement come from his location in the everyday space of the barrio, this space is also shaped by various state agencies and private foundations. Guerrero says that he studied in percussion workshops organized by the Fundación Bigott, a philanthropic organization set up by British American Tobacco, which invested heavily in the field of culture as a way to promote itself after tobacco advertising was outlawed in 1981. He also worked as a cultural promoter under the Chávez administration with the cultural institutions Fundarte and the National Council for Culture (Consejo Nacional de la Cultura, CONAC). This is similar to Peraza, who mentions his cultural work with the Ministry of Education, CONAC, Montessori schools, and the municipality.

The key events in Guerrero's autobiography are not political, like Peraza, but are more focused in the *cotidiano*, the everyday experiences and struggles of those from the barrio. After living for many years in a crowded house with his grandmother, Guerrero moves with his mother and siblings to their own *rancho*, a precariously constructed house in the upper reaches of the barrio Las Torres. He recalls that it cost his mother 4,000 bolívares, it was assigned the number 0017 by the National Guard, and it was like a little matchbox, with a toilet behind it.[68] Guerrero describes the problems of transport for those living in the *ranchos*. They have to wake up at five in the morning or earlier to catch a bus and then train to go to their work. As a result, many have developed "a level of patience, of tolerance in the midst of disorder and noise that all of this generates."[69] Then, Guerrero recounts how in December 1999, the *rancho* collapsed during a storm:

> On December 15 at 9:00 pm, in the year 1999, a large tree behind our house at the top of Los Mercedores and Las Torres collapsed. It had been raining a lot for the three days prior. The *rancho* was inundated with water and mud. I was out of it, stunned in this moment. I didn't want to leave the *rancho* and lose everything. Before the walls collapsed, I rushed out, thanks to Wuilfredo, a neighbor and Morao's brother-in-law, who

shook me out of it and made me react by letting out a loud scream. Five minutes passed after I left the *rancho* and suddenly, in fractions of a second, the walls fell in of what was my home. I was in shorts and without a shirt, with the rubber boots that I had on in this moment. All of our belongings were now in the mud.[70]

The collapse of his home is a defining moment in Guerrero's life, not because of the change or awakening it produces in him, but because of the way it alters his life circumstances, forcing him to live with many others in a makeshift camp that was to become his home. It is these daily struggles—of housing, transport, sanitation, and then dislocation—as well as the collective space of the barrio and the cultural activities he is involved with that shape the specific form of consciousness and agency that undergirds his narrative.

Community-based activism extends to Guerrero's time in the relocation camp in the Parque Recreacional Sur. After facing depression, isolation, and dependency on his mother, he began working with the Unified Social Fund (FUS) to organize people in the camp. He convened assemblies in order to name work commissions, and he gave percussion classes to children in the camp. He taught the children origami, organized sport activities, and managed to find spaces for the children in local schools. In the camp, he ended up meeting a woman, María Ariza, who became his long-term partner.

Toward the end of his narrative, Guerrero recounts that he and María were given an apartment in the nearby northern state of Miranda by the housing authority. He had also won a grant from Fundarte to give percussion classes in Los Torres. He then ran into problems with the local Consejo Comunal, a form of community-based organization sponsored by the Chávez administration. The Consejo Comunal of Las Torres issued a damaging commentary saying that he had robbed this money. They wrote notices to the community saying that Guerrero was molesting the children. Guerrero defended himself by saying that it was because of his critical and revolutionary attitude toward the members of the Consejo Comunal that they were harassing him, and he ends the autobiography by affirming his firm defense of the "Bolivarian process led by Comandante Hugo Chávez Frías."[71] Interestingly, this is his only mention of the Bolivarian process or Chávez in the whole autobiography. From knowing Guerrero personally, I can say that he is a fervent Chavista, but the writing of his life history in terms other than the model provided by Chávez also points to the greater importance of everyday cultural organizing in Guerrero's life.

The understanding of culture in Guerrero's narrative differs in important ways from that found in the mission statement and training manuals of the Misión Cultura. Rather than seeing culture as something to be rescued, quantified, classified, or put in the service of various ends, Guerrero sees culture as a space for encounter and collaboration. He gives a detailed description of the Cruz de Mayo fiesta, which was re-created in the barrio Las Torres for the first time in 1983. The ability to have the fiesta depended on the networks of collaboration that existed between families in the barrio, which would allow them to house visitors and serve them food, make toilets available for the evening, and other necessities that arose. Guerrero says that each passing year they put together a more beautiful altar, with an alcove made of bamboo and palms, flowers, fruits, and harvests from the land that represent the multicolors of nature, abundance, and light that illuminate the path forward. He describes the impact of the event in the following terms:

> We were able to invite many Afro-Venezuelan musical groups from Caracas.... Also attending were social and community organizations, social fighters and revolutionary youth from distinct places and distinct organizations. We try to convert the Velorio de Cruz into a great meeting of brothers, of friendship and solidarity and full of commitment to struggle. It is not only the magical-religious, the mystical, the deity, and the devotion to the Cruz de Mayo. It also implies organization, the search for spaces to share as a community, and recognize each other as brothers united by a single topographical identity, with the same needs and sharing the same reality.[72]

There are many definitions of culture in Guerrero's description. There is culture as spirituality, culture as a way of being, culture as a means of organization, culture as the space of collective life, and culture as a vehicle for identity. Culture is intrinsically connected with the everyday life of the barrio, Fanon's zone of occult instability, from where alternate modes of subject-making and radical forms of agency can become available.

CONCLUSION

Can the forms of storytelling emerging out of a post-neoliberal context such as Venezuela provide an alternative to the other modes of curated stories that I have examined in this book? I have shown the unexpected convergences between revolutionary subjectivity as modeled on the life story of Chávez and the upwardly mobile, entrepreneurial, and self-reliant subject of neoliberal discourse. Linear revolutionary subjectivity and neoliberal subjectivity share a basis in the same sovereign liberal independent subject as formed in the eighteenth-century Enlightenment. Like the other workshops examined in this book, the Misión workshops encourage participants to narrate their stories as subjects who move from humble beginnings to become model citizens capable of participation in civic life. Like the other storytelling trainings, the Misión Cultura trainings also aim to use stories to direct people away from independent political organizing and toward state-supporting forms of civic and electoral participation. The life story workshops promote the idea that people should come to understand themselves as part of a state-led nationalist project.

Yet while promoting this linear revolutionary subjectivity, the Misión Cultura also presents alternative models of narrating one's story. The workbook materials offer examples of nonlinear models, and dialectical understandings of knowledge creation from thinkers such as Paulo Freire and Eduardo Galeano among others, that counter the messianic construction of personal narrative. Without strict templates and protocols, the workshops and materials offer up the possibility for longer, noncurated narratives that can explore the varied dimensions of a person's life, rather than being limited to a few moments of political awakening or self-discovery. These alternative models are taken up by actors from organized and grassroots social movements, with their bases in barrios and poor rural communities, who use the stories as a tool of organizing and a means of creating alternative models of subjectivity and consciousness.

What is it that distinguishes this alternative model that has its makings in post-neoliberal contexts such as Venezuela and Bolivia? The stories explicitly reconnect the personal details of a life story to the political and collective registers. They show the individual as embedded within local networks of family and community, as the product of historical forces, and as acting on those forces through political involvement. We caught glimpses of these alternative stories among the Afghan women, domestic workers, and undocumented students. But in a context like mid-2000s Venezuela of organized social movements and a post-neoliberal state, we can see the availability and mobilization of this kind of storytelling on a larger scale. The impetus does not come from the government alone, or from the nomenclature of revolution, but from the broad presence of organized groups building spaces of popular power.

The last two micro narratives explored in this chapter are defined by the strength of local barrio-based movements that take everyday struggles over housing, transport, food, and sanitation as the core of their organizing work. As compared to the self-reliant, independent leader who has "no commitment to anyone," the interdependence of residents in urban and rural spaces constitutes a different kind of revolutionary subject who takes culture, place, and interpersonal relations as the basis for their political struggles. Rather than being integrated into the Bolivarian project or limiting the scope of their vision to winning elections, these actors seek to build a base of popular power. This is not to romanticize such spaces as existing outside the dominant, because popular spaces are also subject to hierarchy, corruption, and absorption into the dominant praxis. In fact, the balance of forces under Chávez's successor Maduro shifted power away from these popular movements and more into the hands of Bolivarian party elites. But this study of the earlier Chávez era shows how an essential element of alternative storytelling projects is their ability to build autonomous collective spaces of resistance that can forge new representations, and through their sheer strength in organized movements can have their force be felt in the dominant political and mediatic spheres.

Epilogue

New Movements, New Stories?

O ne of my aims in this book has been to unpack the question of how and why contemporary modes of storytelling came to be guided by utilitarian logics and forms of liberal and neoliberal subject-making. I have used the examples of an online storytelling project for Afghan women, domestic workers telling their stories in the legislature and media, storytelling trainings for undocumented youth, and a state-sponsored storytelling project for barrio residents in Venezuela as specific sites to examine this question. In this Epilogue, I reprise the major arguments of the book, and I elaborate on my theoretical observations. I also reflect on one of my key concerns: how can we find a way beyond curated storytelling?

HISTORICAL MATERIALISM AS METHOD

To study the construction of curated stories, and their impacts and uses, requires a method of historical materialism, of locating the object within a set of historically produced political-economic conditions. What is presented as a story—a two-minute recruitment narrative, a ten-minute legal testimony—is already the result of a process of editing and selection that disavows the messiness of everyday lives. The individual is always already part of the social; the everyday is enmeshed with the geopolitical. These scales cannot be easily disentangled. Rather than taking stories and the prototypical story form as givens, in this book I have interrogated the conditions of production of both narrative and genre.

My analysis is indebted to a Foucaultian account of neoliberal governmentality, as the knowledges and techniques concerned with the regulation of everyday conduct. Theories of neoliberal governmentality can help us to understand how storytelling comes to be based on market logics and neoliberal subjectivities that foreclose more critical alternatives. Yet in the detailed specifics of the sites that I examined, this Foucaultian approach came up against its limits. In rendering each person in economic terms as little capitals seeking to maximize their individual gains, the concept of neoliberal subjectivity leaves us without the tools to understand why these individuals sometimes group together in classes to seek upward mobility and middle-class status, or how they might create oppositional class-based movements. The importance of capital as a social and historical force is denied a role in class formation and subject production.[1] In the various sites that I explored, we saw inconsistencies and moments of failure, but the totalizing framework of neoliberal governmentality does not equip us to theorize internal contradictions,[2] which could provide the grounds for moving beyond the hegemonic paradigm.

Grappling with and analyzing the empirical details of each case in the book requires suturing a Foucaultian account of neoliberal governmentality with Marxian and Gramscian accounts of class formation, agency, and contradiction. Through telling their stories, upwardly mobile Afghan women, niche immigrant workers, and high-achieving undocumented students did not only present themselves as individual strivers, but they were encouraged to see themselves in class terms, as part of new and elite class strata. The binary forms of identification available to these actors often required them to differentiate themselves from the majority of undocumented, rural, anonymous peoples and African Americans, many of whom were stigmatized as terrorists or criminals.

Gramscian frameworks that focus on processes of class formation give us the tools to understand how these actors were integrated into strategies developed by dominant groups. I have used Gramsci's concept of *trasformismo* to discuss how storytelling was part of a broader strategy in the Obama era to draw Muslim populations and domestic migrant rights groups into projects of statecraft, advocacy, civic education, and electoral participation, and to absorb and demobilize mass antiwar and migrant rights protests. The focus on class strategies allows us to locate agency not simply within an order of reason, but in the actual actors themselves—foundations, legislators, advocates, mentors, workers, students—all acting according to their own sets of logics and constraints within a shifting field. Mentors and funders encouraged Afghan women to use their stories to promote voting in the controversial national elections in Afghanistan. Advocates showcased domestic workers' stories in the media and legislature in order to lobby for bills of protection, while undocumented students were trained by immigrant rights organizations to tell their stories to recruit voters for the Democratic Party and promote controversial immigration legislation.

In Venezuela, barrio residents were encouraged by trainers to use cultural practices like storytelling as part of an electoral strategy. Rather than mass mobilizations that could put pressure on the government and challenge the broader conditions of exploitation, these storytelling activities narrowed the field of action to the voting booth and legislature, thereby reducing the range of independent actions available to groups.

At a time of growing concern about the role of the United States as human rights violator and aggressor both domestically and abroad, the stories were also used to promote the image of the United States as a benefactor nation. Afghan women, and the readers of their stories, often reinforced images of the United States as a global crusader for women's rights. In hearings for the domestic workers bill, legislators presented the United States as a nation of immigrants that provided upward mobility for all those generations of immigrants who come through. Hearings for the DREAM Act promoted nationalist mythologies of America as the land of the free and a refuge of freedom for those escaping backward and illiberal nations. All of these settings promoted the idea of the American Dream, as the possibility for upward mobility through hard work and enterprise. By tying stories to electoral and legislative campaigns and by reinterpreting them through the lens of nationalist mythologies, a range of groups participated in a process of *trasformismo* that absorbed and defused the discontent being expressed globally and domestically toward American-supported neoliberal and imperialist policies.

THE CONTRADICTIONS OF MOBILIZING STORIES

The Gramscian lens allows us to understand not just how power is produced but also the contradictions inherent in class strategies that can enable forms of resistance. Some of the storytelling I examined in the book revealed dissonance between the personal experiences of the teller and the dominant framings given by facilitators. I gave the example of an event in New York where the Afghan writer Marzia framed her stories with a dominant narrative about how much the US-led intervention has helped Afghan women, but then she shared a poem based on her own personal experience about the realities of poverty, powerful warlords, and cruelties that have been generated by the war. One of the trainers for a Dreamers workshop, Michelle Rudy, talked about using stories to register people to vote for Obama so that he can pass immigration reform, but then she reflected on how Obama betrayed the immigrant rights movement and did not pass immigration reform in his first term. In both of these cases, Marzia and Rudy became emotional; the disconnect between the framings they repeated and the reality of their own experiences was clearly apparent. The Venezuelan barrio resident Sara Elena Pérez narrated a story about coming to political awareness through the Bolivarian project, but the limitations of the available tropes of marriage and motherhood become apparent when she briefly hints at her molestation as a child. The micro narratives often contain double voicings or multiple registers that allow the expression of experiences such as gendered poverty and betrayal that do not fit the macro framings and epic narratives.

Sometimes these tensions crystalize into overt critiques. The Afghan Womens Writing Project had a few writers and readers who criticized the US government for killing Afghans with impunity while claiming to help the country. Afghan writers pointed out the opportunism of Western human rights and feminist networks which glorify a few cases of Afghan women attacked by the Taliban while ignoring others. And one reader objected to the whole enterprise of Westerners trying to read Afghan women's stories online with no context and no sense of their own implication in the abuses that take place. Domestic workers and undocumented youth also spoke of the demand for stories of silenced and invisible immigrants which were being turned into commodities, the good immigrant tropes that pitted them against minorities, and the ways that immigrants were reduced to telling their stories and not given a role to play in strategizing. They were critical of the middle-class leaders who sought to use their stories to build their own political capital and prestige, while the workers and students themselves were seeing few changes in their conditions.

Some of these workers and youth began refusing to tell their stories at all, preferring to remain illegible rather than achieve recognition in limited ways. The domestic worker Christine Lewis spoke about how domestic workers were increasingly cautious when invited to tell their stories: "They don't want to tell their stories, or they choose who they may tell the stories to."[3] Yosimar Reyes also spoke about feeling bamboozled by the constant requests to come out of the shadows and tell his story of being undocumented. Reyes speaks to a similar desire to remain illegible to the dominant order; he tells stories about his grandmother that he knows cannot be heard within mainstream narratives.

The tensions, criticisms, and refusals that we see in this book show the process of neoliberalization through storytelling as much more contested and flexible than Foucaultian accounts have allowed for. The concept of neoliberal governmentality is crucial to understand how certain kinds of curated stories have emerged in tandem with a free market economy, but neoliberalism itself is open to challenge and reformulation. Although neoliberalism may be ascendant as a mode of governance and economics, it is not seamlessly reproduced. Disaggregating actors, logics, and class processes through my empirical investigations has been one way to show the contested and contradictory ways that neoliberalism is created and re-created.

HISTORICIZING THE PRESENT

If we identify neoliberalism as the force underlying contemporary modes of curated storytelling, then will the rolling back of neoliberalism lead to different kinds of storytelling? Although neoliberalism has been unevenly adopted in various parts of the globe, in recent years there has been a more sustained critique of austerity and free trade policies. Protests and mass movements crystallized most significantly in Latin America, where governments came to power and explicitly reversed certain neoliberal economic policies. What does this mean for the kinds of stories that are told? Can we see a return to more deeply contextualized and alternative stories in places that are going against the neoliberal model?

The case of Venezuela under the radical leftist leader Hugo Chávez that I examine in the last chapter of the book would suggest that an anti-neoliberal agenda alone is not enough to produce alternative stories and subjectivities. There are striking similarities between the life stories of Chávez and Obama used as models in storytelling trainings. Both are underdogs who come from humble backgrounds to attain the highest levels of office in their country; they are proud of their black and mixed-race heritage that is an affront to the white political establishment. And although Chávez's autobiography is based on a model of revolutionary subjectivity, just like Obama's story, it enunciates the idea of the sovereign liberal subject who through moments of individual choice and self-reliance becomes an enlightened subject capable of participation in civic life. Both revolutionary subject-making in the Bolivarian frame and neoliberal subject-making in the US context resecure the sovereignty of the autonomous liberal subject.

The liberal subjecthood that undergirds curated storytelling dates back to the transition to liberal economies during the eighteenth century. Many of the cultural tropes and myths deployed in contemporary narratives have their genesis in this era of colonialism and slavery. The tropes of bad masters and individual victims that were mobilized by domestic worker advocates in media interviews, legislative debates, and storytelling campaigns have their genealogies in slavery and colonialism. Myths of domesticity were used both in an earlier era of slavery and the contemporary moment of globalized economies to mask exploitative labor relations. Likewise, the images in the Afghan Women's Writing Project of Afghan women as silenced victims and Islamic societies as patriarchal and repressive are Orientalist constructions that were used to eradicate the cultures of colonized peoples. The idea that marginal subjects can attain their freedom through hard work, civic duty, and self-improvement also dates back to this modern liberal era and its uses of autobiography to give aesthetic form to narratives of progress.[4] The tropes and genres used in present narratives are situated within long genealogies that date back to the emergence of Western liberalism and its forms of subjection and narrative.

It is not enough for counterhegemonic projects to roll back neoliberal orders; subversive stories require a challenging of the foundations of liberal modernity on which these orders rest. We saw such a challenge in the stories by some domestic workers, barrio residents, and others who rejected tropes of individual victims and loyal mammies, and framed their stories as part of broader collective struggles against exploitative global relations. The domestic workers of DWU participated in events where they told stories about the violence of global inequality in their homelands that had forced them to come to the United States in search of work. They refuted celebratory narratives that presented domestic workers as helping a growing economy. In Venezuela, we saw a broad challenge to liberal individualism coming from grassroots actors. Barrio residents William Peraza and Ricardo Guerrero told personal stories that connected local movements for cultural recognition to class-based demands and collective social struggles. These kinds of storytelling hark back to earlier genres of *testimonio* and narratives in the feminist movement that used personal stories in order to critique broader structures of oppression and to build collective struggles.

These alternative modes of storytelling have also given rise to different kinds of subject-making. Undocumented youth such as Reyes who reject the class projects and ideal citizen subjectivities of mainstream immigrant organizations formulate alternative migrant subjectivities that contest myths of the United States as a land of freedom, and discourses of social mobility and assimilation in favor of recognizing the ties to homelands and to undocumented migrant parents. In his autobiography, Guerrero presents an alternative collective subjectivity that draws on the interdependent space of the barrio and networks of social activism rather than the self-reliant, risk-taking, independent model of revolutionary subjectivity based on the life of Chávez. The spaces of everyday life and experiences of collective struggle can nurture alternative projects, forms of storytelling, and subjectivities.

WHOSE MOVEMENT IS IT?

What is at stake in contemporary modes of curated storytelling? Of those who tell their stories, who are living under the impact of debilitating wars and foreign occupations, trafficked and forced into poverty wage occupations in order to survive, suffering abuse and violent reprisal for speaking out, some are calling for an end to interventionist wars and a restructuring of the global economic order to end the destruction of local livelihoods and concentration of wealth. They have criticized the piecemeal changes sought by advocates as ultimately not bringing about changes in their lives. Against the pragmatists who seek limited changes within a hostile political climate, there are those who believe it is necessary to do the work of building independent sources of power that can launch more critical and contentious actions like strikes and mass mobilizations in order to demand change from below.

In the contest between these competing visions, the stakes are much higher for those who live these conditions than for the middle-class advocates who often lead the movements and workshops. As the domestic worker Patricia Francois said, "The stakes here are big, this is about our very lives. We can't have any more symbolic victories, victories for the professionalized organizers and academics. We, the workers, need real victories."[5] It's not surprising that there is a growing divide between advocates who claim to know what is best for those they represent, and those most deeply affected like Francois, the latter who are beginning to ask the question, "Whose movement is it?"[6] There has increasingly been a push among migrant rights groups, for instance, to create organizations led by those most affected and demand their presence where any decision is to be made regarding their future. "How would *we* define a victory?" asked Francois.[7] Those who experience daily the hardships of being occupied, disenfranchised, exploited, and undocumented stand the most to lose from any decision or legislation regarding their future and are less likely to settle for limited reforms in place of fighting for more substantive changes.

In the transition to a post-Obama era, we are seeing more of a rejection of the politics of *trasformismo*. During Obama's second term in office, the #BlackLivesMatter movement to protest the indiscriminate killing of black people by police and racial injustices more broadly grew into a mass protest movement where multiracial activists under black youth leadership shut down highways, protested outside police conventions, took over malls, confronted politicians, and walked off their campuses and schools. Combined with other struggles by minimum-wage workers, public school teachers, and antideportation activists, and the earlier Occupy Wall Street movement, the climate of ongoing protest produced an election cycle where the antiestablishment candidate Senator Bernie Sanders could actually be a contender for the Democratic nomination. Although Sanders faced hard questioning from #BlackLivesMatter activists and others, his presence owed much to the ways that movements on the ground had shifted the parameters of political debate.

The attempt to channel the energy of grassroots movements into an electoral strategy was also apparent. Democratic candidate Hillary Clinton enlisted mothers or daughters of those killed by police to endorse her candidacy. Democratic strategists raised $25 million for a group called Black Votes Matter, which, just like their earlier attempts to co-opt the migrant rights marches, was focused on attracting black voters in states where they were key constituencies for Democrats to win. Prominent #BlackLivesMatter activists like Shaun King joined the Sanders campaign and Dreamer activists Erika Andiola and Cesar Vargas were employed as staffers. Within the high-profile Sanders campaign, these activists had the ability to push the candidate to take more aggressive stances, to help craft his platforms, and to publicly criticize the policies of the Obama administration on immigration and deportation.

However, others preferred to stay outside of the Democratic Party machine, continuing to build power at the grassroots and put pressure from the outside. During the 2016 electoral cycle, activists spoke about the need to build independent social movements. The #BlackLivesMatter organizer Melina Abdullah specifically argued that democracy must be more than electoral politics: "We know that the revolution won't come at the ballot box and the revolution won't be televised. The revolution will be on the ground, when the people rise up and demand something better, something more imaginative and something more visionary."[8] In a Donald Trump era that has seen the intensification of free market capitalism and rampant xenophobia and racism, these independent movements are more necessary that ever in order to build power on the ground with a vision for deeper change.

If we want different kinds of tropes, subjectivities, storylines, and narratives, we need new kinds of organizing that is going to open the spaces for those. Without broader mass movements we will be constrained to stories that conform to what is acceptable in the narrow vision of the mainstream. In recent years, we have seen rounds of global uprisings, from the Arab and North African revolts and Occupy Wall Street movement in 2011, to direct democracy movements in Spain and Greece and the #BlackLivesMatter movement. Occupy Wall Street popularized the narrative of the 99% and the 1%, a narrative which reshaped people's perceptions of wealth, social inequality, and social redistribution in broad ranging ways. The #BlackLivesMatter movement has made available languages for talking about race, white supremacy, and state violence that did not exist prior.

Collective, grassroots, and global social movement organizing is the key for shifting from the terrain of the probable in which much nonprofit and development work takes place to the terrain of the utopian, where we can start imagining a fundamental restructuring of work, reproduction, and the global economy. It is only with a resurgence of interlocking movements in a range of areas that we can move from curated stories to mobilizing stories that deepen the work of social justice organizing.

NOTES

CHAPTER 1

1. Ayesha Siddiqi, "Does America Deserve Malala?," *Vice*, November 30, 2015, https://www.vice.com/read/does-america-deserve-malala
2. Vinson Cunningham, "Humans of New York and the Cavalier Consumption of Others," *The New Yorker*, November 3, 2015.
3. Justin Sanchez, "Narrative Networks," Defense Advanced Research Projects Agency (DARPA), accessed March 31, 2016, http://www.darpa.mil/program/narrative-networks &id=fd625a4022ec38fde2a8f6f1f4628395&tab=core&_cview=0
4. Walter Benjamin, *Illuminations* (New York: Schocken Books, 1968), p. 9.
5. Jonathan Gottschall, *The Storytelling Animal: How Stories Make Us Human* (New York: Houghton Mifflin Harcourt, 2012).
6. Paul VandeCarr, "Storytelling and Social Change: A Guide for Activists, Organizations and Social Entrepreneurs," Working Narratives, accessed January 5, 2016, http://workingnarratives.org/story-guide/, p. 10.
7. Jonah Sachs, *Winning the Story Wars: Why Those Who Tell (and Live) the Best Stories Will Rule the Future* (Boston: Harvard Business Review Press, 2012), p. 4.
8. Eric Selbin, *Revolution, Rebellion, Resistance: The Power of Story* (London and New York: Zed Books, 2010), p. 43.
9. Frederick Mayer, *Narrative Politics: Stories and Collective Action* (New York: Oxford University Press, 2014), p. 54.
10. Jerome Bruner, *Making Stories: Law, Literature, Life* (Cambridge, MA and London: Harvard University Press, 2002), p. 16.
11. Sachs, *Winning the Story Wars*, p. 20.
12. Brian Upton, *The Aesthetic of Play* (Cambridge, MA: MIT Press, 2015).
13. Thomas DeGloma, *Seeing the Light: The Social Logic of Personal Discovery* (Chicago and London: University of Chicago Press, 2014), p. 21.
14. Francesca Polletta, Pang Ching Bobby Chen, Beth Gharrity Gardner, and Alice Motes, "The Sociology of Storytelling," *Annual Review of Sociology* 37, no. 1 (Summer 2011): 112.
15. Daniel James, *Doña María's Story: Life History, Memory, and Political Identity* (Durham, NC and London: Duke University Press, 2000); Charlotte Linde, *Life Stories: The Creation of Coherence* (Oxford: Oxford University Press, 1993). Following these authors, I recognize that narrative is a discourse unit in story, which refers to the glue that holds the story together. But I also use the term "narrative" in its more popular sense as interchangeable with "story."
16. Patricia Ewick and Susan Silbey, "Subversive Stories and Hegemonic Tales: Toward a Sociology of Narrative," *Law & Society Review* 29, no. 2 (Winter 1995): 212.
17. Alessandro Portelli, *The Death of Luigi Trastulli and Other Stories: Form and Meaning in Oral History* (Albany, NY: SUNY Press, 1990), p. 70.
18. Ibid., 21.
19. Ewick and Silbey, "Subversive Stories and Hegemonic Tales," p. 219.

20. Michael Jackson, *The Politics of Storytelling: Violence, Transgression, and Intersubjectivity* (Copenhagen: Museum Tusculanum Press, 2006), p. 18.

21. "Barack Obama Speech at 2004 DNC Convention," C-SPAN, July 27, 2004, https://www.youtube.com/watch?v=eWynt87PaJ0

22. Erik Nielson and Travis L. Gosa, "Introduction: The State of Hip Hop in the Age of Obama," in *The Hip Hop & Obama Reader*, edited by Erik Nielson and Travis L. Gosa (Oxford and New York: Oxford University Press, 2015), p. 33.

23. William Robinson, *Global Capitalism and the Crisis of Humanity* (Cambridge: Cambridge University Press, 2014), p. 171.

24. Antonio Gramsci, *Selections from the Prison Notebooks of Antonio Gramsci*, edited and translated by Quintin Hoare and Geoffrey Nowell Smith (New York: International Publishers, 1971), p. 59. See also Chris Hesketh and Adam David Morton, "Spaces of Uneven Development and Class Struggle in Bolivia: Transformation or *Trasformismo?*" *Antipode* 46, no. 1 (2014): 149–169.

25. *Changing Course: A New Direction for U.S. Relations with the Muslim World*, 2nd ed., U.S.-Muslim Engagement Project (Washington, DC and Cambridge: Search for Common Ground and the Consensus Building Institute, 2009), accessed June 18, 2015, http://www.usmuslimengagement.org/storage/usme/documents/Changing_Course_Second_Printing.pdf

26. Joseph Nye, "Get Smart: Combining Hard and Soft Power," *Foreign Affairs*, July 1, 2009, https://www.foreignaffairs.com/articles/2009-07-01/get-smart

27. Hisham D. Aidi, *Rebel Music: Race, Empire, and the New Muslim Youth Culture* (New York: Pantheon Books, 2014).

28. Deepa Kumar, *Islamaphobia and the Politics of Empire* (Chicago: Haymarket Books, 2012), p. 132.

29. Alfonso Gonzales, *Reform Without Justice: Latino Migrant Politics and the Homeland Security State* (New York: Oxford University Press, 2014), p. 125.

30. "Narrative Witness: A Caracas-Sarajevo Collaboration," International Writing Program, accessed June 10, 2015, http://www.iwpcollections.org/nw1#nw1-title

31. See Christopher Colvin's work on traumatic storytelling in postapartheid South Africa. For example, Christopher Colvin, "Limiting Memory: The Roots and Routes of Storytelling in Post-Apartheid, Post-TRC South Africa," in *Telling Wounds: Narrative, Trauma and Memory: Working Through the South African Armed Conflicts of the 20th Century*, proceedings of the conference held at the University of Cape Town, July 3–5, 2002, edited by Chris Van der Merwe and Rolf Wolffswinkle (Stellenbosch, South Africa: Van Schaik Content Solutions, 2002); Christopher Colvin, "Trafficking Trauma: Intellectual Property Rights and the Political Economy of Traumatic Storytelling." *Critical Arts: South-North Cultural and Media Studies* 20, no. 1 (2008): 171–182.

32. Gillian Whitlock, *Soft Weapons: Autobiography in Transit* (Chicago and London: University of Chicago Press, 2007).

33. Christian Salmon, *Storytelling: Bewitching the Modern Mind* (London: Verso Books, 2010).

34. George Yúdice, *The Expediency of Culture: Uses of Culture in the Global Era* (Durham, NC and London: Duke University Press, 2003).

35. Stuart Hall, "The Neoliberal Revolution," *Cultural Studies* 25, no. 6 (Fall 2011): 705–728.

36. Joseph Slaughter, "Enabling Fictions and Novel Subjects: The 'Bildungsroman' and International Human Rights Law," *Modern Language Association* 121, no. 5 (2006): 1405–1423; Sidonie Smith, "Self, Subject, and Resistance: Marginalities and Twentieth-Century Autobiographical Practice," *Tulsa Studies in Women's Literature*, 9, no. 1 (1990): 11–24; Lisa Lowe, *The Intimacies of Four Continents* (Durham, NC and London: Duke University Press, 2015).

37. Nikolas Rose, "Governing 'Advanced' Liberal Democracies," in *Foucault and Political Reason: Liberalism, Neoliberalism, and Rationalities of Government*, edited by Andrew Barry, Thomas Osborne, and Nikolas Rose (Chicago: University of Chicago Press, 1996), p. 57.

38. Ibid., 59.

39. Wendy Brown, "Neo-liberalism and the End of Liberal Democracy," *Theory & Event* 7, no. 1 (2003).

40. Valerie Walkerdine and Jessica Ringrose, "Femininities: Reclassifying Upward Mobility and the Neo-liberal Subject," in *The Sage Handbook of Gender and Education*, edited by Christine Skelton, Becky Francis, and Lisa Smulyan (London, SAGE publications, 2006), pp. 31– 46.

CHAPTER 2

1. Some of the details of Menchú's story were later challenged by David Stoll, who claimed to have spoken with some of the figures in her account. See David Stoll, *Rigoberta Menchú and the Story of All Poor Guatemalans* (Boulder, CO and London: Westview Press, 1999).

2. Alberto Moreiras, "The Aura of Testimonio (1995)," in *The Real Thing: Testimonial Discourse and Latin America*, edited by Georg Gugelberger (Durham, NC and London: Duke University Press, 1996), p. 196.

3. John Beverley, *Testimonio: On the Politics of Truth* (Minneapolis: University of Minnesota Press, 2004), p. 41.

4. Sara Evans, *Personal Politics: The Roots of Women's Liberation in the Civil Rights Movement and the New Left* (New York: Vintage Books, 1979), p. 215.

5. Frank Bardacke, *Trampling out the Vintage: Cesar Chavez and the Two Souls of the United Farm Workers* (London and New York: Verso, 2011), p. 74.

6. Wendy Brown, *Undoing the Demos: Neoliberalism's Stealth Revolution* (New York: Zone Books, 2015).

7. The storytelling turn is distinct from what has been referred to as the narrative turn in the social sciences, which dates to about the mid-1990s. Although the narrative turn coincides with the storytelling turn within academia, my concerns are with the usage of storytelling beyond academia—in social advocacy, cultural diplomacy, the legal sphere, and other spheres of social and political life.

8. Jacques Ranciére, "Comments and Responses," *Theory & Event* 6, no. 4 (2003).

9. Nelly Richard, *The Insubordination of Signs: Political Change, Cultural Transformation, and Poetics of the Crisis* (Durham, NC and London: Duke University Press, 2004), p. 65.

10. Greg Grandin and Thomas Klublock, "Editors Introduction," in *Truth Commissions: State Terror, History, and Memory*, a special issue of *Radical History Review*, edited by Greg Grandin and Thomas Klublock, no. 97 (Winter 2007): 1.

11. Ibid., 5.

12. Ibid., 2.

13. Sonali Chakravarti, "Agonism and Victim Testimony," in *Theorizing Post-Conflict Reconciliation: Agonism, Restitution, & Repair*, edited by Alexander Hirsch (New York: Routledge, 2012), p. 17.

14. Naomi Klein, *The Shock Doctrine: The Rise of Disaster Capitalism* (New York: Picador, 2007). Klein acknowledges that the military governments of the Southern Cone experimented with neoliberal economics to different degrees, with Chilean neoliberal reforms far more drastic than Argentina.

15. Julie Taylor, "Body Memories: Aide-Memories and Collective Amnesia in the Wake of the Argentine Terror," in *Body Politics: Disease, Desire, and the Family*, edited by Michael Ryan and Avery Gordon (Boulder, CO: Westview Press, 1994), p. 198.

16. Ibid., 200–201.

17. Fiona C. Ross, *Bearing Witness: Women and the Truth and Reconciliation Commission in South Africa* (London: Pluto Press, 2003), p. 11.

18. Greg Grandin, *Who Is Rigoberta Ménchu?* (London and New York: Verso, 2011), p. 37.

19. Ibid., 40.

20. Elizabeth Oglesby, "Educating Citizens in Postwar Guatemala: Historical Memory, Genocide, and the Culture of Peace," in *Truth Commissions: State Terror, History, and*

Memory, a special issue of *Radical History Review,* edited by Greg Grandin and Thomas Klublock, no. 97 (Winter 2007): 90.

21. Pamela Allen, *Free Space: A Perspective on the Small Groups in Women's Movements* (New York: Times Change, 1970); Sara Evans and Harry Boyte, *Free Spaces: The Sources of Democratic Change in America* (Chicago: The University of Chicago Press, 1986).

22. Nancy Whittier, *The Politics of Child Sexual Abuse: Emotions, Social Movements, and the State* (Oxford: Oxford University Press, 2009), p. 48.

23. Ibid., 52.

24. Norman Fairclough, *Language and Power* (London and New York: Longman, 1989); Janice Peck, "The Mediated Talking Cure: Therapeutic Framing of Autobiography in TV Talk Shows," in *Getting a Life: Everyday Uses of Autobiography,* edited by Sidonie Smith and Julia Watson (Minneapolis and London: University of Minnesota Press, 1996).

25. Peck, "The Mediated Talking Cure," p. 142.

26. Jane M. Shattuc, *The Talking Cure: TV Talk Shows and Women* (New York: Routledge, 1997), pp. 118–119.

27. Didier Fassin and Richard Rechtman, *The Empire of Trauma: An Inquiry into the Condition of Victimhood* (Princeton, NJ: Princeton University Press, 2009).

28. Christopher Colvin, "Traumatic Storytelling after Apartheid," in *Borders and Healers: Brokering Therapeutic Resources in Southeast Africa,* edited by Tracy J. Luedke and Harry G. West (Bloomington: Indiana University Press, 2006), p. 173.

29. Fassin and Rechtman, *The Empire of Trauma,* p. 211.

30. Ibid., 214.

31. Colvin, "Traumatic Storytelling after Apartheid," p. 173.

32. Christopher Colvin, "Brothers and Sisters, Do Not Be Afraid of Me: Trauma, History and the Therapeutic Imagination in the New South Africa," in *Contested Pasts: The Politics of Memory,* edited by Katharine Hodgkin and Susannah Radstone (New York: Routledge, 2003), pp. 156–157.

33. Colvin, "Traumatic Storytelling after Apartheid."

34. Wendy Brown, *States of Injury: Power and Freedom in Late Modernity* (Princeton, NJ: Princeton University Press, 1995), p. 27.

35. Ibid., 27.

36. Ibid., 70.

37. Ibid., 74.

38. Laura Grindstaff, *Money Shot: Trash, Class, and the Making of TV Talk Shows* (Chicago and London: University of Chicago Press, 2002), p. 30.

39. Cited in Ross, *Bearing Witness,* p. 78.

40. Alejandro Castillejo-Cuéllar, "Knowledge, Experience, and South Africa's Scenarios of Forgiveness," in *Truth Commissions: State Terror, History, and Memory,* a special issue of *Radical History Review,* edited by Greg Grandin and Thomas Klublock, no. 97 (2007): 17.

41. Ibid., 17.

42. Ibid., 18.

43. Ibid., 19.

44. Philip Bonner and Noor Nieftagodien, "The Truth and Reconciliation Commission and the Pursuit of 'Social Truth': The Case of Kathorus," in *Commissioning the Past: Understanding South Africa's Truth and Reconciliation Commission,* edited by Deborah Posel and Graeme Simpson (Johannesburg: Witwatersrand University Press, 2002), p. 177.

45. Molly Andrews, *Shaping History: Narratives of Political Change* (Cambridge: Cambridge University Press, 2007), p. 158.

46. Ross, *Bearing Witness,* p. 14.

47. Kimberly Theidon, "Gender in Transition: Common Sense, Women, and War," *Journal of Human Rights* 6, no. 4 (December 2007): 455.

48. Ibid., 463.

49. Allison Crosby and M. Brinton Lykes, "Mayan Women Survivors Speak: The Gendered Relations of Truth Telling in Postwar Guatemala," *International Journal of Transitional Justice* 5, no. 3 (September 2011): 474.

50. Theidon, "Gender in Transition," p. 464.

51. Christopher Colvin, "Limiting Memory: The Roots and Routes of Storytelling in Post-Apartheid, Post-TRC South Africa," in *Telling Wounds: Narrative, Trauma and Memory: Working Through the South African Armed Conflicts of the 20th Century*, proceedings of the conference held at the University of Cape Town, July 3–5, 2002, edited by Chris Van der Merwe and Rolf Wolffswinkle (Stellenbosch, South Africa: Van Schaik Content Solutions, 2002), p. 10.
52. Castillejo-Cuéllar, "Knowledge, Experience," pp. 11–42.
53. Ibid., 24–29.
54. Ibid., 29.
55. Peck, "The Mediated Talking Cure," p. 144.
56. Ibid., 141.
57. Ibid., 146.
58. Grindstaff, *Money Shot*, p. 30.
59. Ibid., 221.
60. Ibid., 224.
61. Klein, *The Shock Doctrine*, p. 157.
62. Francesca Polletta, *It Was Like a Fever: Storytelling in Protest and Politics* (Chicago and London: University of Chicago Press, 2006), p. 124.
63. Whittier, *The Politics of Child Sexual Abuse*, p. 195.
64. Ibid.
65. James Nolan, "Drug Court Stories: Transforming American Jurisprudence," in *Stories of Change: Narratives and Social Movements*, edited by Joseph Davis (Albany, NY: SUNY Press, 2002).
66. Ibid., 170.
67. Brown, *Undoing the Demos*, p. 66.
68. Ibid., 31.
69. Nikolas Rose, *Powers of Freedom: Reframing Political Thought* (Cambridge: Cambridge University Press, 1999), p. 174.
70. Brown, *Undoing the Demos*, p. 36.
71. Paul VanDeCarr, "Storytelling and Social Change: A Guide for Activists, Organizations and Social Entrepreneurs," accessed January 15, 2016, http://workingnarratives.org/story-guide/, p. 13.
72. Neill Coleman, "Making the Case to Invest in Story," Hatch for Good, November 23, 2014, https://www.hatchforgood.org/explore/71/making-the-case-to-invest-in-story
73. Ibid.
74. Andy Goodman, *Storytelling as Best Practice* (Los Angeles: The Goodman Center, 2015).
75. VanDeCarr, "Storytelling and Social Change: A Guide for Activists, Organizations and Social Entrepreneurs," p. 11.
76. Ibid., 10.
77. Paul VanDeCarr, "Storytelling and Social Change: A Strategy Guide for Grantmakers," Working Narratives, accessed September 19, 2014, http://workingnarratives.org/wp-content/uploads/2013/08/Story-Guide.pdf, p. 8.
78. Ibid., 64.
79. John Gledhill, "Neoliberalism," in *A Companion to the Anthropology of Politics*, edited by David Nugent and Joan Vincent (London: Blackwell, 2004), p. 340.
80. VanDeCarr, "Storytelling and Social Change: A Strategy Guide for Grantmakers," p. 9.
81. Ibid., 11.
82. Ibid., 15.
83. Ibid., 43.
84. "Storytelling Project—Turning Anecdotes into Useful Data," GlobalGiving, accessed March 28, 2016, https://www.globalgiving.org/stories/
85. Ibid.
86. VanDeCarr, "Storytelling and Social Change: A Guide for Activists, Organizations and Social Entrepreneurs," p. 7.
87. Ibid., 12.
88. Ibid., 13.

89. Rose, *Powers of Freedom*, p. 174.
90. Julia Paley, *Marketing Democracy: Power and Social Movements in Post-Dictatorship Chile* (Berkeley: University of California Press, 2001), p. 146.
91. Sasha Abramsky, "A Conversation with Marshall Ganz," *The Nation*, February 3, 2011.
92. Marshall Ganz, "Organizing Obama: Campaign, Organizing, Movement," Paper presented at American Sociological Association annual meeting, 2009, p. 2.
93. Ibid., 7.
94. Hahrie Han and Elizabeth McKenna, *Groundbreakers: How Obama's 2.2 Million Volunteers Transformed Campaigning in America* (Oxford: Oxford University Press, 2015), p. 17.
95. Aaron Schutz and Marie G. Sandy, "Campaign Versus Community Organizing: Storytelling in Obama's 2008 Presidential Campaign," in *Collective Action for Social Change: An Introduction to Community Organizing*, edited by Aaron Schutz and Marie G. Sandy (New York: Palgrave, 2012).
96. http://www.barackobama.com/about/, accessed September 22, 2014.
97. Zelda Bronstein, "'Politics' Fatal Therapeutic Turn," *Dissent*, Summer 2011, https://www.dissentmagazine.org/article/politics-fatal-therapeutic-turn
98. Bakari Kitwana and Elizabeth Méndez Berry, "It's Bigger Than Barack: Hip Hop Political Organizing, 2004–2013," in *The Hip Hop & Obama Reader*, edited by Erik Nielson and Travis L. Gosa (Oxford and New York: Oxford University Press, 2015), p. 59.
99. Ibid., 61.
100. James Jasper, "Emotions and Social Movements: Twenty Years of Theory and Research," *Annual Review of Sociology* 37 (April 2011): 285–304.
101. Ganz, "Organizing Obama," p. 3.
102. Ibid., 6.
103. Schutz and Sandy, "Campaign Versus Community Organizing," p. 119.
104. Han and McKenna, *Groundbreakers*, p. 18.
105. "Story of Self," NOI Organizing Toolbox, uploaded on June 22, 2010, https://www.youtube.com/watch?v=H0wq5VVxAFk
106. Zack Exley, "Stories and Numbers—a Closer Look at Camp Obama," *Huffington Post*, August 29, 2007.
107. "Susan's Story of Us (Camp Obama: Burbank)," CampObama, uploaded on July 30, 2007, https://www.youtube.com/watch?v=Z-WEM-taoG8
108. Francesca Polletta, James Jasper, and Jeff Goodwin, *Passionate Politics: Emotions and Social Movements* (Chicago: University of Chicago Press, 2001).
109. Ibid., 9.

CHAPTER 3

1. CIA Red Cell Special Memorandum, "CIA Report into Shoring up Afghan War Support in Western Europe," Wikileaks, March 11, 2010, https://file.wikileaks.org/file/cia-afghanistan.pdf
2. Joseph S. Nye, "Get Smart: Combining Hard and Soft Power," *Foreign Affairs*, July 1, 2009, pp. 162–163.
3. Marnia Lazreg, *Torture and the Twilight of Empire: From Algiers to Baghdad* (Princeton, NJ: Princeton University Press, 2007).
4. Deepa Kumar, *Islamophobia and the Politics of Empire* (Chicago: Haymarket Books, 2012), p. 131.
5. Leila Ahmed, *Women and Gender in Islam: Historical Roots of a Modern Debate* (New Haven, CT: Yale University Press, 1992); Meyda Yeğenoğlu, *Colonial Fantasies: Towards a Feminist Reading of Orientalism* (Cambridge: Cambridge University Press, 1998).
6. Ahmed, *Women and Gender in Islam*, p. 151.
7. Edward Said, *Orientalism* (New York: Vintage Books, 1979).
8. Yeğenoğlu, *Colonial Fantasies*, p. 72.

9. Chandra Talpade Mohanty, "Under Western Eyes: Feminist Scholarship and Colonial Discourses," *boundary 2* 12, no. 3 (1984): 333–358.

10. Yeğenoğlu, *Colonial Fantasies*, p. 121.

11. Dohra Ahmad, "Not Yet Beyond the Veil: Muslim Women in American Popular Literature," *Social Text* 27, no. 2 (2009): 105–131; Lila Abu-Lughod, *Do Muslim Women Need Saving?* (Cambridge, MA: Harvard University Press, 2013).

12. Said, *Orientalism*; Laura Nader, *Culture and Dignity: Dialogues Between the Middle East and the West* (West Sussex, UK: John Wiley & Sons, 2012).

13. Amy Farrell and Patrice McDermott, "Claiming Afghan Women: The Challenge of Human Rights Discourse for Transnational Feminism," in *Just Advocacy? Women's Human Rights, Transnational Feminisms, and the Politics of Representation*, edited by Wendy S. Hesford and Wendy Kozol (New Brunswick, NJ: Rutgers University Press, 2005), pp. 46–47.

14. Nader, *Culture and Dignity*.

15. Masha Hamilton, "History and Mission," Afghan Women's Writing project, accessed May 15, 2015, http://awwproject.org/discover-awwp/history-mission/

16. Ibid.

17. Roya, "Feathers of Freedom, Washed Away," Afghan Women's Writing Project, March 20, 2010, http://awwproject.org/2010/03/feathers-of-freedom-washed-away/

18. Gayatri Chakravorty Spivak, "The Rani of Sirmur: As Essay in Reading the Archives," *History and Theory* 24, no. 3 (1985): 247–272; Gayatri Chakravorty Spivak, "Can the Subaltern Speak?," in *Marxism and the Interpretation of Culture*, edited by Cary Nelson and Lawrence Grossberg (London: Macmillan, 1988), pp. 271–313.

19. Farrell and McDermott, "Claiming Afghan Women," p. 51.

20. Masha Hamilton. "Zarmeena," Afghan Women's Writing Project, accessed May 13, 2015, http://awwproject.org/about/zarmeena/

21. Shilpa Kameswaran, "War, Women, and Writing: The Story of the Afghan Women's Writing Project," *Delphi Quarterly*, accessed May 13, 2015, http://delphiquarterly.com/recent-issues/current-issue-2-2/interview-with-the-afghan-womens-writing-workshop/

22. Margaret Mills, "Victimhood as Agency: Afghan Women's Memoirs," in *Orientalism and War*, edited by Tarak Barkawi and Ketih Stanski (Oxford: Oxford University Press, 2013), p. 198.

23. Kumar, *Islamophobia and the Politics of Empire*, p. 39.

24. Elaheh Rostami-Povey, *Afghan Women: Identity and Invasion* (London and New York: Zed Books, 2007).

25. UNESCO Office in Kabul, "Enhancement of Literacy in Afghanistan Program," accessed May 13, 2015, http://www.unesco.org/new/en/kabul/education/enhancement-of-literacy-in-afghanistan-ela-program/

26. Women's Voices Now, accessed May 13, 2015, http://womensvoicesnow.org/images/uploads/E_TITUS_WVN_VOL.1_NO.10.pdf

27. Kameswaran, "War, Women, and Writing."

28. Lyse Doucet, "Dangerous 'Truth': The Kabul Women's Poetry Club," BBC News, October 21, 2013, http://www.bbc.com/news/world-asia-24608666

29. George W. Bush Institute Publications, "Amplifying the Voice of Afghan Women," October 22, 2013, http://www.bushcenter.org/blog/2013/10/22/amplifying-voice-afghan-women-afghan-women%E2%80%99s-writing-project

30. "What AWWP Means: Our Mentors Speak," Afghan Women's Writing Project, accessed August 24, 2015, http://awwproject.org/about/what-awwp-means-our-teachers-speak/

31. Ibid.

32. Ibid.

33. Ibid.

34. Srimati Basu, "V is for Veil, V is for Ventriloquism: Global Feminisms in the Vagina Monologues," *Frontiers: A Journal of Women Studies* 31, no. 1 (2010): 55.

35. Benedicte Grima, *The Performance of Emotions among Paxtun Women: "The Misfortunes Which Have Befallen Me"* (Austin: University of Texas Press, 1992).

36. Julie Billaud, *Kabul Carnival: Gender Politics in Postwar Afghanistan* (Philadelphia: University of Pennsylvania Press, 2015).
37. Mills, "Victimhood as Agency," p. 4.
38. Abu-Lughod, *Do Muslim Women Need Saving?*, p. 91.
39. Sally Kitch, *Contested Terrain: Reflections with Afghan Women Leaders* (Chicago: University of Illinois Press, 2014).
40. Leeda, "Eight Daughters for Sale, the Oldest First," Afghan Women's Writing Project, December 18, 2012, http://awwproject.org/2012/12/eight-daughters-for-sale-the-oldest-first/
41. Marzila, "Exchange for a Cow, Part II," Afghan Women's Writing Project, April 25, 2013, http://awwproject.org/2013/04/exchange-for-a-cow-part-2/
42. Basu, "V is for Veil, V is for Ventriloquism," p. 44.
43. Gillian Whitlock, *Soft Weapons: Autobiography in Transit* (Chicago and London: University of Chicago Press, 2007), p. 58.
44. Marzia, "Afghan Women's Rights: Will History Repeat Itself," Afghan Women's Writing Project, January 14, 2013, http://awwproject.org/2013/01/afghan-womens-rights-will-history-repeat-itself/
45. Zainab, "Teach the Children," Afghan Women's Writing Project, December 8, 2011, http://awwproject.org/2011/12/teach-the-children/
46. Deniz Kandiyoti, "Old Dilemmas or New Challenges? The Politics of Gender and Reconstruction in Afghanistan," *Development and Change* 38, no. 2 (2007): 176.
47. Emaan, "Hijab: The Beauty of Muslim Women," Afghan Women's Writing Project, June 29, 2010, http://awwproject.org/2010/06/hijab-the-beauty-of-muslim-women/
48. Safia, "Forced Marriage—Shame of Divorce," Afghan Women's Writing Project, October 18, 2010, http://awwproject.org/2010/10/forced-marriage-%E2%80%93-shame-of-divorce/
49. Fatima F, "Why Parents Must Stop Marrying Girls Early," Afghan Women's Writing Project, September 3, 2013, http://awwproject.org/2013/09/why-parents-must-stop-marrying-girls-early/
50. Roya, "1 + 1 = 1," Afghan Women's Writing Project, November 8, 2009, http://awwproject.org/2009/11/111/
51. Hamilton, "History and Mission."
52. Ibid.
53. Mills, "Victimhood as Agency," p. 198.
54. Eric Bennett, *Workshops of Empire: Stegner, Engle, and American Creative Writing During the Cold War* (Iowa City: University of Iowa Press, 2015).
55. Billaud, *Kabul Carnival*.
56. Ibid.
57. Abu-Lughod, *Do Muslim Women Need Saving?*, p. 44.
58. Ibid., 103.
59. Fattemeh, "The Evening I Will Never Forget," Afghan Women's Writing Project, May 20, 2009, http://awwproject.org/2009/05/the-evening-i-will-never-forget/
60. Seeta, "The Burqa Bride," Afghan Women's Writing Project, June 18, 2010, http://awwproject.org/2010/06/the-burqa-bride/
61. Sabira, "To Laugh," Afghan Women's Writing Project, January 27, 2011, http://awwproject.org/2011/01/to-laugh/
62. Shogofa, "The Mirror," Afghan Women's Writing Project, January 25, 2011, http://awwproject.org/2011/01/the-mirror/
63. Mimi Thi Nguyen, "The Biopower of Beauty: Humanitarian Imperialisms and Global Feminisms in an Age of Terror," *Signs* 36, no. 2 (2011): 369.
64. Shakila, "The Different Daughter" Afghan Women's Writing Project, January 13, 2011, http://awwproject.org/2011/01/the-different-daughter/
65. Nguyen, "The Biopower of Beauty," p. 370.
66. Karl Eikenberry, "Inverting the International Interference Paradigm: Afghan Women Seek Support," WikiLeaks, December 2, 2009, https://wikileaks.org/plusd/cables/09KABUL3849_a.html

67. Hillary Rodham Clinton, "Remarks at the US-Afghan Women's Council 10th Anniversary Celebration Luncheon," March 21, 2012, http://www.state.gov/secretary/20092013clinton/rm/2012/03/186618.htm

68. Rostami-Povey, *Afghan Women*, pp. 40–41.

69. Anand Gopal, *No Good Men among the Living: America, the Taliban, and the War Through Afghan Eyes* (New York: Metropolitan Books, 2014).

70. Malalai Joya, *A Woman Among Warlords: The Extraordinary Story of an Afghan Who Dared to Raise Her Voice* (New York: Scribner, 2009), p. 2.

71. Ibid., 3.

72. Rostami-Povey, *Afghan Women*.

73. Marzia, "What I Expect from My New President," Afghan Women's Writing Project, March 30, 2014, http://awwproject.org/2014/03/what-i-expect-from-my-new-president/

74. Nasima, "A Reminder of the Last Afghan Elections," Afghan Women's Writing Project, March 13, 2014, http://awwproject.org/2014/03/a-reminder-of-the-last-afghan-elections/

75. Nasima, "The Violence Lifted from My Shoulders When I Voted," Afghan Women's Writing Project, April 10, 2015, http://awwproject.org/2014/04/the-violence-lifted-from-my-shoulders-when-i-voted/

76. Anonymous, "Paying the Price for Democracy in Afghanistan," Afghan Women's Writing Project, March 20, 2014, http://awwproject.org/2014/03/paying-the-price-for-democracy-in-afghanistan/

77. Sitara B, "Who Can Win? What the Campaign Slogans Don't Say," March 28, 2014, http://awwproject.org/2014/03/who-can-win-what-the-campaign-slogans-dont-say/

78. Gopal, *No Good Men among the Living*.

79. Safia, "Forced Marriage."

80. Gopal, *No Good Men among the Living*.

81. Ibid., 183.

82. Billaud, *Kabul Carnival*, pp. 148–149.

83. Afghan Women's Writing Project, "Remembering Tabasom," April 23, 2012, http://awwproject.org/2012/04/remembering-tabasom/

84. Freshta, "American Soldiers: Here to Protect, or Violate?" Afghan Women's Writing Project, April 7, 2010, http://awwproject.org/2010/04/american-soldiers-here-to-protect-or-violate/

85. Shafiqa, "Ocean of Disappointment," Afghan Women's Writing Project, September 25, 2010, http://awwproject.org/2010/09/ocean-of-disappointment/

86. Shogofa, "Dear President Obama," Afghan Women's Writing Project, May 9, 2010, http://awwproject.org/2010/05/dear-president-obama/

87. Shogofa, "When Can I See?" Afghan Women's Writing Project, July 22, 2010, http://awwproject.org/2010/07/when-can-i-see/

88. Sitara, "How to Change Afghanistan," Afghan Women's Writing Project, October 11, 2012, http://awwproject.org/2012/10/how-to-change-afghanistan/

89. Abu-Lughod, *Do Muslim Women Need Saving?*, p. 114.

90. Fatima H, "The Bravest Girls in the World," Afghan Women's Writing Project, November 1, 2012, http://awwproject.org/2012/11/the-bravest-girls-in-the-world/

91. Wendy Brown, "Civilizational Delusions: Secularism, Tolerance, Equality," *Theory & Event* 15, no. 2 (2012).

92. "What AWWP Means: Our Mentors Speak."

93. Ibid.

94. Roya, "Feathers of Freedom, Washed Away."

95. Safia, "Forced Marriage."

96. Marzila, "Exchange for a Cow, Part II."

97. Sabira, "Shouting for Their Rights," Afghan Women's Writing Project, March 17, 2010, http://awwproject.org/2010/03/shouting-for-their-rights/

98. Sitara, "How to Change Afghanistan."

99. Huma Ahmed-Ghosh, "A History of Women in Afghanistan: Lessons Learnt for the Future or Yesterdays and Tomorrow: Women in Afghanistan," *Journal of International*

Women's Studies 4, no. 3 (2003): 1–14; Gillian Wylie, "Women's Rights and 'Righteous War:' An Argument for Women's Autonomy in Afghanistan." *Feminist Theory* 4, no. 2 (2003): 217–223.

100. From the biography of Linda Fisher in the program for "Readings from the Afghan Women's Writing Project," October 20, 2014, p. 2.
101. Basu, "V is for Veil, V is for Ventriloquism."
102. Ibid., 32.
103. Forte Poesy, "AWWP + Forte Poesy: Night of Poetry and Song," May 18, 2014, https://www.youtube.com/watch?v=kmOLIOFu3Ok
104. Sitara, "A Tale of Two Teenagers: Malala and Anisa," Afghan Women's Writing Project, August 12, 2013, http://awwproject.org/2013/08/a-tale-of-two-teenagers-malala-and-anisa/
105. Marzila, "Exchange for a Cow, Part II."
106. Mohanty, "Under Western Eyes."
107. Shahnaz Khan, "Between Here and There: Feminist Solidarity and Afghan Women," *Genders* 33 (2001): 1–26.
108. Ahmed, *Women and Gender in Islam.*
109. Roya, "The Meaning of Democracy," Afghan Women's Writing Project, July 27, 2010, http://awwproject.org/2010/07/the-meaning-of-democracy/
110. Wendy Brown, "Civilizational Delusions: Secularism, Tolerance, Equality." *Theory & Event* 15, no. 2 (2012).

CHAPTER 4

1. In this book, I differentiate between the terms "immigrant" and "migrant," using "immigrant" to refer to the advocacy-based movements that seek upward mobility and higher class status. As Alicia Schmidt Camacho has argued, while the immigrant is on a path to citizenship and permanent status in the host country, the term migrant indicates the circular nature of migration that more accurately describes if not the realities for many migrants today, at least their desires to keep a close connection with their homeland and a possible return. See Alicia Schmidt Camacho, *Migrant Imaginaries: Latino Cultural Politics in the US-Mexico Borderlands* (New York and London: New York University Press, 2008).
2. Thavolia Glymph, *Out of the House of Bondage: The Transformation of the Plantation Household* (Cambridge: Cambridge University Press, 2008), p. 74; Walter Johnson, *Soul by Soul: Life Inside the Antebellum Slave Market* (Cambridge, MA: Harvard University Press, 1999).
3. Ann Laura Stoler and Karen Strassler, "Memory-Work in Java: A Cautionary Tale," *Carnal Knowledge and Imperial Power: Race and the Intimate in Colonial Rule* (Berkeley: University of California Press, 2002), pp. 162–203.
4. Wendy Brown, *Undoing the Demos: Neoliberalism's Stealth Revolution* (New York: Zone Books, 2015).
5. Nancy Fraser, "From Redistribution to Recognition? Dilemmas of Justice in a 'Post-Socialist' Age," *New Left Review* I/212 (July-August 1995): 68–93.
6. Ibid., 79.
7. Ibid., 89.
8. Marie Marquardt, Timothy Steigenga, Philip Williams, and Manuel Vásquez, *Living Illegal: The Human Face of Unauthorized Immigration* (New York and London: The New Press, 2011).
9. Samuel Huntington, "The Hispanic Challenge," *Foreign Policy* March-April (2004): 30–45.
10. Janice Fine, "Community Unions and the Revival of the American Labor Movement," *Politics & Society* 33, no. 1 (2005): 153–199.
11. Alfonso Gonzales, *Reform Without Justice: Latino Migrant Politics and the Homeland Security State* (New York: Oxford University Press, 2014), p. 50.
12. Ibid., 128–129.
13. Walter Nicholls, *The DREAMers: How the Undocumented Youth Movement Transformed the Immigrant Rights Debate* (Stanford, CA: Stanford University Press, 2013), p. 10.

14. Nicholas De Genova, *Working the Boundaries: Race, Space, and "Illegality" in Mexican Chicago* (Durham, NC and London: Duke University Press, 2005).
15. Saskia Sassen, "Global Cities and Survival Circuits," in *Global Woman: Nannies, Maids, and Sex Workers in the New Economy*, edited by Barbara Ehrenreich and Arlie Hochschild (New York: Henry Holt and Company, 2012), pp. 254–274.
16. Ibid.
17. Barbara Ehrenreich and Arlie Hochschild, "Introduction" in *Global Woman: Nannies, Maids, and Sex Workers in the New Economy*, edited by Barbara Ehrenreich and Arlie Hochschild (New York: Henry Holt and Company, 2012), pp. 1–13.
18. Sassen, *Global Woman: Nannies, Maids, and Sex Workers in the New Economy*, pp. 264–265.
19. Ibid., 258.
20. Monisha Das Gupta, "The Neoliberal State and the Domestic Workers Movement in New York City," *Canadian Woman Studies* 22, no. 3/4 (2003): 220.
21. Silvia Federici, *Revolution at Point Zero: Housework, Reproduction, and Feminist Struggle* (Brooklyn, NY: PM Press, 2012), p. 73.
22. Ai-jen Poo and Eric Tang, "Domestic Workers Organize in the Global City," in *The Fire This Time: Young Activists and the New Feminism*, edited by Vivien Labaton and Dawn Lundy Martin (Toronto: Anchor, 2004), p. 155.
23. Petra Foundation, "Fellows," accessed February 11, 2016, http://www.petrafoundation.org/fellows/nahar-alam/
24. Notes from member workshops and trainings were made available to me from the DWU archives in New York by former DWU director Priscilla Gonzalez.
25. Domestic Workers United, "Breaking Down the Domestic Work Industry," Training handout, undated. DWU archives.
26. Domestic Workers United SC Retreat, "Building a Movement," February 22, 2004. DWU archives.
27. Domestic Workers United, "Leadership Training Program: Theory of Change and Role of an Organization," July 21, 2006. DWU archives.
28. Author interview with Ninaj Raoul, February 6, 2015.
29. Fine, "Community Unions and the Revival of the American Labor Movement," 153–199.
30. Harmony Goldberg, "'Prepare to Win:' Domestic Workers United's Strategic Transition following Passage of the New York Domestic Workers' Bill of Rights," in *New Labor in New York: Precarious Workers and the Future of the Labor Movement*, edited by Ruth Milkman and Ed Ott (Ithaca, NY and London: Cornell University Press, 2014), pp. 266–288.
31. Ai-jen Poo, "Organizing with Love: Lessons from the New York Domestic Workers Bill of Rights Campaign," *Left Turn: Notes from the Global Intifada*, December 1, 2010, http://www.leftturn.org/Organizing-with-Love
32. Ai-jen Poo and Andrea Cristina Mercado, "What's Next for the Domestic Workers Movement?" *The Nation*, July 13, 2015, http://www.thenation.com/article/whats-next-for-the-domestic-workers-movement/
33. Interview with Raoul.
34. Courtney Frantz and Ruth Milkman interview with Linda Oalican, July 6, 2015.
35. Author interview with Silvia Medina, December 17, 2012.
36. Tera Hunter *To Joy My Freedom: Southern Black Women's Lives and Labors after the Civil War* (Cambridge, MA: Harvard University Press, 1997).
37. Ibid., 97.
38. Premilla Nadasen, *Household Workers Unite: The Untold Story of African American Women Who Built a Movement* (Boston: Beacon Press, 2015), p. 116.
39. Erica Kohl-Arenas, *The Self-Help Myth: How Philanthropy Fails to Alleviate Poverty* (Berkeley: University of California Press, 2016), p. 74.
40. Ford Foundation, "Glossary of Grant-Making Approaches," accessed May 18, 2016, http://web.archive.org/web/20150906075606/http://www.fordfoundation.org/pdfs/grants/glossary-of-approaches.pdf
41. This total was calculated by comparing figures from NDWA's 2013 Form 990 (federal tax return) found in Mike Tigas and Sisi Wei, "ProPublica Nonprofit Explorer," accessed April 9, 2016, projects.propublica.org/nonprofits with figures from Ford Foundation, "Grants

Database," accessed February 16, 2016, www.fordfoundation.org/work/our-grants/grants-database; and figures from foundations' 990 forms as well as data on individual grants, both found in the Foundation Center, "Foundation Directory Online Professional Grants Database," accessed December 20, 2014, fconline.foundationcenter.org

42. This figure is the total of all grants made by NDWA to other organizations, as listed on NDWA's 2013 Form 990 (federal tax return), found in Tigas and Wei, "ProPublica Nonprofit Explorer." It does not include grants of less than $5,000.

43. Ford Foundation Form 990 tax returns, 2008–2011.

44. For more information on this, see Courtney Frantz and Sujatha Fernandes, "Whose Movement Is It? Strategic Funding, Worker Centers, and Foundation Influence," *Critical Sociology*, 2016, pp. 1–16.

45. Peggie Smith, "Regulating Paid Household Work: Class, Gender, Race, and Agendas of Reform" *American University Law Review* 48, no. 4 (1999): 851–923.

46. By 2014, NDWA began acting directly as a labor broker, providing middle- and upper-class families access to the labor of migrant women. NDWA started up a nanny referral business called Care Tango, with its own CEO, and employers were referred to as "consumers" rather than allies. In their promotional materials, NDWA states, "Through our decades of working together with domestic workers and consumers, we created a business model that ensures that domestic workers are receiving high quality jobs and that families have access to quality care that meets their specific needs."

47. See the following trainings "Household Management 101 & 102" conducted by DWU, accessed February 12, 2015, http://www.domesticworkersunited.org/index.php/en/workforce-trainings/item/93-household-management-101-102

48. Poo, "Organizing with Love."

49. Author interview with Jennifer Bernard, October 25, 2012.

50. The Human Rights Tribunal was held on October 8, 2005.

51. Interview with Raoul.

52. Nahar Alam and Chitra Aiyar, "The Power of Complicated Stories," *Samar: South Asian Magazine for Action and Reflection*, Issue 40: Circles of Gender Justice, May 31, 2013, http://samarmagazine.org/archive/articles/430

53. Author interview with Linda Oalican, August 20, 2014.

54. Steven Greenhouse, "Legislation Pushed to Require Minimum Wage for Domestic Workers," *New York Times*, June 1, 2007, http://www.nytimes.com/2007/06/01/nyregion/01nanny.html?pagewanted=print&_r=0

55. Smith, "Regulating Paid Household Work," p. 895.

56. Federici, *Revolution at Point Zero*, p. 73.

57. Terri Nilliasca, unpublished research proposal on childcare and the domestic workers movement, viewed on September 10, 2015.

58. Lucy Kaylin, "Domestic Help," *New York Times*, September 23, 2007, http://www.nytimes.com/2007/09/23/opinion/nyregionopinions/23CIkaylin.html?pagewanted=print

59. Editorial, "Women's Work," *New York Times*, June 8, 2008, http://www.nytimes.com/2008/06/08/opinion/08sun2.html?scp=1&sq=women%27s+work&st=nyt

60. Glymph, *Out of the House of Bondage*, p. 65.

61. Russ Buettner, "For Nannies, Hope for Workplace Protection," *New York Times*, June 2, 2010, http://www.nytimes.com/2010/06/03/nyregion/03nanny.html

62. Interview with Raoul.

63. Jennifer Gonnerman, "The Nanny Uprising," *New York Magazine*, June 6, 2010, http://nymag.com/news/features/66471/

64. Francesca Polletta, "Storytelling in Social Movements," in *Culture, Social Movements, and Protest*, edited by Hank Johnston (Surrey, UK and Burlington, VT: Ashgate Publishing, 2009), p. 51.

65. Madeleine Fullard and Nicky Rousseau, *Truth Telling, Identities and Power in South Africa and Guatemala*, International Center for Research and Justice, research brief, accessed March 14, 2013, http://ictj.org/sites/default/files/ICTJ-Identities-TruthCommissions-ResearchBrief-2009-English.pdf

66. Author interview with Patricia Francois, September 4, 2012.

67. National Domestic Workers Alliance, "NY Domestic Worker Wins Justice, Finally," June 14, 2012, http://www.domesticworkers.org/es/news/2012/ny-domestic-worker-wins-justice-finally

68. Mikhail Bakhtin, *The Dialogic Imagination: Four Essays,* translated by Caryl Emerson and Michael Holquist (Austin: University of Texas Press, 1981).

69. Carl Gutiérrez-Jones, *Critical Race Narratives: A Study of Race, Rhetoric, and Injury* (New York and London: New York University Press, 2001).

70. Edward V. Schneier, John Brian Murtaugh, and Antoinette Pole, *New York Politics: A Tale of Two States* (Armonk, NY and London: M.E. Sharpe, 2010), p. 326.

71. Ibid., 219.

72. Interview with Medina.

73. Author interview with Christine Lewis, September 20, 2012.

74. New York State Assembly Standing Committee on Labor, "Notice of Public Hearing: Domestic Working Circumstances and Conditions," accessed May 18, 2016, assembly.state.ny.us/comm/Labor/20081110/

75. New York State Assembly Standing Committee on Labor, "Domestic Working Circumstances and Conditions: Hearing before the Standing Committee on Labor," accessed May 18, 2016, nysl.cloudapp.net/awweb/main.jsp?flag=browse&smd=1&aw did=1. All of the testimonies in this section are taken from here.

76. Polletta, "Storytelling in Social Movements," p. 41.

77. Glymph, *Out of the House of Bondage.*

78. Francesca Polletta, Pang Ching Bobby Chen, Beth Gharrity Gardner, and Alice Motes, "The Sociology of Storytelling," *Annual Review of Sociology* 37, no. 1 (2011): 120.

79. New York State Assembly Standing Committee on Labor, "Domestic Working Circumstances and Conditions," 9–10.

80. Tamara Mose Brown, *Raising Brooklyn: Nannies, Childcare, and Caribbeans Creating Community* (New York and London: New York University Press, 2011).

81. Bonnie Honig, "Immigrant America? How Foreignness 'Solves' Democracy's Problems," *Social Text* 56, no. 1 (1998): 3.

82. New York State Senate, June 1, 2010 session, accessed May 18, 2016, www.youtube.com/watch?v=1EdzvlpvEHc

83. New York State Senate Majority, Domestic Workers' News Conference, June 1, 2010, accessed May 18, 2016, www.youtube.com/watch?v=xdik4E02Uu8

84. These testimonies were shared in both the news conference and the senate debate: New York State Senate Majority, Domestic Workers' News Conference, June 1, 2010; New York State Senate, NYS Senate Session, June 1, 2010.

85. Honig, "Immigrant America?," 5.

86. Ibid., 2.

87. New York State Senate Majority, Domestic Workers' News Conference, June 1, 2010.

88. Jennifer Gordon, "Campaign for the Unpaid Wages Prohibition Act: Latino Immigrants Change New York Wage Law," *Carnegie Paper* No. 4, August 1999.

89. Poo, "Organizing with Love."

90. Terri Nilliasca, "Some Women's Work: Domestic Work, Class, Race, Heteropatriarchy, and the Limits of Legal Reform," *Michigan Journal of Race and Law* 16 (2011): 397.

91. Ibid., 405.

92. Das Gupta, "The Neoliberal State and the Domestic Workers Movement in New York City"; Monisha Das Gupta, *Unruly Immigrants: Rights, Activism, and Transnational South Asian Politics in the United States* (Durham, NC and London: Duke University Press, 2006).

93. Das Gupta, *Unruly Immigrants,* p. 226.

94. Domestic Workers United, "Why Legislators Should Support the Domestic Workers Bill of Rights." Talking points handout, DWU archives.

95. Political education workshop, "Whose Movement Is It?" CUNY Graduate Center, March 18, 2016, author's notes.

96. Working group on "Narratives and Strategies of Domestic Worker Activism," CUNY Graduate Center, March 20, 2015, author's notes.

97. Ibid.
98. National Domestic Workers Alliance and National Employment Law Project, "Winning Dignity and Respect: A Guide to the Domestic Workers Bill of Rights," accessed March 3, 2015, https://ctpcsw.files.wordpress.com/2010/07/from-marla-shiller-winning-dignity-respect-9-27-13.pdf
99. Interview with Raoul.
100. Association of Black Women Historians, "An Open Statement to The Fans of *The Help*," accessed October 27, 2014, http://www.abwh.org/index.php?option=com_content&view=article&id=2%3Aopen-statement-the-help
101. Linda Holmes, "Actor Wendell Pierce Takes to Twitter to Talk about 'The Help,'" *NPR*, August 16, 2011, http://www.npr.org/blogs/monkeysee/2011/08/16/139669564/actor-wendell-pierce-takes-to-twitter-to-talk-about-the-help
102. "Meet Today's Help," National Domestic Workers Alliance (NDWA), accessed March 10, 2014, www.domesticworkers.org/bethehelp. The video has since been taken down from this website.
103. David Montgomery, "Activists Bolster Political Causes with 'The Help' and 'A Better Life,'" *The Washington Post*, February 29, 2012, http://articles.washingtonpost.com/2012-02-29/lifestyle/35443532_1_day-laborer-pablo-alvarado-social-media
104. Ibid.
105. Tamara Nopper, "Be The Help Campaign and Black Disappearance among the Multiracial Left," February 28, 2012, http://tamaranopper.com/2012/02/28/be-the-help-campaign-black-disappearance-among-the-multiracial-left/
106. Melissa Harris-Perry, "The Help Doesn't Help," *NBC News*, February 25, 2012, http://www.nbcnews.com/video/mhp/46523913#46523913
107. Ann Hornaday, "Review of *The Help*," *The Washington Post*, August 10, 2011, http://www.washingtonpost.com/gog/movies/the-help,1175294/critic-review.html
108. Cited in Nopper, "Be The Help Campaign and Black Disappearance among the Multiracial Left."
109. Christine Lewis, Panel on Narrating Labor Struggles, Center for the Humanities, CUNY Graduate Center, April 17, 2013.
110. Interview with Lewis.
111. "Narratives and Strategies of Domestic Worker Activism."
112. Pen World Voices Festival, "Say It Loud! Stories from New York's Worker-Writers," New York, May 9, 2015, accessed May 18, 2016 https://www.youtube.com/watch?v=sBXOztRGXYw
113. Alam and Aiyar, "The Power of Complicated Stories."
114. Joan Tronto, *Caring Democracy: Markets, Equality, and Justice* (New York, NYU Press, 2013), p. 9.

CHAPTER 5

1. Peter Orner, *Underground America: Narratives of Undocumented Lives* (San Francisco: McSweeney's Books, 2008).
2. Wendy Brown, "Neo-liberalism and the End of Liberal Democracy," *Theory & Exam* 7, no. 1 (2003).
3. Martha Escobar, "No One Is Criminal," in *Abolition Now! Ten Years of Strategy and Struggle Against the Prison Industrial Complex*, edited by Publications Collective (New York: AK Press, 2008), pp. 57–69.
4. Walter Nicholls, *The DREAMers: How the Undocumented Youth Movement Transformed the Immigrant Rights Debate* (Stanford, CA: Stanford University Press, 2013), pp. 31–32.
5. Susan Coutin, *Legalizing Moves: Salvadoran Immigrants' Struggle for US Residency* (Ann Arbor: University of Michigan Press, 2003), p. 118.
6. Ibid., 119.
7. Nicholls, *The DREAMers*, p. 35.
8. Cong. Rec. October 24, 2007: S13303. Congressional Record–Senate.

9. Phyllis Chock, "'Illegal Aliens' and 'Opportunity:' Myth-Making in Congressional Testimony," *American Ethnologist* 18, no. 2 (1991): 279.

10. Cong. Rec. May 18, 2007: 1–57. Comprehensive Immigration Reform: The Future of Undocumented Immigrant Students. Further testimonies from this hearing are taken from here.

11. Chock, "'Illegal Aliens' and 'Opportunity,'" 281.

12. Dick Durbin United States Senator Illinois, accessed October 24, 2014, http://www.durbin.senate.gov/public/index.cfm/hot-topics?ID=43eaa136-a3de-4d72-bc1b-12c3000f0ae9

13. Benita Veliz, "Dreamers' Stories," Website of Dick Durbin, United States Senator, Illinois, accessed June 15, 2015, http://www.durbin.senate.gov/issues/immigration-and-the-dream-act/dreamers-stories

14. Chock, "'Illegal Aliens" and "Opportunity,"' p. 285.

15. Cong. Rec. December 8, 2010: H8214. House Floor Consideration of Senate Amendments to Dream Act of 2010. Congressional Record–House.

16. Eithne Luibhéid, *Queer Migrations: Sexuality, US Citizenship, and Border Crossings* (Minnesota: University of Minnesota Press, 2005).

17. *Underground Undergrads: UCLA Undocumented Immigrant Students Speak Out* (Los Angeles: UCLA Center for Labor Research and Education, 2008).

18. Nicholls, *The DREAMers.*

19. Thomas Piñero Shields, "DREAMers Rising: Constituting the Undocumented Student Immigrant Movement" (PhD dissertation, Brandeis University, 2014).

20. Escobar, "No One Is Criminal."

21. Nativo Lopez cited in Alfonso Gonzalez, *Reform Without Justice: Latino Migrant Politics and the Homeland Security State* (New York and Oxford: Oxford University Press, 2014), p. 70.

22. Ibid., 125.

23. Ibid., 4.

24. Ibid., 126.

25. William Robinson and Xuan Santos, "Global Capitalism, Immigrant Labor, and the Struggle for Justice," *Class, Race, and Corporate Power* 2, no. 3 (2014): 12.

26. Shields, "DREAMers Rising," p. 136.

27. Ibid., 143.

28. Center for Community Change, 2009 Annual Report.

29. Author interview with Mohammad Abdollahi, August 20, 2014.

30. Dream Team Los Angeles, *Yes CA! Youth Empowerment Summit, California Leadership Workshop Guide* (April 2010), pp. 49–50.

31. Ibid., 6–7.

32. "Why Do We Tell Our Story," New Organizing Institute, accessed June 12, 2015, https://www.youtube.com/watch?v=mAxQWH2uuQE

33. "Sean Story Self, Us and Now," New Organizing Institute, accessed June 12, 2015, https://www.youtube.com/watch?v=qJF07cond3Q

34. Gonzalez, *Reform Without Justice*, p. 129.

35. National Organizing Institute (NOI), *Power Shift Organizing Training—Northeast*, March 18–20, 2011, p. 39.

36. Shields, "DREAMers Rising," pp. 139–140.

37. "Tony Fierro Testimony," accessed June 12, 2015, https://www.youtube.com/watch?v=4nNo3jOujXE

38. Francesca Polletta, "Storytelling in Social Movements," in *Culture, Social Movements, and Protest*, edited by Hank Johnston (Surrey, UK and Burlington, VT: Ashgate Publishing, 2009), pp. 33–54.

39. Hahrie Han and Elizabeth McKenna, *Groundbreakers: How Obama's 2.2 Million Volunteers Transformed Campaigning in America* (Oxford: Oxford University Press, 2015).

40. Dream Team Los Angeles, *Yes CA!*, p. 5.

41. Ibid., 14.

42. "Role Play Ithaca Immigration Training," New Organizing Institute, accessed June 12, 2015, https://www.youtube.com/watch?v=1wfyWEhOLIc

43. ICE refers to the Immigration and Customs Enforcement Agency. ICE raids are actions carried out by ICE officers in homes and workplaces to find undocumented people, with the intention to detain and deport them.

44. "The Keeping Families Together Day of Action," Center for Community Change Action, accessed December 23, 2014, https://www.youtube.com/watch?v=79G9vNQ0ie4

45. Thomas Swerts, "Non-Citizen Citizenship: A Comparative Ethnography of Undocumented Activism in Chicago and Brussels" (PhD dissertation, University of Chicago, 2014), p. 203.

46. "Story of US & Now," New Organizing Institute, accessed June 12, 2015, https://www.youtube.com/watch?v=if5fVgXqxxY

47. Author interview with Andrea Leon Schettini, August 26, 2014.

48. Interview with Abdollahi.

49. Gonzalez, *Reform Without Justice*, p. 135.

50. Nicholls, *The DREAMers*, p. 78.

51. Ibid., 79.

52. Promise Arizona. Live the Promise, Paz Movement Building Training, Training Guide, August 28, 2010, p. 8.

53. Nicholls, *The DREAMers*, p. 83.

54. Neidi Dominguez Zamorano, Jonathan Perez, Jorge Perez, Nency Meza, and Jorge Gutierrez, "DREAM Movement: Challenges with the Social Justice Elite's Military Option and the Immigration Reform 'Leaders,'" *Dissent*, September 20, 2010, http://www.truth-out.org/archive/component/k2/item/91872-dream-movement-challenges-with-the-social-justice-elites-military-option-arguments-and-the-immigration-reform-leaders

55. Nicholls, *The DREAMers*, p. 92.

56. Sally Kohn, "DREAM Act Students Causing a Nightmare," *Daily Kos*, October 12, 2010, http://www.dailykos.com/story/2010/10/12/909688/-DREAM-Act-Students-Causing-a-Nightmare#

57. Paulina Gonzalez, "Winning the Dream: Part Two of the 'Strategy and Organizing Behind the Successful Dream Act Movement,'" Organizing Upgrade, August 13, 2012, http://organizingupgrade.com/index.php/blogs/malkia-cyril/item/606-winning-the-dream-part-ii

58. Nicholls, *The DREAMers*, p. 127.

59. "Our Stories—Our Power: Queer, Undocumented, and Unafraid," Irene Vasquez, accessed December 22, 2014, https://www.youtube.com/watch?v=ndx1hjblOO8&list=UUmqpFPtPA8UCbdiLqk75vOw

60. Nicholls, *The DREAMers*, p. 125.

61. "HRC, Don't Push Us Back in the Closet," United We Dream, accessed December 22, 2014, https://www.youtube.com/watch?v=Kz7IlSInMcE

62. "Dream Warrior: Cristina Jimenez," United We Dream, accessed June 12, 2015, https://www.youtube.com/watch?v=aSEtbWBwefE

63. Alicia Schmidt Camacho, *Migrant Imaginaries: Latino Cultural Politics in the US-Mexico Borderlands* (New York and London: New York University Press, 2008).

64. Prerna Lal, "Deconstructing the Dreamer Status," June 3, 2011, http://prernalal.com/2011/06/deconstructing-the-dreamer-status/

65. Yosimar Reyes and Julio Salgado, "The Legalities of Being," Dreamers Adrift, accessed December 22, 2014, http://dreamersadrift.com/all-videos/page/4

66. Daniel Altschuler, "The Dreamers" Movement Comes of Age,' *Dissent*, May 16, 2011, https://www.dissentmagazine.org/online_articles/the-dreamers-movement-comes-of-age

67. Zé Garcia, "Speech: Desirable Undesirables," accessed October 27, 2014, http://whoseimmigrationreform.com/2014/02/22/ze-garcia/

68. Subhash Kateel and Aarti Shahani, "Families for Freedom Against Deportation and Delegalization," in *Keeping Out The Other: A Critical Introduction to Immigration Enforcement Today*, edited by David Brotherton and Philip Kretsedemas (New York: Columbia University Press, 2008).

69. Ibid., 264.

70. Garcia, "Speech: Desirable Undesirables."

71. Black Alliance for Just Immigration, accessed October 27, 2014, http://www.blackalliance.org/mission-and-history/
72. Marybeth Onyeukwu, "(Re)Imagining Immigrant Rights: Remembering Mike Brown, Renisha McBride, Eric Garner, Rekia Boyd, John Crawford, Kimani Gray and Countless Others," DC Center for Immigrant Justice, August 15, 2014, http://www.dcij.org/2014/08/15/reimagining-immigrant-rights-remembering-mike-brown-renisha-mcbride-eric-garner-rekia-boyd-john-crawford-kimani-gray-and-countless-others/
73. Interview with Abdollahi.
74. Victor Narro, "Perspectives: Employing a Spiritual Framework to Advance the Immigrant Rights Movement," Law at the Margins, accessed December 23, 2014, http://lawatthemargins.com/perspectives-employing-a-spiritual-framework-to-advance-the-immigrant-rights-movement-forward/
75. Sonia Guinansaca, "Mamita Mala—One Bad Mami," Word Press blog, accessed February 22, 2016, https://lamamitamala.wordpress.com/2015/11/20/from-sonia-guinansaca-re-tedxcuny/

CHAPTER 6

1. *Trabajo con Autobiografía*, Fundación Misión Cultura, December 2006, p. 5.
2. Sujatha Fernandes, *Who Can Stop the Drums: Urban Social Movements in Chávez's Venezuela* (Durham, NC and London: Duke University Press, 2010). In my book *Who Can Stop the Drums?*, I differentiate between the anti-neoliberal orientation of the Chávez government and its post-neoliberal character, as a hybrid state formation that has mounted certain challenges to the neoliberal paradigm but which remains subject to the internal and external constraints of global capital.
3. Alessandro Portelli, *The Death of Luigi Trastulli and Other Stories: Form and Meaning in Oral History* (Albany, NY: SUNY Press, 1990).
4. Lynn Stephen, *We Are the Face of Oaxaca: Testimony and Social Movements* (Durham, NC and London: Duke University Press, 2013); Marcia Stephenson, "Forging an Indigenous Counterpublic Sphere: The Taller de Historia Oral Andina in Bolivia," *Latin American Research Review* 37, no. 2 (2002): 99–118.
5. Fernandes, *Who Can Stop the Drums*, p. 81.
6. Fundación Misión Cultura, accessed May 11, 2013, http://www.misioncultura.gob.ve/mculturaweb/index.php
The conversion is calculated at the 2005 exchange rate of 2150 bolívares to the US dollar.
7. Michelle Leigh Farrell, "La Historia Local de la Misión Cultura: Un Componente Clave en el Proyecto Contemporáneo Nacional Venezolano," Paper presented at Latin American Studies Association annual meeting, 2010.
8. Fernandes, *Who Can Stop the Drums*.
9. Fundación Misión Cultura, http://www.misioncultura.gob.ve/mculturaweb/index.php
10. James Scott, *Seeing Like a State: How Certain Schemes to Improve the Human Condition Have Failed* (New Haven, CT and London: Yale University Press, 1998).
11. Fundación Misión Cultura, http://www.misioncultura.gob.ve/mculturaweb/index.php
12. Chris Hesketh and Adam David Morton, "Spaces of Uneven Development and Class Struggle in Bolivia: Transformation or *Trasformismo*," *Antipode* 46, no. 1 (January 2013): 1–21.
13. *Trabajo con Autobiografía*, p. 13.
14. Ibid., 5.
15. Ibid.
16. Daniel James, *Doña María's Story: Life History, Memory, and Political Identity* (Durham, NC and London: Duke University Press, 2000), p. 162.
17. Hugo Chávez, "Soy Sencillamente un Revolucionario," in *Chávez Nuestro*, edited by Rosa Miriam Elizade and Luis Báez (Casa Editora Abril, La Habana: 2004).
18. Josefina María Saldaña-Portillo, *The Revolutionary Imagination in the Americas and the Age of Development* (Durham, NC and London: Duke University Press, 2003), p. 67.

19. Ibid.
20. Chávez, "Soy Sencillamente un Revolucionario," p. 310.
21. Ibid.
22. Ibid., 331.
23. Ibid., 335.
24. Ibid., 322.
25. Germán Damas Carrera, *El Culto a Bolívar: Esbozo para un Estudio de la Historia de las Ideas en Venezuela* (Caracas: Universidad Central de Venezuela, 1970).
26. Fernando Coronil and Julie Skurski, "Dismembering and Remembering the Nation: The Semantics of Political Violence in Venezuela," *Comparative Politics in Society and History* 33, no. 2 (1991): 296–297.
27. Yolanda Salas, *Bolívar y La Historia en la Conciencia Popular* (Caracas: Universidad Simón Bolívar, 1987).
28. Chávez, "Soy Sencillamente un Revolucionario," p. 354.
29. Ibid., 342.
30. Magdalena Valdavieso, "Confrontación, Machismo y Democracia: Representaciones del "Heroísmo" en la Polarización Política en Venezuela," *Revista Venezolana de Economía y Ciencias Sociales* 10, no. 2 (2004): 140.
31. Chávez, "Soy Sencillamente un Revolucionario," p. 350.
32. Ibid., 339.
33. Ibid., 343.
34. Ibid.
35. Ibid., 356.
36. Ibid., 359.
37. Ibid.
38. Ileana Rodríguez, *Women, Guerillas, and Love: Understanding the War in Central America* (Minneapolis: University of Minnesota Press, 1996), p. 61.
39. *Trabajo con Autobiografía*, p. 15.
40. Stephenson, "Forging an Indigenous Counterpublic Sphere," p. 108.
41. *Trabajo con Autobiografía*, p. 7.
42. Ibid.,17.
43. Ibid., 5.
44. Eric Selbin, *Revolution, Rebellion, Resistance: The Power of Story* (London and New York: Zed Books, 2010).
45. I obtained the text of her personal narrative from the website ClubEnsayos, where it was uploaded in its entirety.
46. Chávez, "Soy Sencillamente un Revolucionario," p. 317.
47. James, *Doña María's Story*, p. 165.
48. Ibid., 211.
49. Ibid.
50. Saldaña-Portillo, *The Revolutionary Imagination*, p. 166.
51. Ibid., 189.
52. Ibid., 167.
53. James, *Doña María's Story*, p. 159.
54. William Peraza, "Autobiografía de William Peraza," February 2006, http://www.ccpc.org.ve/prueba/index.php?title=Autobiograf%C3%ADa_de_William_Peraza
55. I know Guerrero personally from an earlier time doing field research in Caracas, and he gave me a copy of this narrative. The writing of his text took a long time, much longer than the three months suggested by the mission directors. Although he finished it in 2014 when there had been a transition of leadership to President Nicolás Maduro, it was mostly written during the government of Hugo Chávez, hence the reference in the text to Chávez and not Maduro.
56. Ricardo José Guerrero, Autobiografía, Fundación Misión Cultura, 2014, p. 6.
57. Ibid., 9.
58. Ibid.
59. Ibid., 45.

60. Ibid., 16.
61. Ibid., 29.
62. Ibid., 30.
63. Margaret Mills, "Victimhood as Agency: Afghan Women's Memoirs," in *Orientalism and War*, edited by Tarak Barkawi and Ketih Stanski (Oxford: Oxford University Press, 2013), p. 198.
64. Autobiografía, Ricardo José Guerrero, Fundación Misión Cultura, 2014, p. 14.
65. Ibid., 31.
66. Ibid., 35.
67. Margaret Mills, "Victimhood as Agency," p. 198.
68. Autobiografía, Ricardo José Guerrero, Fundación Misión Cultura, 2014, p. 42.
69. Ibid., 61.
70. Ibid., 74.
71. Ibid., 83.
72. Ibid., 56.

EPILOGUE

1. Wendy Brown, *Undoing the Demos: Neoliberalism's Stealth Revolution* (New York: Zone Books, 2015), p. 75.
2. See Jodi Dean, "Neoliberalism's Defeat of Democracy," *Critical Inquiry*, accessed March 28, 2016, http://criticalinquiry.uchicago.edu/neoliberalisms_defeat_of_democracy/
3. Author interview with Christine Lewis, September 20, 2012.
4. Lowe, Lisa, *The Intimacies of Four Continents* (Durham, NC and London: Duke University Press, 2015), p. 51.
5. Political education workshop, "Whose Movement Is It?" CUNY Graduate Center, March 18, 2016, introductory comments by Patricia François.
6. This phrase was first used by Linda Oalican from Damayan and is the title of a piece by Terri Nilliasca, "Perspectives: Whose Movement? Domestic Workers Bill of Rights Four Years Later," Law at the Margins, http://lawatthemargins.com/perspectives-whose-movement-domestic-workers-bill-of-rights-four-years-later/
7. "Whose Movement Is It?", introductory comments by Francois.
8. Democracy Now!, "'We Are Pushing Real Revolution': Black Lives Matter on Why They Don't Have Faith in Any Candidate," March 9, 2016, http://www.democracynow.org/2016/3/9/we_are_pushing_real_revolution_black

BIBLIOGRAPHY

Abramsky, Sasha. "A Conversation with Marshall Ganz." *The Nation*, February 3, 2011.

Abu-Lughod, Lila. *Do Muslim Women Need Saving?* (Cambridge, MA: Harvard University Press, 2013).

Afghan Women's Writing Project. "Remembering Tabasom." April 23, 2012. http://awwproject.org/2012/04/remembering-tabasom/

Ahmad, Dohra. "Not Yet Beyond the Veil: Muslim Women in American Popular Literature." *Social Text* 27, no. 2 (2009): 105–131.

Ahmed, Leila. *Women and Gender in Islam: Historical Roots of a Modern Debate* (New Haven, CT: Yale University Press, 1992).

Ahmed-Ghosh, Huma. "A History of Women in Afghanistan: Lessons Learnt for the Future or Yesterdays and Tomorrow: Women in Afghanistan." *Journal of International Women's Studies* 4, no. 3 (2003): 1–14.

Aidi, Hisham D. *Rebel Music: Race, Empire, and the New Muslim Youth Culture* (New York: Pantheon Books, 2014).

Alam, Nahar, and Chitra Aiyar. "The Power of Complicated Stories." *Samar: South Asian Magazine for Action and Reflection*, Issue 40: Circles of Gender Justice, May 31, 2013. http://samarmagazine.org/archive/articles/430

Alessandro Portelli. *The Death of Luigi Trastulli and Other Stories: Form and Meaning in Oral History* (Albany, NY: SUNY Press, 1990).

Allen, Pamela. *Free Space: A Perspective on the Small Groups in Women's Movements* (New York: Times Change, 1970).

Altschuler, Daniel. "The Dreamers Movement Comes of Age." *Dissent*. May 16, 2011. https://www.dissentmagazine.org/online_articles/the-dreamers-movement-comes-of-age

Andrews, Molly. *Shaping History: Narratives of Political Change* (Cambridge, MA: Cambridge University Press, 2007).

Anonymous. "Paying the Price for Democracy in Afghanistan." Afghan Women's Writing Project. March 20, 2014. http://awwproject.org/2014/03/paying-the-price-for-democracy-in-afghanistan/

Association of Black Women Historians. "An Open Statement to The Fans of *The Help*." Accessed October 27, 2014. http://aalbc.com/reviews/the_help_historical_context.html

Bakhtin, Mikhail. *The Dialogic Imagination: Four Essays*. Translated by Caryl Emerson and Michael Holquist (Austin: University of Texas Press, 1981).

Bardacke, Frank. *Trampling out the Vintage: Cesar Chavez and the Two Souls of the United Farm Workers* (London and New York: Verso, 2011).

Basu, Srimati. "V is for Veil, V is for Ventriloquism: Global Feminisms in the Vagina Monologues." *Frontiers: A Journal of Women Studies* 31, no. 1 (2010): 31–62.

Benjamin, Walter. *Illuminations* (New York: Schocken Books, 1968).

Bennett, Eric. *Workshops of Empire: Stegner, Engle, and American Creative Writing during the Cold War* (Iowa City: University of Iowa Press, 2015).

Beverley, John. *Testimonio: On the Politics of Truth* (Minneapolis: University of Minnesota Press, 2004).

Billaud, Julie. *Kabul Carnival: Gender Politics in Postwar Afghanistan* (Philadelphia: University of Pennsylvania Press, 2015).

Black Alliance for Just Immigration. "Mission and History." Accessed October 27, 2014. http://www.blackalliance.org/mission-and-history/

Bonner, Philip, and Noor Nieftagodien. "The Truth and Reconciliation Commission and the Pursuit of 'Social Truth': The Case of Kathorus," in *Commissioning the Past: Understanding South Africa's Truth and Reconciliation Commission*, edited by Deborah Posel and Graeme Simpson (Johannesburg: Witwatersrand University Press, 2002), pp. 173–203.

Bronstein, Zelda. "'Politics' Fatal Therapeutic Turn." *Dissent*, Summer 2011. https://www.dissentmagazine.org/article/politics-fatal-therapeutic-turn

Brown, Tamara Mose. *Raising Brooklyn: Nannies, Childcare, and Caribbeans Creating Community* (New York and London: New York University Press, 2011).

Brown, Wendy. "Civilizational Delusions: Secularism, Tolerance, Equality." *Theory & Event* 15, no. 2 (2012).

———. "Neo-liberalism and the End of Liberal Democracy." *Theory & Event* 7, no. 1 (2003).

———. *States of Injury: Power and Freedom in Late Modernity* (Princeton, NJ: Princeton University Press, 1995).

———. *Undoing the Demos: Neoliberalism's Stealth Revolution* (New York: Zone Books, 2015).

Bruner, Jerome. *Making Stories: Law, Literature, Life* (Cambridge, MA and London: Harvard University Press, 2002).

Buettner, Russ. "For Nannies, Hope for Workplace Protection." *New York Times*, June 2, 2010. http://www.nytimes.com/2010/06/03/nyregion/03nanny.html

Camacho, Alicia Schmidt. *Migrant Imaginaries: Latino Cultural Politics in the US-Mexico Borderlands* (New York and London: New York University Press, 2008).

CampObama. "Susan's Story of Us (Camp Obama: Burbank)." March 21, 2014. https://www.youtube.com/watch?v=Z-WEM-taoG8

Carrera, Germán Damas. *El Culto a Bolívar: Esbozo para un Estudio de la Historia de las Ideas en Venezuela* (Caracas: Universidad Central de Venezuela, 1970).

Castillejo-Cuéllar, Alejandro. "Knowledge, Experience, and South Africa's Scenarios of Forgiveness," in *Truth Commissions: State Terror, History, and Memory*, a special issue of *Radical History Review*, edited by Greg Grandin and Thomas Klublock, no. 97 (Winter 2007): 11–42.

Center for Community Change Action. "The Keeping Families Together Day of Action." March 22, 2013. https://www.youtube.com/watch?v=79G9vNQ0ie4

Chakravarti, Sonali. "Agonism and Victim Testimony," in *Theorising Post-Conflict Reconciliation: Agonism, Restitution, & Repair*, edited by Alexander Hirsch (New York: Routledge, 2012), pp. 11–26.

Chávez, Hugo. "Soy Sencillamente un Revolucionario," in *Chávez Nuestro*, edited by Rosa Miriam Elizade and Luis Báez (Casa Editora Abril, La Habana: 2004), pp. 305–370.

Chock, Phyllis. "'Illegal Aliens' and 'Opportunity': Myth-Making in Congressional Testimony." *American Ethnologist* 18, no. 2 (1991): 279–294.

CIA Red Cell Special Memorandum, "CIA Report into Shoring up Afghan War Support in Western Europe," Wikileaks, March 11, 2010. https://file.wikileaks.org/file/cia-afghanistan.pdf

Clinton, Hillary Rodham. "Remarks at the US-Afghan Women's Council 10th Anniversary Celebration Luncheon." March 21, 2012. http://www.state.gov/secretary/ 20092013clinton/rm/2012/03/186618.htm

Coleman, Neill. "Making the Case to Invest in Story." *Hatch for Good*, November 23, 2014. https://www.hatchforgood.org/explore/71/making-the-case-to-invest-in-story

Cong. Rec. October 24, 2007: S13303. Congressional Record–Senate.

Cong. Rec. May 18, 2007: 1–57. Comprehensive Immigration Reform: The Future of Undocumented Immigrant Students.

Cong. Rec. December 8, 2010: H8214. House Floor Consideration of Senate Amendments to Dream Act of 2010. Congressional Record–House.

Colvin, Christopher. "Brothers and Sisters, Do Not Be Afraid of Me: Trauma, History and the Therapeutic Imagination in the New South Africa." In *Contested Pasts: The Politics of Memory*, edited by Katharine Hodgkin and Susannah Radstone (New York: Routledge, 2003), pp. 153–167.

———. "Limiting Memory: The Roots and Routes of Storytelling in Post-Apartheid, Post-TRC South Africa," in *Telling Wounds: Narrative, Trauma and Memory, Working Through the South African Armed Conflicts of the 20th Century*. Proceedings of the conference held at the University of Cape Town, July 3–5 2002, edited by Chris Van der Merwe and Rolf Wolffswinkle (Stellenbosch, South Africa: Van Schaik Content Solutions, 2002), p. 10.

———. "Trafficking Trauma: Intellectual Property Rights and the Political Economy of Traumatic Storytelling." *Critical Arts: South-North Cultural and Media Studies* 20, no. 1 (2008): 171–182.

———. "Traumatic Storytelling after Apartheid," in *Borders and Healers: Brokering Therapeutic Resources in Southeast Africa*, edited by Tracy J. Luedke and Harry G. West (Bloomington: Indiana University Press, 2006), pp. 166–184.

Coronil, Fernando, and Julie Skurski. "Dismembering and Remembering the Nation: The Semantics of Political Violence in Venezuela," *Comparative Politics in Society and History* 33, no. 2 (1991): 296–297.

Coutin, Susan. *Legalizing Moves: Salvadoran Immigrants' Struggle for US Residency* (Ann Arbor: University of Michigan Press, 2003).

Crosby, Allison, and M. Brinton Lykes. "Mayan Women Survivors Speak: The Gendered Relations of Truth Telling in Postwar Guatemala." *International Journal of Transitional Justice* 5, no. 3 (2011): 456–476.

Cunningham, Vinson. "Humans of New York and the Cavalier Consumption of Others." *The New Yorker*, November 3, 2015.

Das Gupta, Monisha. *Unruly Immigrants: Rights, Activism, and Transnational South Asian Politics in the United States* (Durham, NC and London: Duke University Press, 2006).

———. "The Neoliberal State and the Domestic Workers' Movement in New York City," *Canadian Woman Studies* 22, no. 3 (2003): 78–85.

Dean, Jodi. "Neoliberalism's Defeat of Democracy," *Critical Inquiry*. Accessed March 28, 2016. http://criticalinquiry.uchicago.edu/neoliberalisms_defeat_of_democracy/

De Genova, Nicholas. *Working the Boundaries: Race, Space, and "Illegality" in Mexican Chicago* (Durham, NC and London: Duke University Press, 2005).

DeGloma, Thomas. *Seeing the Light: The Social Logic of Personal Discovery* (Chicago and London: University of Chicago Press, 2014).

Democracy Now!, "'We Are Pushing Real Revolution': Black Lives Matter on Why They Don't Have Faith in Any Candidate," March 9, 2016. http://www.democracynow.org/2016/ 3/9/we_are_pushing_real_revolution_black

Doucet, Lyse. "Dangerous 'Truth': The Kabul Women's Poetry Club," *BBC News*, October 21, 2013. http://www.bbc.com/news/world-asia-24608666

Dream Team Los Angeles. *Yes CA! Youth Empowerment Summit*, California Leadership Workshop Guide, April 2010.

Durbin, Dick. "United States Senator Illinois." http://www.durbin.senate.gov/public/index.cfm/hot-topics?ID=43eaa136-a3de-4d72-bc1b-12c3000f0ae9

Editorial board. "Women's Work" *New York Times*, June 8, 2008. http://www.nytimes.com/2008/06/08/opinion/08sun2.html?scp=1&sq=women%27s+work&st=nyt

Ehrenreich, Barbara, and Arlie Hochschild. "Introduction," in *Global Woman: Nannies, Maids, and Sex Workers in the New Economy*, edited by Barbara Ehrenreich and Arlie Hochschild (New York: Henry Holt and Company, 2002), pp. 1–13.

Eikenberry, Karl. "Inverting the International Interference Paradigm: Afghan Women Seek Support." WikiLeaks. December 2, 2009. https://wikileaks.org/plusd/cables/09KABUL3849_a.html

Eisenstein, Zillah. *Against Empire: Feminisms, Racism, and the West* (New York: Zed Books, 2004).

Emaan. "Hijab: The Beauty of Muslim Women." Afghan Women's Writing Project. June 29, 2010. http://awwproject.org/2010/06/hijab-the-beauty-of-muslim-women/

Escobar, Martha. "No One Is Criminal," in *Abolition Now! Ten Years of Strategy and Struggle Against the Prison Industrial Complex*, edited by Publications Collective (New York: AK Press, 2008), pp. 57–69.

Evans, Sara. *Personal Politics: The Roots of Women's Liberation in the Civil Rights Movement and the New Left* (New York: Vintage Books, 1979).

Evans, Sara, and Harry Boyte. *Free Spaces: The Sources of Democratic Change in America* (Chicago: The University of Chicago Press, 1986).

Ewick, Patricia, and Susan Silbey. "Subversive Stories and Hegemonic Tales: Toward a Sociology of Narrative." *Law & Society Review* 29, no. 2 (1995): 197–226.

Exley, Zack. "Stories and Numbers—a Closer Look at Camp Obama." *Huffington Post*, August 29, 2007.

Fairclough, Norman. *Language and Power* (London and New York: Longman, 1989).

Farrell, Amy, and Patrice McDermott. "Claiming Afghan Women: The Challenge of Human Rights Discourse for Transnational Feminism," in *Just Advocacy? Women's Human Rights, Transnational Feminisms, and the Politics of Representation*, edited by Wendy S. Hesford and Wendy Kozol (New Brunswick, NJ: Rutgers University Press, 2005), pp. 33–55.

Farrell, Michelle Leigh. "La Historia Local de la Misión Cultura: Un Componente Clave en el Proyecto Contemporáneo Nacional Venezolano." Paper presented at Latin American Studies Association annual meeting, 2010.

Fassin, Didier, and Richard Rechtman. *The Empire of Trauma: An Inquiry into the Condition of Victimhood* (Princeton, NJ: Princeton University Press, 2009).

Fatima F. "The Bravest Girls in the World." Afghan Women's Writing Project. November 1, 2012. http://awwproject.org/2012/11/the-bravest-girls-in-the-world/

———. "Why Parents Must Stop Marrying Girls Early." Afghan Women's Writing Project. September 3, 2013. http://awwproject.org/2013/09/why-parents-must-stop-marrying-girls-early/

Fattemeh. "The Evening I Will Never Forget." Afghan Women's Writing Project. May 20, 2009. http://awwproject.org/2009/05/the-evening-i-will-never-forget/

Federici, Silvia. *Revolution at Point Zero: Housework, Reproduction, and Feminist Struggle* (Oakland, CA: PM Press, 2012).

Fernandes, Sujatha. *Who Can Stop the Drums: Urban Social Movements in Chávez's Venezuela* (Durham, NC and London: Duke University Press, 2010).

Fine, Janice. "Community Unions and the Revival of the American Labor Movement." *Politics & Society* 33, no. 1 (2005): 153–199.

————. *Worker Centers: Organizing Communities at the Edge of the Dream* (Ithaca, NY: Cornell University Press, 2006).

Ford Foundation. "Glossary of Grant-Making Approaches." Accessed May 18, 2016. http://web.archive.org/web/20150906075606/http://www.fordfoundation.org/pdfs/grants/glossary-of-approaches.pdf

————. "Grants Database." Accessed February 16, 2016. www.fordfoundation.org/work/our-grants/grants-database

Forte Poesy. "AWWP + Forte Poesy: Night of Poetry and Song." May 18, 2014. https://www.youtube.com/watch?v=kmOLIOFu3Ok

Foundation Center. "Foundation Directory Online Professional Grants Database." Accessed December 20, 2014. fconline.foundationcenter.org

Frantz, Courtney, and Sujatha Fernandes. "Whose Movement Is It? Strategic Funding, Worker Centers, and Foundation Influence." *Critical Sociology*, 2016, pp 1–16.

Fraser, Nancy. "From Redistribution to Recognition? Dilemmas of Justice in a 'Post-Socialist' Age." *New Left Review* I/212 (July-August 1995): 68–93.

Freshta. "American Soldiers: Here to Protect, or Violate?" Afghan Women's Writing Project. April 7, 2010. http://awwproject.org/2010/04/american-soldiers-here-to-protect-or-violate/

Fullard, Madeleine, and Nicky Rousseau. *Truth Telling, Identities and Power in South Africa and Guatemala*. International Center for Research and Justice, research brief. 2009. http://ictj.org/sites/default/files/ICTJ-Identities-TruthCommissions-ResearchBrief-2009-English.pdf

Fundación Misión Cultura. Accessed May 11, 2013. http://www.misioncultura.gob.ve/mculturaweb/index.php

————. *Trabajo con Autobiografía*. December 2006.

Ganz, Marshall. "Organizing Obama: Campaign, Organizing, Movement." Paper presented at American Sociological Association annual meeting, 2009.

Garcia, Zé. "Speech: Desirable Undesirables." Accessed October 27, 2014. http://whoseimmigrationreform.com/2014/02/22/ze-garcia/

George W. Bush Institute Publications. "Amplifying the Voice of Afghan Women." October 22, 2013. http://www.bushcenter.org/blog/2013/10/22/amplifying-voice-afghan-women-afghan-women%E2%80%99s-writing-project

Gledhill, John. "Neoliberalism," in *A Companion to the Anthropology of Politics*, edited by David Nugent and Joan Vincent Nugent (London: Blackwell, 2004), pp. 332–348.

GlobalGiving. "Storytelling Project—Turning Anecdotes into Useful Data." Accessed March 28, 2016. https://www.globalgiving.org/stories/

Goldberg, Harmony. "'Prepare to Win:' Domestic Workers United's Strategic Transition following Passage of the New York Domestic Workers' Bill of Rights," in *New Labor in New York: Precarious Workers and the Future of the Labor Movement*, edited by Ruth Milkman and Ed Ott (Ithaca, NY and London: Cornell University Press, 2014), pp. 266–288.

Gonnerman, Jennifer. "The Nanny Uprising." *New York Magazine*. June 6, 2010. http://nymag.com/news/features/66471/

Gonzalez, Alfonso. *Reform Without Justice: Latino Migrant Politics and the Homeland Security State* (New York and Oxford: Oxford University Press, 2014).

Gonzalez, Paulina. "Winning the Dream: Part Two of the 'Strategy and Organizing Behind the Successful Dream Act Movement'". Organizing Upgrade. August 13, 2012. http://organizingupgrade.com/index.php/blogs/malkia-cyril/item/606-winning-the-dream-part-ii

Goodman, Andy. *Storytelling as Best Practice* (Los Angeles: The Goodman Center, 2015).

Gopal, Anand. *No Good Men among the Living: America, the Taliban, and the War Through Afghan Eyes* (New York: Metropolitan Books, 2014).

Gordon, Jennifer. "Campaign for the Unpaid Wages Prohibition Act: Latino Immigrants Change New York Wage Law." *Carnegie Paper* no. 4, August 1999.

Gottschall, Jonathan. *The Storytelling Animal: How Stories Make Us Human* (New York: Houghton Mifflin, 2012).

Gramsci, Antonio. *Selections from the Prison Notebooks of Antonio Gramsci*, ed. and trans. Quintin Hoare and Geoffrey Nowell Smith (New York: International Publishers, 1971).

Grandin, Greg. *Who Is Rigoberta Ménchu?* (London and New York: Verso, 2011).

Grandin, Greg, and Thomas Klublock. "Editors' Introduction," in *Truth Commissions: State Terror, History, and Memory*, a special issue of *Radical History Review*, edited by Greg Grandin and Thomas Klublock, no. 97 (Winter 2007): 1–10.

Greenhouse, Steven. "Legislation Pushed to Require Minimum Wage for Domestic Workers." *New York Times*, June 1, 2007. http://www.nytimes.com/2007/06/01/nyregion/01nanny.html?pagewanted=print&_r=0

Grima, Benedicte. *The Performance of Emotions Among Paxtun Women: "The Misfortunes Which Have Befallen Me"* (Austin: University of Texas Press, 1992).

Grindstaff, Laura. *Money Shot: Trash, Class, and the Making of TV Talk Shows* (Chicago and London: University of Chicago Press, 2002).

Guerrero, Ricardo José. "Autobiografía." (Fundación Misión Cultura, 2014).

Guinansaca, Sonia. "MamitaMala—OneBadMami." WordPress blog. November 20, 2015. https://lamamitamala.wordpress.com/2015/11/20/from-sonia-guinansaca-re-tedxcuny/

Gutiérrez-Jones, Carl. *Critical Race Narratives: A Study of Race, Rhetoric, and Injury* (New York and London: New York University Press, 2001).

Hall, Stuart. "The Neoliberal Revolution." *Cultural Studies* 25, no. 6 (2011): 705–728.

Hamilton, Masha. "History and Mission." Afghan Women's Writing Project. Accessed May 15, 2015. http://awwproject.org/discover-awwp/history-mission/

———. "Zarmeena." Afghan Women's Writing Project. Accessed May 13, 2015. http://awwproject.org/about/zarmeena/

Han, Hahrie, and Elizabeth McKenna. *Groundbreakers: How Obama's 2.2 Million Volunteers Transformed Campaigning in America* (Oxford: Oxford University Press, 2015).

Harris-Perry, Melissa. "'The Help' Doesn't Help." *NBC News*. February 25, 2012. http://www.nbcnews.com/video/mhp/46523913#46523913

Henderson, Lynne. "Legality and Empathy." *Michigan Law Review* 85, no. 7 (1987): 1574–1653.

Hesketh, Chris, and Adam David Morton. "Spaces of Uneven Development and Class Struggle in Bolivia: Transformation or *Trasformismo*," *Antipode* 46, no. 1 (2013): 1–21.

Holmes, Linda. "Actor Wendell Pierce Takes to Twitter to Talk about 'The Help.'" *NPR*, August 16, 2011. http://www.npr.org/blogs/monkeysee/2011/08/16/139669564/actor-wendell-pierce-takes-to-twitter-to-talk-about-the-help

Honig, Bonnie. "Immigrant America? How Foreignness 'Solves' Democracy's Problems." *Social Text* 56, no. 3 (1998): 1–27.

Hornaday, Ann. "Review of *The Help*." *The Washington Post*, August 10, 2011. http://www.washingtonpost.com/gog/movies/the-help,1175294/critic-review.html

Hunter, Tera. *To Joy My Freedom: Southern Black Women's Lives and Labors after the Civil War* (Cambridge, MA: Harvard University Press, 1997).

Huntington, Samuel. "The Hispanic Challenge," *Foreign Policy* (March-April 2004): 30–45.

International Writing Program. "Narrative Witness: A Caracas-Sarajevo Collaboration." Accessed June 10, 2015. http://www.iwpcollections.org/nw1#nw1-title

Jackson, Michael. *The Politics of Storytelling: Violence, Transgression, and Intersubjectivity* (University of Copenhagen: Museum Tusculanum Press, 2006).

James, Daniel. *Doña María's Story: Life History, Memory, and Political Identity* (Durham, NC and London: Duke University Press, 2000).

Jasper, James. "Emotions and Social Movements: Twenty Years of Theory and Research." *Annual Review of Sociology* 37 (April 2011): 285–304.

Joya, Malalai. *A Woman among Warlords: The Extraordinary Story of an Afghan Who Dared to Raise Her Voice* (New York: Scribner, 2009).

Kameswaran, Shipla. "War, Women, and Writing: The Story of the Afghan Women's Writing Project." *Delphi Quarterly*. Accessed May 13, 2015. http://delphiquarterly.com/recent-issues/current-issue-2-2/interview-with-the-afghan-womens-writing-workshop/

Kandiyoti, Deniz. "Old Dilemmas or New Challenges? The Politics of Gender and Reconstruction in Afghanistan." *Development and Change* 38, no. 2 (2007): 169–199.

Kateel, Subhash, and Aarti Shahani. "Families for Freedom Against Deportation and Delegalization" in *Keeping Out The Other: A Critical Introduction to Immigration Enforcement Today*, edited by David Brotherton and Philip Kretsedemas (New York: Columbia University Press, 2008), pp. 258–287.

Kaylin, Lucy. "Domestic Help." *New York Times*, September 23, 2007. http://www.nytimes.com/2007/09/23/opinion/nyregionopinions/23CIkaylin.html?pagewanted=print

Khan, Shahnaz. "Between Here and There: Feminist Solidarity and Afghan Women." *Genders* 33 (2001): 1–26.

Kitch, Sally. *Contested Terrain: Reflections with Afghan Women Leaders* (Chicago: University of Illinois Press, 2014).

Kitwana, Bakari, and Elizabeth Méndez Berry. "It"s Bigger Than Barack: Hip Hop Political Organizing, 2004–2013," in *The Hip Hop & Obama Reader*, edited by Erik Nielson and Travis L. Gosa (Oxford and New York: Oxford University Press, 2015), pp. 54–69.

Klein, Naomi. *The Shock Doctrine: The Rise of Disaster Capitalism* (New York: Picador, 2007).

Kohl-Arenas, Erica. *The Self-Help Myth: How Philanthropy Fails to Alleviate Poverty* (Berkeley: University of California Press, 2016).

Kohn, Sally. "DREAM Act Students Causing a Nightmare." *Daily Kos*. October 12, 2010. http://www.dailykos.com/story/2010/10/12/909688/-DREAM-Act-Students-Causing-a-Nightmare#

Kumar, Deepa. *Islamophobia and the Politics of Empire* (Chicago: Haymarket Books, 2012).

Lal, Prerna. "Deconstructing the Dreamer Status." June 3, 2011. http://prernalal.com/2011/06/deconstructing-the-dreamer-status/

Lazreg, Marnia. *Torture and the Twilight of Empire: From Algiers to Baghdad* (Princeton, NJ: Princeton University Press, 2007).

Lederman, Arline. "The *Zan* of Afghanistan: A 35-Year Perspective on Women in Afghanistan," in *Women for Afghan Women: Shattering Myths and Claiming the Future*, edited by Sunita Mehta (New York: Palgrave Macmillan, 2002), pp. 46–58.

Leeda. "Eight Daughters for Sale, the Oldest First." Afghan Women's Writing Project. December 18, 2012. http://awwproject.org/2012/12/eight-daughters-for-sale-the-oldest-first/

Lowe, Lisa. *The Intimacies of Four Continents* (Durham, NC and London: Duke University Press, 2015).

Luibheid, Eithne. *Queer Migrations: Sexuality, US Citizenship, and Border Crossings* (Minneapolis: University of Minnesota Press, 2005).

Marquardt, Marie, Timothy Steigenga, Philip Williams, and Manuel Vásquez. *Living Illegal: The Human Face of Unauthorized Immigration* (New York and London: The New Press, 2011).

Marzia. "Afghan Women's Rights: Will History Repeat Itself." Afghan Women's Writing Project. January 14, 2013. http://awwproject.org/2013/01/afghan-womens-rights-will-history-repeat-itself/

———. "What I Expect from My New President." Afghan Women's Writing Project. March 30, 2014. http://awwproject.org/2014/03/what-i-expect-from-my-new-president/

Marzila. "Exchange for a Cow, Part II." Afghan Women's Writing Project. April 25, 2013. http://awwproject.org/2013/04/exchange-for-a-cow-part-2/

Mayer, Frederick. *Narrative Politics: Stories and Collective Action* (New York: Oxford University Press, 2014).

Milkman, Ruth. "Introduction," in *Working for Justice: The L.A. Model of Organizing and Advocacy*, edited by Ruth Milkman, Joshua Bloom, and Victor Narro (Ithaca, NY: Cornell University Press, 2010), pp. 1–22.

Mills, Margaret. "Victimhood as Agency: Afghan Women's Memoirs," in *Orientalism and War*, edited by Tarak Barkawi and Ketih Stanski (Oxford: Oxford University Press, 2013), pp. 197–221.

Mohanty, Chandra Talpade. "Under Western Eyes: Feminist Scholarship and Colonial Discourses." *boundary 2* 12, no. 3 (1984): 333–358.

Montgomery, David. "Activists Bolster Political Causes with 'The Help' and 'A Better Life,'" *The Washington Post*. February 29, 2012. http://articles.washingtonpost.com/2012-02-29/lifestyle/35443532_1_day-laborer-pablo-alvarado-social-media

Moreiras, Alberto. "The Aura of Testimonio (1995)." In *The Real Thing: Testimonial Discourse and Latin America*, edited by Georg Gugelberger (Durham, NC and London: Duke University Press, 1996), pp. 192–224.

Murphy, Jane. "Lawyering for Social Change: The Power of the Narrative in Domestic Violence Law Reform." *Hofstra Law Review* 21, no. 4 (1993): 1243–1293.

Muslim Engagement Project. *Changing Course: A New Direction for U.S. Relations with the Muslim World*, 2nd ed. (Washington, DC and Cambridge: Search for Common Ground and the Consensus Building Institute, 2009). Accessed June 18, 2015. http://www.usmuslimengagement.org/storage/usme/documents/Changing_Course_Second_Printing.pdf

Nader, Laura. *Culture and Dignity: Dialogues Between the Middle East and the West* (West Sussex. UK: John Wiley & Sons, 2012).

Narro, Victor. "Perspectives: Employing a Spiritual Framework to Advance the Immigrant Rights Movement." Law at the Margins. Accessed December 23, 2014. http://lawatthemargins.com/perspectives-employing-a-spiritual-framework-to-advance-the-immigrant-rights-movement-forward/

Nasima. "A Reminder of the Last Afghan Elections." Afghan Women's Writing Project. March 13, 2014. http://awwproject.org/2014/03/a-reminder-of-the-last-afghan-elections/

———. "The Violence Lifted from My Shoulders When I Voted." Afghan Women's Writing Project. April 10, 2014. http://awwproject.org/2014/04/the-violence-lifted-from-my-shoulders-when-i-voted/

National Domestic Workers Alliance. "NY Domestic Worker Wins Justice, Finally." June 14, 2012. http://www.domesticworkers.org/es/news/2012/ny-domestic-worker-wins-justice-finally

National Domestic Workers Alliance and National Employment Law Project. "Winning Dignity and Respect: A Guide to the Domestic Workers Bill of Rights." September 2013. https://ctpcsw.files.wordpress.com/2010/07/from-marla-shiller-winning-dignity-respect-9-27-13.pdf

New Organizing Institute. "Role Play, Ithaca Immigration Training." January 28, 2010. https://www.youtube.com/watch?v=1wfyWEhOLIc

———. "Sean Story Self, Us and Now." November 18, 2010. https://www.youtube.com/watch?v=qJF07cond3Q

———. "Why Do We Tell Our Story." Ithaca Immigration Training. January 29, 2010. https://www.youtube.com/watch?v=mAxQWH2uuQE

Nguyen, Mimi Thi. "The Biopower of Beauty: Humanitarian Imperialisms and Global Feminisms in an Age of Terror." *Signs* 36, no. 2 (2011): 359–383.

Nicholls, Walter. *The DREAMers: How the Undocumented Youth Movement Transformed the Immigrant Rights Debate* (Stanford, CA: Stanford University Press, 2013).

Nielson, Erik, and Travis L. Gosa. "Introduction: The State of Hip Hop in the Age of Obama," in *The Hip Hop & Obama Reader*, edited by Erik Nielson and Travis L. Gosa (Oxford and New York: Oxford University Press, 2015), pp. 1–28.

Nilliasca, Terri. "Perspectives: Whose Movement? Domestic Workers Bill of Rights Four Years Later," LawattheMargins.http://lawatthemargins.com/perspectives-whose-movement-domestic-workers-bill-of-rights-four-years-later/

———. "Some Women's Work: Domestic Work, Class, Race, Heteropatriarchy, and the Limits of Legal Reform." *Michigan Journal of Race and Law* no. 16 (2011): 377–410.

NOI Organizing Toolbox. "Story of Self." March 21, 2014. https://www.youtube.com/watch?v=H0wq5VVxAFk

Nolan, James. "Drug Court Stories: Transforming American Jurisprudence," in *Stories of Change: Narratives and Social Movements*, edited by Joseph Davis (Albany: SUNY Press, 2002), pp. 149–178.

Nopper, Tamara. "Be The Help Campaign and Black Disappearance among the Multiracial Left." February 28, 2012. http://tamaranopper.com/2012/02/28/be-the-help-campaign-black-disappearance-among-the-multiracial-left/

Nye, Joseph. "Get Smart: Combining Hard and Soft Power." *Foreign Affairs*, July 1, 2009. https://www.foreignaffairs.com/articles/2009-07-01/get-smart

Obama, Barack. "Speech at 2004 DNC Convention." C-SPAN. July 27, 2004. https://www.youtube.com/watch?v=eWynt87PaJ0

Oglesby, Elizabeth. "Educating Citizens in Postwar Guatemala: Historical Memory, Genocide, and the Culture of Peace," in *Truth Commissions: State Terror, History, and Memory*, a special issue of *Radical History Review*, edited by Greg Grandin and Thomas Klublock, no. 97 (Winter 2007): 77–98.

Orner, Peter. *Underground America: Narratives of Undocumented Lives* (San Francisco: McSweeney's Books, 2008).

Paley, Julia. *Marketing Democracy: Power and Social Movements in Post-Dictatorship Chile* (Berkeley: University of California Press, 2001).

Peck, Janice. "The Mediated Talking Cure: Therapeutic Framing of Autobiography in TV Talk Shows," in *Getting a Life: Everyday Uses of Autobiography*, edited by Sidonie Smith and Julia Watson (Minneapolis and London: University of Minnesota Press, 1996), pp. 134–155.

Peraza, William. "Autobiografía de William Peraza." February 2006. http://www.ccpc.org.ve/prueba/index.php?title=Autobiograf%C3%ADa_de_William_Peraza

Petra Foundation. "Fellows." Accessed February 11, 2016. http://www.petrafoundation.org/fellows/nahar-alam/

Polletta, Francesca. *It Was Like a Fever: Storytelling in Protest and Politics* (Chicago and London: University of Chicago Press, 2006).

———. "Storytelling in Social Movements," in *Culture, Social Movements, and Protest*, edited by Hank Johnston (Surrey, UK and Burlington, VT: Ashgate Publishing, 2009), pp. 33–54.

Polletta, Francesca, James Jasper, and Jeff Goodwin. *Passionate Politics: Emotions and Social Movements* (Chicago: University of Chicago Press, 2001).

Polletta, Francesca, Pang Ching Bobby Chen, Beth Gharrity Gardner, and Alice Motes. "The Sociology of Storytelling." *Annual Review of Sociology* 37, no. 1 (2011): 109–130.

Poo, Ai-jen. "Organizing with Love: Lessons from the New York Domestic Workers Bill of Rights Campaign." *Left Turn: Notes from the Global Intifada*. December 1, 2010. http://www.leftturn.org/Organizing-with-Love

Portelli, Alessandro. *The Death of Luigi Trastulli and Other Stories* (Albany, NY: SUNY Press, 1990).

Promise Arizona. *Live the Promise, Paz Movement Building Training*. Training Guide. August 28, 2010.

Ranciére, Jacques, "Comments and Responses." *Theory and Event* 6, no. 4 (2003).

Reyes, Yosimar, and Julio Salgado. "The Legalities of Being." Dreamers Adrift. October 12, 2012. http://dreamersadrift.com/all-videos/page/4

Richard, Nelly. *The Insubordination of Signs: Political Change, Cultural Transformation, and Poetics of the Crisis* (Durham, NC and London: Duke University Press, 2004).

Robinson, William. *Global Capitalism and the Crisis of Humanity* (Cambridge: Cambridge University Press, 2014).

Robinson, William, and Xuan Santos. "Global Capitalism, Immigrant Labor, and the Struggle for Justice." *Class, Race, and Corporate Power* 2, no. 3 (2014): 1–16.

Rodríguez, Ileana. *Women, Guerillas, and Love: Understanding the War in Central America* (Minneapolis: University of Minnesota Press, 1996).

Rose, Nikolas. *Powers of Freedom: Reframing Political Thought* (Cambridge: Cambridge University Press, 1999).

Ross, Fiona C. *Bearing Witness: Women and the Truth and Reconciliation Commission in South Africa* (London: Pluto Press, 2003).

Rostami-Povey, Elaheh. *Afghan Women: Identity and Invasion* (London and New York: Zed Books, 2007).

Roya. "1 + 1 = 1." Afghan Women's Writing Project. November 8, 2009. http://awwproject. org/2009/11/111/

———. "Feathers of Freedom, Washed Away." Afghan Women's Writing Project. March 30, 2010. http://awwproject.org/2010/03/feathers-of-freedom-washed-away/

———. "The Meaning of Democracy." Afghan Women's Writing Project. July 27, 2010. http:// awwproject.org/2010/07/the-meaning-of-democracy/

Sabira. "Shouting For Their Rights." Afghan Women's Writing Project. March 17, 2010. http:// awwproject.org/2010/03/shouting-for-their-rights/

———. "To Laugh." Afghan Women's Writing Project. January 17, 2011. http://awwproject. org/2011/01/to-laugh/

Sachs, Jonah. *Winning the Story Wars: Why Those Who Tell (and Live) the Best Stories Will Rule the Future* (Boston: Harvard Business Review Press, 2012).

Safia. "Forced Marriage—Shame of Divorce." Afghan Women's Writing Project. October 18, 2010. http://awwproject.org/2010/10/forced-marriage-%E2%80%93-shame-of-divorce/

Said, Edward. *Orientalism* (New York: Vintage Books, 1979).

Salas, Yolanda. *Bolívar y La Historia en la Conciencia Popular* (Caracas: Universidad Simón Bolívar, 1987).

Saldaña-Portillo, Josefina María. *The Revolutionary Imagination in the Americas and the Age of Development* (Durham, NC and London: Duke University Press, 2003).

Salmon, Christian. *Storytelling: Bewitching the Modern Mind* (London: Verso Books, 2010).

Sanchez, Justin. "Narrative Networks." Defense Advanced Research Projects Agency (DARPA). Accessed March 31, 2016. http://www.darpa.mil/program/narrative-networks

Sassen, Saskia. "Global Cities and Survival Circuits," in *Global Woman: Nannies, Maids, and Sex Workers in the New Economy*, edited by Barbara Ehrenreich and Arlie Hochschild (New York: Henry Holt and Company, 2002), pp. 254–274.

———. "The Other Workers in the Advanced Corporate Economy." *The Scholar and Feminist Online* 8, no. 1 (Fall 2009). http://sfonline.barnard.edu/work/sassen_01.htm

Schneier, Edward V., John Brian Murtaugh, and Antoinette Pole. *New York Politics: A Tale of Two States* (Armonk, NY and London: M.E. Sharpe, 2010).

Schutz, Aaron, and Marie G. Sandy. "Campaign Versus Community Organizing: Storytelling in Obama's 2008 Presidential Campaign," in *Collective Action for Social Change: An Introduction to Community Organizing*, edited by Aaron Schutz and Marie G. Sandy (New York: Palgrave, 2012), pp. 111–127.

Scott, James. *Seeing Like a State: How Certain Schemes to Improve the Human Condition Have Failed* (New Haven, CT and London: Yale University Press, 1998).

Seeta. "The Burqa Bride." Afghan Women's Writing Project. June 18, 2010. http://awwproject.org/2010/06/the-burqa-bride/

Selbin, Eric. *Revolution, Rebellion, Resistance: The Power of Story* (London and New York: Zed Books, 2010).

Shafiqa. "Ocean of Disappointment." Afghan Women's Writing Project. September 25, 2010. http://awwproject.org/2010/09/ocean-of-disappointment/

Shakila. "The Different Daughter." Afghan Women's Writing Project. January 13, 2011. http://awwproject.org/2011/01/the-different-daughter/

Shattuc, Jane M. *The Talking Cure: TV Talk Shows and Women* (New York: Routledge, 1997).

Shields, Thomas Piñero. "DREAMers Rising: Constituting the Undocumented Student Immigrant Movement." (PhD dissertation, Brandeis University, 2014).

Shogofa. "Dear President Obama." Afghan Women's Writing Project. May 9, 2010. http://awwproject.org/2010/05/dear-president-obama/

————. "The Mirror." Afghan Women's Writing Project. January 25, 2011. http://awwproject.org/2011/01/the-mirror/

————. "When Can I See?" Afghan Women's Writing Project. July 22, 2010. http://awwproject.org/2010/07/when-can-i-see/

Siddiqi, Ayesha. "Does America Deserve Malala?," *Vice*, November 30, 2015. https://www.vice.com/read/does-america-deserve-malala

Sitara B. "A Tale of Two Teenagers: Malala and Anisa." Afghan Women's Writing Project. August 12, 2013. http://awwproject.org/2013/08/a-tale-of-two-teenagers-malala-and-anisa/

————. "How to Change Afghanistan." Afghan Women's Writing Project. October 11, 2012. http://awwproject.org/2012/10/how-to-change-afghanistan/

————. "Who Can Win? What the Campaign Slogans Don't Say." March 28, 2014. http://awwproject.org/2014/03/who-can-win-what-the-campaign-slogans-dont-say/

Slaughter, Joseph. "Enabling Fictions and Novel Subjects: The 'Bildungsroman' and International Human Rights Law," *Modern Language Association* 121, no. 5 (2006): 1405–1423.

Smith, Peggie. "Regulating Paid Household Work: Class, Gender, Race, and Agendas of Reform." *American University Law Review* 48, no. 4 (1999): 851–923.

Smith, Sidonie. "Self, Subject, and Resistance: Marginalities and Twentieth-Century Autobiographical Practice," *Tulsa Studies in Women's Literature* 9, no. 1 (1990): 11–24.

Spivak, Gayatri Chakravorty. "Can The Subaltern Speak?" in *Marxism and the Interpretation of Culture*, edited by Cary Nelson and Lawrence Grossberg (London: Macmillan, 1988), pp. 271–313.

————. "The Rani of Sirmur: As Essay in Reading the Archives," *History and Theory*, 24, no. 3 (1985): 247–272.

Stabile, Carole, and Deepa Kumar. "Unveiling Imperialism: Media, Gender, and the War on Afghanistan." *Media, Culture, and Society* 27, no. 5 (2005): 765–782.

Stephen, Lynn. *We Are the Face of Oaxaca: Testimony and Social Movements* (Durham, NC and London: Duke University Press, 2013).

Stephenson, Marcia. "Forging an Indigenous Counterpublic Sphere: The Taller de Historia Oral Andina in Bolivia," *Latin American Research Review* 37, no. 2 (2002): 99–118.

Stoll, David. *Rigoberta Menchú and the Story of All Poor Guatemalans* (Boulder, CO and London: Westview Press, 1999).

Swerts, Thomas. "Non-Citizen Citizenship: A Comparative Ethnography of Undocumented Activism in Chicago and Brussels" (PhD dissertation, the University of Chicago, 2014).

Taylor, Julie. "Body Memories: Aide-Memories and Collective Amnesia in the Wake of the Argentine Terror," in *Body Politics: Disease, Desire, and the Family*, edited by Michael Ryan and Avery Gordon (Boulder, CO: Westview Press, 1994), pp. 192–203.

Theidon, Kimberly. "Gender in Transition: Common Sense, Women, and War." *Journal of Human Rights* 6 (2007): 453–478.

Tigas, Mike, and Sisi Wei. "ProPublica Nonprofit Explorer." Accessed April 9, 2016. projects. propublica.org/nonprofits

Titus, Elizabeth. "Who Else but the Women?" *The WVoice* 1, no. 10. November 12, 2013. http://www.womensvoicesnow.org/who_else_but_the_women

Underground Undergrads: UCLA Undocumented Immigrant Students Speak Out (Los Angeles: UCLA Center for Labor Research and Education, 2008).

UNESCO. "Enhancement of Literacy in Afghanistan Program." Accessed May 13, 2015. http://www.unesco.org/new/en/kabul/education/enhancement-of-literacy-in-afghanistan-ela-program/

United We Dream. "Dream Warrior: Cristina Jimenez." June 12, 2015. https://www.youtube.com/watch?v=aSEtbWBwefE

———. "HRC, Don't Push Us Back in the Closet." March 28, 2013. https://www.youtube.com/watch?v=Kz7IlSInMcE

Upton, Brian. *The Aesthetic of Play* (Cambridge, MA: MIT Press, 2015).

Urbanbaby. "Workplace Protection for Nannies—Thoughts?" [Online discussion group]. June 3, 2010. http://www.urbanbaby.com/talk/posts/51992609

Valdavieso, Magdalena. "Confrontación, Machismo y Democracia: Representaciones del 'Heroísmo' en la Polarización Política en Venezuela," *Revista Venezolana de Economía y Ciencias Sociales* 10, no. 2 (2004): 137–154.

Van de Carr, Paul. "Storytelling and Social Change: A Guide for Activists, Organizations and Social Entrepreneurs." *Working Narratives*. Accessed January 5, 2016. http://working-narratives.org/story-guide/

———. "Storytelling and Social Change: A Strategy Guide for Grantmakers." *Working Narratives*. Accessed September 19, 2014. http://workingnarratives.org/wp-content/uploads/2013/08/Story-Guide.pdf

Van Wii, Sara. "Amplifying the Voice of Afghan Women: Afghan Women's Writing Project," 22 October 2013. http://www.bushcenter.org/blog/2013/10/22/amplifying-voice-afghan-women-afghan-women%E2%80%99s-writing-project

Vasquez, Irene. "Our Stories—Our Power: Queer, Undocumented, and Unafraid." June 11, 2012. https://www.youtube.com/watch?v=ndx1hjblOO8&list=UUmqpFPtPA8UCb diLqk75vOw

Veliz, Benita. "Dreamers' Stories." Website of Dick Durbin, United States Senator, Illinois. Accessed June 15, 2015. http://www.durbin.senate.gov/issues/immigration-and-the-dream-act/dreamers-stories

Von Eschen, Penny. *Satchmo Blows Up the World: Jazz Ambassadors Play the Cold War* (Cambridge. MA: Harvard University Press, 2006).

Walkerdine, Valerie, and Jessica Ringrose. "Femininities: Reclassifying Upward Mobility and the Neo-liberal Subject." In *The Sage Handbook of Gender and Education*, edited by Christine Skelton, Becky Francis, and Lisa Smulyan (London, SAGE publications, 2006), pp. 31–46.

Whitlock, Gillian. *Soft Weapons: Autobiography in Transit* (Chicago and London: University of Chicago Press, 2007).

Whittier, Nancy. *The Politics of Child Sexual Abuse: Emotions, Social Movements, and the State* (Oxford: Oxford University Press, 2009).

Wylie, Gillian. "Women's Rights and 'Righteous War:' An Argument for Women's Autonomy in Afghanistan." *Feminist Theory* 4, no. 2 (2003): 217–223.

Yeğenoğlu, Meyda. *Colonial Fantasies: Towards a Feminist Reading of Orientalism* (Cambridge: Cambridge University Press, 1998).

Yúdice, George. *The Expediency of Culture: Uses of Culture in the Global Era* (Durham and London: Duke University Press, 2003).

Zainab. "Teach The Children." Afghan Women's Writing Project. December 8, 2011. http://awwproject.org/2011/12/teach-the-children/

Zamorano, Neidi Dominguez, Jonathan Perez, Jorge Perez, Nency Meza, and Jorge Gutierrez. "DREAM Movement: Challenges with the Social Justice Elite's Military Option and the Immigration Reform 'Leaders,'"*Dissent*, September 20, 2010. http://www.truth-out.org/archive/component/k2/item/91872-dream-movement-challenges-with-the-social-justice-elites-military-option-arguments-and-the-immigration-reform-leaders

INDEX